THE SPORTING RIFLE:
A User's Handbook

THE SPORTING RIFLE:

A User's Handbook

by

Robin Marshall-Ball

SWAN·HILL
PRESS

For my children, Jennifer, Lorraine, and Stuart.

Copyright © 1986, 1989, 1995 by Robin Marshall-Ball

First published in the UK in 1995
by Swan Hill Press
an imprint of Airlife Publishing Ltd
First published by Pelham Books in 1986
and revised in 1989

British Library Cataloguing in Publication Data
A catalogue record for this book
is available from the British Library

ISBN 1 85310 584 8

Printed and bound in Great Britain by
Butler & Tanner Ltd, Frome and London

Swan Hill Press

An imprint of Airlife Publishing Ltd
101 Longden Road, Shrewsbury SY3 9EB

CONTENTS

ACKNOWLEDGEMENTS

IN writing a book of this nature I have received much help from a great many people. I gratefully acknowledge the assistance I have been given by Roger Hale, David Lloyd, Lea MacNally, Brian Martin, Richard Prior, and all the rifle-makers, in this country and abroad, who supplied me with much technical information. I am also grateful to Brian Hughes of the B.A.S.C. for his advice and technical help.

I would like to thank my wife, Shelagh, for her infinite patience and encouragement while the book was being prepared, and my father for his valuable recollections from over thirty years of hunting big game in India.

Finally, I would like to single out Clive Wordley of Marlborough Guns, Urchfont, without whose patience, interest, and deep fund of rifle-shooting lore, this book would not have been written.

PART ONE

THE RIFLE

1. History and Evolution of the Sporting Rifle

FOR two centuries after the introduction of gunpowder to the western hemisphere, around 1100 AD, its existence had very little effect on the traditions of hunting. The earliest published formulae for gunpowder were often vague and cryptic and the resulting mixtures were unreliable or burned too slowly to be useful as an explosive propellant. Indeed, the whole history of the development of firearms seems to have been hampered and even at times halted by religious opposition to the work of alchemists in their attempts to produce a reliable gunpowder and to the blacksmiths, bell-founders and locksmiths who strove to improve the weapons.

Even as late as the fifteenth century, hunting for sport was still dominated by the longbow and crossbow, which were far more effective and accurate than firearms. Compared to these powerful and easily-handled weapons, the early firearms were crude, noisy, unreliable and unwieldy. Most of the early guns were scaled-down cannons which required mounting on a forked stick or resting against a tree or wall in order to absorb the recoil. These 'hand guns' took the form of a crude and heavy metal tube which was sealed at one end and loaded from the other. Ignition was provided by either a flame or a glowing cord being placed in the touch hole to fire the powder. As a consequence, firing one of these weapons was a slow and laborious business and the hand gun was obviously not a suitable weapon for hunting deer, boar or wolf.

Nevertheless, its usefulness as a military weapon saw the slow development of the firearm as a weapon that could be successfully used by a foot soldier. By 1471 there are accounts of King Edward IV retaining a force of three hundred Flemish soldiers armed with 'Hange gonnes'. The weapons used by these soldiers were probably more developed than the simple tube in that the barrel was now mounted on a crossbow stock and fired from the shoulder – the harquebus had evolved.

It was already well understood that a crossbow bolt achieved stability in flight by the spin it was given from the airflow over the fins, and experimenters reasoned that as this spin promoted far greater accuracy in a crossbow bolt, then the same effect may be possible on a harquebus ball if it was induced to spin by scoring a spiral groove inside the barrel. Following this line of

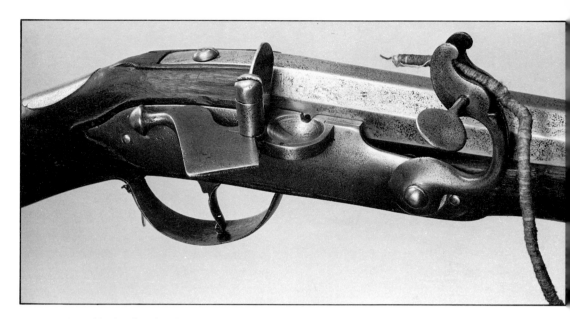

Matchlock rifle: the glowing 'match' ignited the powder in the pan and the resulting flash ignited the main charge. (*H.M. Tower of London Armoury*)

experimentation the first rifle was probably made during the last half of the fifteenth century. That rifles existed by 1477 can be inferred from the announcement of a harquebus shooting-contest at Eichstadt, Bavaria, at which shots were taken at a range of 200 paces – far beyond the accurate range of a smooth-bored weapon.

The earliest rifle which is still in existence is one of 24 bore, (.577in) which is dated around 1500 and was once owned by Maximillian I. Its powder measure gives a load of 115 grains of weak powder driving a ball of 292 grains. The ballistics are similar to those delivered from muzzle-loading rifles made nearly three hundred years later. Even so, the method of ignition was still very slow and unreliable restricting the rifle to use against stationary targets; and indeed, the sport of target shooting became well established in the time before the Thirty Years War (1618–48). In addition to the difficulty in loading, the rifle was also costly to manufacture and the inherent disadvantages of its ignition system meant that it was seldom looked on as a military weapon. The fact that it required a glowing fuse to be at hand whenever firing was imminent meant that a considerable amount of care was required to tend the match. During night-time manoeuvres, the soldiers were often betrayed by their glowing matches and the occasional shower of sparks, and on damp rainy days the match would often go out. In windy weather, sparks from the match were known to prematurely fire the weapons and even the powder store.

The invention of the wheel-lock around 1515 was a significant improvement on the older matchlock. In this new mechanism, a serrated steel wheel was rotated against a small piece of pyrites, and the resulting shower of sparks ignited the priming powder in a pan which then set off the main charge. With this system ignition was more certain and all the problems which were inherent

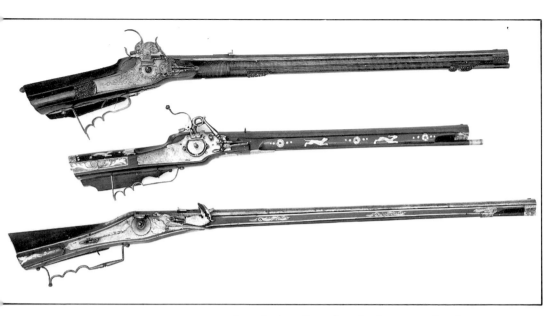

Three examples of early wheel-lock rifles. The complicated mechanism meant that they were expensive to make. (*H.M. Tower of London Armoury*)

in the matchlock were cured. Despite this, it did not readily catch on as a military weapon because the wheel-lock was very much more expensive to produce; but within the field of target shooting and hunting, it rapidly became very popular. Here then, was a weapon which could be hand held and was sufficiently accurate to merit serious consideration for use against live game. The new ignition system was also more dependable than the matchlock and the lock time – that is, the delay between pulling the trigger and the gun firing – was reduced, and the resulting weapon was recognised as the first real challenge to the crossbow and longbow for hunting deer, boar and wolf. The appearance and ready acceptance of the wheel-lock rifle sounded the death-knell of the stringed hunting weapons and heralded the future total domination of firearms in the pursuit of wild game. The sporting rifle had arrived.

During the rest of the sixteenth century development was hampered, not as in the past by religious opposition, but by the turmoil of the Thirty Years War which left much of the German arms industry in ruins. It was then left to the firearms manufacturers based in places such as Brescia and Gardone in Italy, and also in Holland to make two refinements which considerably widened the field in which rifles could be used.

Firstly, it became standard practice after about 1550 to use milled or 'canned' powder. This had the effect of preserving air spaces within the powder even after it had been rammed down during loading. In doing so the effect was to increase the strength of the powder by approximately one-third and to ensure a more consistent ignition with fewer misfires.

The second development was brought about by the quest for an ignition system which was both reliable and cheap. Using the wheel-lock as a starting point, a much simplified mechanism actually scraped the piece of pyrites on a strip of rough steel to produce the required shower of sparks. This lock, being far cheaper and simpler to make than the wheel-lock, was first produced by the Dutch and quickly taken up by makers in other European countries. It became known as the 'snaphaunce'. From the time of its appearance around 1580 this mechanism at last began to supplant the matchlock on military weapons and the firmly established reputation for long-range accuracy of the rifle over the infantry musket began to draw the attention of the more far-sighted military planners of the era.

Both the wheel-lock and the snaphaunce possessed one inherent disadvantage in that crystalline pyrite (well known as fool's gold) is prone to shatter when roughly treated, and the search was made in the latter part of the sixteenth and early seventeenth centuries for a more durable alternative. The obvious answer was to use flint and a number of experimental forms of flintlocks appeared before the final form was arrived at in 1630. This mechanism, initially termed the 'French lock', was to totally dominate all forms of shooting for the next two hundred years. Within this period the military flintlock was to develop into a range of weapons from accurate long-range rifles to close-range volley muskets. On the sporting side, the rifle was to evolve into many varied styles and calibres to suit a wide range of shooting situations and quarry species, and the sporting shotgun was to develop into a weapon of grace and beauty.

Initially though, the development of the flintlock in its final form stimulated great interest within military circles and the flintlock musket was quickly adopted as the standard infantry arm. In addition, many military strategists began to incorporate rifle shooters into their armies – either as separate entities as *chasseurs* or rifle companies to be used for skirmishing and minor actions, or within the main body of infantry as riflemen. By 1680 rifles were adopted for use by mounted cavalry and the English Life Guards, for instance, were equipped with eight carbines per company. The use of rifles from horseback required a more easily handled weapon and the carbine – a short-barrelled form of rifle – evolved.

If its acceptance by the military was astonishingly rapid, the flintlock was far less readily adopted by the sporting fraternity. Compared to the wheel-lock, the flintlock's lock-time was generally slower, and the flint generated fewer sparks than the wheel-lock's pyrites. This meant that, of the two, it was the wheel-lock which was deemed to be more reliable. However, the simplicity of the flint ignition system, together with increasingly slim and graceful lines that were possible on a gun using the flint system, caused the flintlock rifle to gradually supplant the earlier mechanism as the standard sporting weapon.

One of the major problems associated with these early rifles is that of loading. Once the charge of powder has been tipped down the barrel, the bullet – invariably a lead ball – would have to be seated on top of the powder, and this is where the difficulty lay. In order that the ball was induced to spin in flight it would have to 'take the rifling' as it was being loaded. To do this the ball had to be very slightly larger than the actual bore diameter of the rifle and consequently seating the ball correctly on the powder involved using a steel

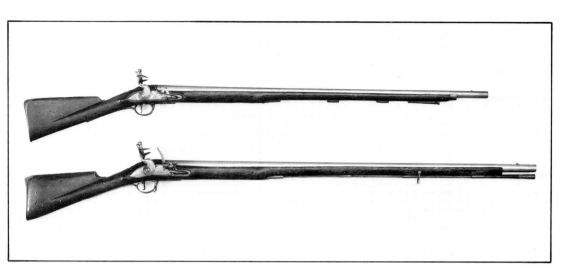

Two examples of flintlock weapons, which were far more reliable than matchlocks and cheaper to produce than wheel-locks. (*H.M. Tower of London Armoury*)

ramrod and a hammer and literally hammering the ball into place. This process often took considerably longer than loading a smooth-bored weapon and its disadvantage in the heat of battle is obvious.

This situation was considerably eased by the introduction, in the mid-seventeenth century, of the 'greased patch'. When it was realised that it was the actual spin of the ball and not the grooves left on it by the rifling that gave the rifle ball its accuracy, the practice of wrapping a ball in a small patch of greased cloth or thin leather greatly eased its passage down the barrel when loading, and gave the ball the required spin when it was fired. The rifle ball no longer had to be oversized, loading required far less force, and was thus greatly speeded up.

By 1700 the sporting rifle had developed a variety of calibres and styles. In central Europe there had evolved the light rifle for use against small game up to and including roe deer. For these the calibres ranged between .30in and .40in and they were deemed sufficiently accurate for these small targets up to about a hundred yards. Light rifles were also made for larger game, in calibres ranging up to .70in and, despite the heavy bullet, the rifles remained reasonably well balanced and portable so that they could be used in stalking sports. At the same time the driven shoot or 'battue' was already an established form of shooting and for these events the preference was for a heavier rifle. The shooters were placed in strategic hides and game driven towards them by a team of beaters. In these circumstances, portability was not as important as possessing a weapon that would cope with anything that appeared within a rather short range. Initially, this demanded a heavy rifle of large calibre, but later evolved into the 'drilling' combination shotgun/rifles which still remain popular on the continent today.

Throughout all this time England had shown a marked lack of interest in the development of rifles whether for sporting or military use, and the whole field of rifle making was dominated by the gunmakers of Germany, Austria,

Holland and northern Italy. Towns like Suhl, Brescia, Gardone and Herstal can trace a history of gunmaking back to the sixteenth century and are still in the forefront of European gunmaking today.

In England, the military preference was for a weapon that provided a 'hail of lead' at close quarters rather than long-range accuracy. In accordance with this the British Army adopted a weapon which, in its own way, was a departure from tradition. Designed to work even after a period of continuous firing despite powder residues fouling the barrel; designed also to provide rapid fire at close quarters and to have practically foolproof loading, the 'Brown Bess' Tower musket became the standard weapon of the British forces and was to remain so until as late as 1830. The fact that it lasted over a hundred years as the standard weapon speaks for the deadly effectiveness of the disciplined volley fire from the serried ranks of redcoats, but in terms of individual accuracy, the weapon was woefully lacking. At eighty yards the soldier was lucky to hit a human-sized target while at a hundred yards the task was considered impossible. Compared to this, the European rifleman could strike a fifteen-inch square at 200 yards with monotonous regularity.

Despite this, the smooth-bored musket remained the standard military weapon on both sides of the Channel and the European rifle was seen still as a predominantly sporting weapon. Rifle shooting, against both game and inanimate targets, was firmly established and different styles of rifle evolved to fulfil the variety of game and competition that existed. The evolution of the sporting rifle in Europe slowed to almost a standstill and future development was triggered by the expansion, during the mid and late eighteenth century, of the colonial empires of the European countries. During this period the emphasis for important developments in the sporting rifle shifted first to the Americas and then back to Britain as she expanded her Empire through Africa and Asia.

During the initial colonisation of the North American continent the settlers took with them examples of matchlock guns, wheel-locks and the early flintlocks. Around the settled eastern seaboard these weapons were to prove adequate for defence against the indigenous Indians. As the pioneer colonists spread into the interior, however, there arose a demand for a lighter, more accurate and more reliable rifle. Often these early pioneers lived by what they shot with their rifles, and they created a demand for an easily portable weapon of small bore which would use relatively small amounts of powder. Rate of fire was unimportant, accuracy the overriding consideration.

To answer these demands a rifle was developed which took on an almost standardised design. The calibre averaged around .45in and the stock was pared down to save weight. The rifling averaged about one turn in seven feet: the slow twist had the effect of allowing a heavier powder charge to drive the ball at a higher velocity while still taking the rifling. This prevented the tendency of the ball to strip when being pushed out at high velocity and also increased the effective range. An outstanding feature of this new type of rifle was its abnormally long barrel. Although made to this pattern in many states, this long-barrelled frontier rifle gained fame as the 'Kentucky rifle'.

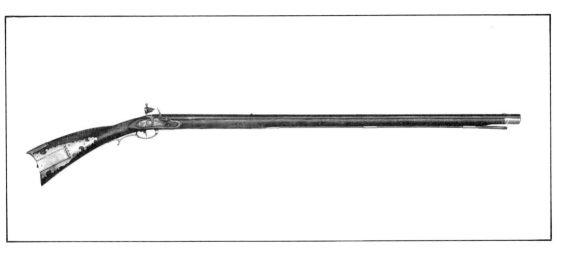

An early flintlock Kentucky rifle. As a long-range weapon, the Kentucky rifle proved to be far superior to the British army musket. (*H.M. Tower of London Armoury*)

The Kentucky rifle was far more than just a sporting rifle: to the frontiersman it was the tool on which he depended for survival and as such the American rifleman developed a higher degree of accuracy than had hitherto been seen. An experienced user would certainly be capable of placing ten shots in a 4-in group at a hundred yards, and the high velocity (often exceeding 2000 fps) meant that the trajectory varied little up to about 120 yards. Against the British infantry at the start of the War of Independence, the user of a well-made Kentucky rifle could pick off a man with reasonable certainty at 400 yards. As a weapon of war, though, it had severe limitations. For one thing it had a slow loading rate, and, perhaps more importantly, it tended to 'foul up' with powder residue after only a few shots. Even so, the use of this rifle caused the American militia to develop tactics which were unconventional for their day – raids and skirmishes with much sniping and long-range firing. The British, used to set-piece actions and lengthy manoeuvres, found this new strategy difficult to answer and it is fair to say that the Kentucky rifle made a significant contribution to the eventual American victory.

By the turn of the nineteenth century, the pace at which rifle development was progressing began to quicken. In America experiments proved that elongated bullets greatly improved the overall accuracy of the Kentucky rifle and these were adopted for sporting shooting and target competitions. For the frontiersman though, they were less practical as great care was needed to seat them on the powder charge without damaging their shape.

In Britain, the early years of the nineteenth century saw a succession of factors which led to the development of a particularly British style of rifle. Experiments in the early 1800s led to the standardisation of powder so that henceforth ballistics could be more uniform and predictable. After the end of the American War of Independence much had been done in Britain to increase the popularity of rifle shooting and by the end of the Napoleonic Wars skill with a rifle was a valued social advantage. The subsequent opening up of trade routes, particularly with India in the first instance, saw a great leap forward in

British rifle making. Big game hunting became the sport of the middle classes who went 'out east' to administer the new-found Empire, and the guns they took with them were of an unusual design.

Like the double-barrelled shotgun, the double rifle was first looked upon as being unsporting but it gradually gained acceptance, particularly as the new British explorers in Asia or Africa were, for the first time, being faced with large and very dangerous game. The English double rifle, like the American Kentucky rifle before it, was the product of the demands of explorers who pushed back the frontiers of the Empire. The designs evolved from experience in the shooting of game, first for the pot and later for sport, and bore no relation to the military weapons of the time. These were, purely and simply, sporting rifles.

Here, for the first time, there seemed to be a clear divergence of interest between the requirements of the target shooter and that of the big-game hunter. The former naturally placed accuracy as a top priority, regardless of such considerations as calibres and velocity. The latter, on the other hand, placed a higher value on velocity, penetration and killing power, and this is where the problem lay. A rifle would shoot most accurately with a well-fitting ball or bullet propelled by a light charge of powder. In order to increase its killing power, however, the usual method was to increase the powder charge thereby increasing the velocity; but this then caused 'stripping' whereby the soft lead ball would be travelling at too high a speed up the barrel to take the spin of the rifling. Even in big-game hunting rifles, velocities had to be controlled at a moderate level to prevent stripping, and so the only other way to increase power was to build larger calibre weapons.

The way in which modern shotguns are categorised by their bore sizes is a leftover from the days when the calibres of all firearms were denoted by the number of lead balls, each exactly fitting the interior diameter of the barrel, which were required to make up 1lb in weight. Thus, a 16-bore weapon, whether a smooth-bored shotgun or a rifle, was one in which a lead ball exactly fitting the barrel weighed one ounce. From this it can be seen that the smaller the bore number, the larger the weapon.

The search for greater knock-down power led to some ferocious weapons being produced, and by all accounts they seemed to be necessary. In one instance during the 1830s R. Gordon-Cummings took on an elephant while armed with a 12-bore rifle made by Dicksons and a 6-bore rifle from a Dutch maker. After thirty-five shots from the 12-bore he switched to the larger rifle and only after another five did he observe the unfortunate elephant begin to show signs of a 'delapidated condition'.

In the light of such experiences, it is hardly surprising that rifles around the 10-bore were considered the norm, with even larger calibres for dangerous game. Sir Samuel Baker, in his expedition to Ceylon, carried a 4-bore rifle by Gibbs and an 8-bore by Blisset as his back-up. The 4-bore was a formidable weapon weighing all of 21lb, but the rifle he demanded for Africa was even better: made by Holland and Holland, it fired a shell weighing eight ounces and powered by ten drams of powder. Even though he was a large framed and

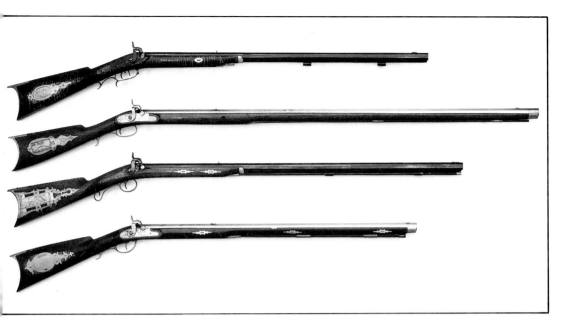

Four examples of percussion rifles. By far the best of muzzle-loading designs, percussion rifles were quickly superseded by breech-loading rifles. (*H.M. Tower of London Armoury*)

muscular man, this rifle frightened him and he seldom fired it – in later life he blamed his 2-bore for the incurable gun flinch he had developed.

In 1807 the sporting rifle underwent its first fundamental change for two hundred years. A Reverend Forsyth in Scotland devised a composition based on a fulminate of mercury which would ignite when subjected to a sharp blow. The implication of this discovery was quickly seized upon by many gunmakers and there followed a decade of feverish invention and experimentation before a completely new ignition system was established. The percussion rifle and shotgun first appeared in the 1820s and the flintlock, after 200 years of unchallenged superiority and dominance, was finally superseded and fell rapidly from use.

The advantages of the percussion system were immediately obvious. The percussion cap was placed on the nipple which channelled the flash directly into the powder charge when the cap was struck. Ignition was practically instantaneous and the more rapid burn of the main charge led to greater velocity and less fouling. The percussion cap brought the first really reliable method of firing a weapon and its popularity continued even after it was superseded by cartridge firing breech-loading mechanisms.

However, the more efficient combustion of the main charge did tend to increase velocity and therefore cause an increase in bullet stripping. Two methods of barrel boring and rifling were devised which went some way towards solving the problem. In England experiments were made to ascertain the best method of preventing bullet stripping and the conclusion arrived at by many rifle-makers was the 'two-groove' system. The internal bore of a rifle of this kind would have the rifling take the form of two deep recessed grooves

Cross-section of a two-groove rifle barrel. The 'fin' on the side of the bullet fitted the groove and allowed heavier powder charges to be used without the risk of the bullet stripping in the rifle.

which matched the 'fins' on the ball or conical bullet. When carefully loaded, either type of projectile could be driven at a higher velocity without the danger of stripping and it was James Purdey who first used the term 'express' rifle to describe his two-groove rifles of 40-bore. The only apparent drawback with this system was the recoil which was often quite ferocious.

In both Britain and America experiments with 'progressive' rifling were carried out and a very high degree of accuracy was achieved from rifles bored in this way. It was reasoned that stripping could be avoided if the ball or bullet was started on a slow spin which progressively increased through the length of the barrel. In practice this worked reasonably well: there was less strain on the bullet and the accuracy obtained was better than anything that had previously been achieved. But although the progressive twist achieved success in target competitions, it was less successful in sporting rifles where any increase in powder would upset the delicate balance between the bullet's grip on the rifling in the barrel and the speed at which this began to break down and the bullet began to strip.

In America the flintlock Kentucky rifle gave way to a percussion-action rifle of shorter barrel and generally heavier bore. This new design, often referred to as the Plains rifle, retained the same slow twist as its predecessor and was considered suitable for any game likely to be encountered on the North American plains. With a heavy octagonal barrel about 30in long, the bore size averaged around .54in and accuracy was judged to be good enough to put shots into a 12-in circle at 200 yards. Though it was the mainstay weapon in the great push westwards across the American continent, and remained popular as a sporting rifle even after the introduction of breech-loading rifles, it never really became popular in Europe. Though proven to be effective against the North American buffalo it was still far too underpowered to effectively match the sort of dangerous animals that the European white hunter had to contend with in Africa and Asia.

In Britain three separate styles of weapon evolved during the height of the percussion era. For shooting small game there was the specialist 'rook and rabbit' rifle. This was a low velocity, lightly loaded rifle, accurate up to about seventy yards and seldom called upon to shoot beyond that range. The calibre varied around 70-bore (approx. 40in). To make a narrower bored weapon would increase the problems of loading with a thin and consequently delicate ramrod as well as increasing the problems of powder fouling between shots. These weapons were usually made as single-barrel rifles and were bored with multigroove rifling intended for use with a 'patched' ball. Light and easily handled, they produced little recoil and they did much to establish the sport of small-game rifle shooting and vermin control which has continued to the present day.

Prince Albert, Prince Consort to Queen Victoria, focused public attention on the joys of stalking deer in the Scottish Highlands, and the new vogue for deer stalking produced the first specialist stalking rifles. These again were single-barrel weapons, though later the double rifle came to be accepted, and the calibre ranged around 16-bore (.66in). Firing a one-ounce ball at moderate velocity, they were stated to be accurate up to about 200 yards, though shots were more often taken at half this distance. For long days stalking on 'the hill' the rifle had to be soundly made, weatherproof and portable: all these qualities were found in the purpose-built medium calibre stalking rifles of the time.

For those travelling overseas, the big-game rifle (or rifles) became almost an essential part of the tropical kit. These heavy weapons ranged from about 12-bore up to 4-bore and used a formidable array of conical bullets or lead balls. Even so, their powder charges had to remain relatively light in order to induce the heavy projectile to take up the rifling when it was fired. To encourage this, special slow burning powders were developed to give the bullet a steady 'push' up the barrel, and longer barrels were required to develop sufficient velocity. Initially, as with the stalking rifle, these heavy-calibre weapons were made with single barrels, and indeed throughout this period of Empire exploration single-shot heavy rifles continued to be made in some quantity. When using these weapons, it was assumed that a gun-bearer would be close at hand to provide the back-up rifle for a quick second shot. However, when faced with a wounded and angry rhino, bison or big cat, it soon became clear that a double rifle gave the shooter a decided advantage, and weapons of this type rapidly became the most popular of all sporting rifles.

The double big-game rifle is considered by many to be the pinnacle in the art of gunmaking. Certainly they were costly to produce and required many hours of careful regulating if they were to be anything like accurate. In a single-barrel rifle it is a comparatively simple matter to align the sights and the barrel so that the weapon shoots to the point of aim at a given distance. In a double rifle, on the other hand, it is extremely difficult to align both barrels so that they have the same point of impact at, say, a hundred yards, and this is where the true skill and patience of a gunmaker is tested to the utmost. In addition, a double rifle is far more sensitive to the effects of recoil and to atmospheric temperature than its single-barrel counterpart. When firing a single-barrel rifle, the barrel (it is hoped) lies along the central long axis of the weapon and the recoil gives a straight back push against the shoulder. In a double rifle, however, the barrels lie on either side of the long axis so that the left barrel will 'pull' the shot to the left and the right to the right. In making both barrels shoot to the same point of aim the gunmaker would need to compensate for this tendency. Account also

Black powder produces a great deal of smoke when it is fired, often obscuring the target for a few seconds. When shooting dangerous game at close quarters the result could be dramatic. (*Firle Pigeon and Gun Club*)

had to be taken of the fact that high temperatures alter the rate at which the propellant powders burn. In the hot tropical regions the powder would burn more rapidly, giving increased velocity which in turn reduced the effect of the 'sideways pull' of each barrel when fired. The net result of this was that if the rifle was regulated in Britain to shoot at one aiming point, under tropical conditions the right barrel would shoot to the left and vice versa. One further problem was that a double barrel could only be regulated to shoot to one point while using a stated and specific bullet weight and powder charge. Any deviation from this would throw the impact point of each barrel apart. Once regulated, therefore, the shooter had to stick to the stated load if the rifle was to remain on zero.

With all the foregoing to consider, it is hardly surprising that the double rifle, even from the very best makers, never achieved the target accuracy that was possible with the single-barrelled weapon. Still, a well-made double would group into a 4-in circle at a hundred yards and this was more than adequate for the purpose for which the rifle was intended.

Before the advent of the two-groove rifling system, many hunters felt that double rifles lacked the knock-down power needed when dealing with dangerous game and for a short while they took to very heavy, large-bored 'ball guns'. These were smooth-bored double-barrel weapons of between 8- and 4-bore which, because they were not rifled, could take large charges of powder. At short range a lead ball weighing between two and four ounces propelled by a heavy charge of powder certainly proved to be devastating enough to cope with charging elephants. The one problem, of course, was that any smooth-bored gun was inaccurate at ranges of over fifty yards so their use was restricted to often very hair-raising close encounters. To add further to the excitement, the powder produced a great deal of smoke when the rifle was fired so the shooter often lost sight of his target after the first shot. Accounts by such famous hunters as Sir Samuel Baker re-tell instances when the first indication of an unsuccessful initial shot at a charging beast was when its very angry face appeared through the smoke!

At the time when James Purdey was developing his first express rifles of 40-bore on the two groove system, experiments with ways in which lead could be 'hardened' had made some progress. A new compound of hardened lead, in which pewter containing tin was added to soft lead, produced a bullet which was less prone to stripping. When used in the newly developed two-groove express rifles these bullets allowed progressively heavier charges of powder to be used, thereby producing higher velocities, flatter trajectories and increased knock-down power. After 1856, when the Purdey express 40-bore first appeared, the term was used for any calibre rifle which produced these higher velocities and greater striking energies. The same power was obtainable from the smaller calibre express rifle as from the large bored big-game rifles and ball guns. The way was now clear to develop these smaller-bored weapons to their full potential and the 4- and 8-bore rifles were soon abandoned in favour of an express rifle of between 40- and 70-bore.

The last half of the nineteenth century witnessed the gunmaking industries of Britain, Europe and North America in a turmoil of experimentation and development which produced an amazing variety of weapons, and the pace at which firearms technology advanced reached a peak which has not been equalled since. In 1850 the standard firearm for both military and sporting use was a rifled muzzle loader using the percussion ignition system, yet by 1900 practically every form of modern sporting rifle had been developed, the muzzle loaded powder charge and ball had given way to a range of solid drawn brass rifle cartridges of both centrefire and rimfire ignition systems, and a variety of jacketed and hollow-point bullets were advertised as approaching velocities of 3000 fps in some calibres. The new nitro-cellulose based powders were rapidly superseding the old black powder and the new propellants were generating muzzle energies which were unheard of only fifty years before.

In the early part of this period a small number of rifles were constructed on the 'capping breech-loader' principle. These weapons, fired by a percussion cap in the same way as a muzzle loader, could nevertheless be loaded from the breech end. The advantages of this were that the bullet was not flattened or pushed out of shape by the action of a ramrod, thus greatly aiding accuracy, and powder fouling ceased to be a problem as the fresh bullet pushed all the fouling out of the barrel before it when the rifle was fired. Of the capping breech-loader systems devised, perhaps the two most successful were those by Prince and by Callisher and Terry.

In Prince's design the barrel unlocked and slid forward to expose the breech for loading. Into this was inserted the bullet and powder charge (the latter was contained in a paper cartridge). The barrel was then slid backwards onto the action and locked and the percussion cap placed in position. The flash from the cap was sufficient to penetrate the paper and ignite the powder.

The Callisher and Terry rifle is an early example of a bolt action weapon, again using the paper-cased powder charge but with modifications which allowed the rifling to be cleared of fouling during the rifle's discharge. While neither of these rifles received widespread acclaim, they were nevertheless important milestones in that they made more people aware of the advantages of a breech-loading rifle.

In 1851, the Lefauchaux double pinfire shotgun was first exhibited at the Paris Exhibition, and, despite initial and sometimes bitter opposition, took the shotgun world by storm. From this design there evolved progressively improved pinfire, then centrefire breech-loading shotguns which culminated, by the turn of the century, in the hammerless ejector boxlock and sidelock double shotguns, many of which are still in use today.

The rifle-shooting fraternity were less impressed. For one thing, the Lefauchaux design could barely withstand the light pressures exerted by shotgun cartridges, let alone the heavy punishment of the express rifle. For another, the percussion rifle had, they believed, reached a pinnacle of elegance and reliability which could not be matched by the new-fangled breech loader. Any heavy charges tended to damage the hinge under the barrels so that they would not fit tight to the standing breech – the rifle was said to have 'shot loose' and the barrels to have 'blown off the face' of the action.

Despite this, many of the more progressive gunmakers introduced improvements which, within the decade, were to see the drop-down breech-loading double become established as a rifle as well as a shotgun. Though as yet the double's construction was still too weak for the express rifles, medium velocity deer-stalking rifles were produced using pinfire ammunition and these gained acceptance as suitable weapons for use in the Scottish Highlands.

At the same time as the design of double breech-loading rifles was progressing, so were efforts made to improve on the pinfire cartridge. There were three major flaws in the design of this type of ammunition. The pin, protruding as it did from the base of the cartridge, was susceptible to detonation if it was handled carelessly. In addition, there was a tendency for gas to leak past the pin when the weapon was fired; as this blew back just in front of the shooter's face, the ammunition was not a great success. Finally, when the rifle was loaded, the pin had to be carefully aligned with the recess in the breech-end of the barrel and this was found to be fiddly and time consuming.

Many experiments were carried out to try to find a better system. Charles Lancaster produced some double rifles on his oval-bore rifling system. These cartridges were detonated by his 'base fire' patent system whereby the cartridge

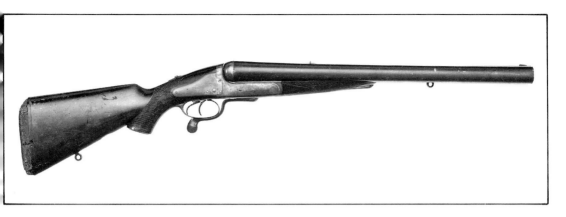

A massive four-bore elephant rifle built with two-groove rifling and firing a 4 oz conical bullet. (H.M. *Tower of London Armoury*)

was struck in the centre of its base. Made in the deer-stalking calibre of .498, it achieved some popularity before it was superseded by a better development. In 1861 George Daw produced a centrefire shotgun cartridge in which the cap was recessed centrally in the base. That he copied the design from Pollet in France and Schneider in Germany may have resulted in his failure to secure the patent and this contributed to its rapid and almost universal acceptance as the ideal shotgun ignition system. This time, the riflemen were not far behind. Coming as it did at the same time as the powerful and reliable under-lever, screw-grip method of locking the barrels of a double gun in place, it meant that by the early 1870s the double-barrelled centrefire sporting rifle had appeared, and was being built in all bore sizes from rook-and-rabbit calibres to elephant guns.

Now that bullets could be made to fit the bore exactly and there was no risk of them being distorted by a ramrod, the two-groove rifling system was no longer necessary. The rifling in these new breech loaders evolved to one in which the broad but shallow grooves and lands were of equal width. In addition, the restrictions placed on small calibres by the ramrod were removed and there was a general trend towards smaller calibres for shooting small game and deer in Britain. The .360in became a popular deer calibre and small-game rifles were made as small as .250in. Overseas though, old preferences died hard and many double and single barrelled 8- and 4-bores were made for this market. Such weapons, now shooting as well if not better than the old two-groove percussion rifle, and with the additional advantage of ease and speed of loading, could deliver a tremendous knock-down blow to any game. Lord de Grey illustrated this by scoring a left and right at rhino using a double 4-bore rifle in 1883.

Gradually, these large-bore rifles were replaced by more modest calibres and by the mid 1880s the most useful began to emerge as the leaders for their particular brand of sport. Express rifles in the range from .577in to .450in were classed in the medium-to-heavy league according to the type of cartridge they used. By now, the paper cases had been replaced by drawn brass cases of varying shape and length, and the rifle's power could no longer be assessed merely by the bore diameter. A .450 using a parallel brass case would only be suitable for medium-to-small game whereas an express rifle of the same calibre using a 'bottlenecked' case would be powerful enough for most large game. Medium or deer-stalking calibres ranged down to the popular .360, and the rook-and-rabbit rifles developed a wide variety of smaller calibres.

With the ability to produce a wide range of velocities from the various calibres came the need to develop different bullets to suit a variety of targets. Heavy, thick-skinned game required a bullet which would have the ability to penetrate deep into the animal before dissipating its energy; yet the same kind of bullet would pass straight through a 'soft-skinned' animal such as a tiger, without doing too much harm. Similarly, a bullet used for deer stalking, designed to break up quickly, would probably fail to penetrate one of the large cats, leaving it with a surface wound and a very angry frame of mind. Bullet selection was therefore second only in importance to the actual rifle and a wide range of bullets were produced in hard lead and soft lead as solids, hollow-points, round nosed and flat (bluff) nosed – each with its own merits for a particular kind of target.

The double rifle of this period achieved a grace and elegance which was as much as expression of the engraver's artistry as the gunmaker's skill. Though following the lead set by the shotguns, the rifle did tend to put more emphasis on the strength of the action – not surprisingly, as the chamber pressures and recoil were so much greater than in a shotgun. The rotary underbolt locking system therefore persisted in the rifle long after the shotgun had gone over to top-lever opening, and back-action locks were usually preferred to the more stylish bar-action as this provided a more robust action body. Stocks were usually furnished with a pistol grip and, in the heavier rifles, recoil pads were fitted on the butt and cheekpiece. After 1880 the traditional Damascus barrels made from alternating strips of steel and iron were replaced by those made of steel, and in this respect the rifle actually led the shotgun in development. Steel as a material had two decided advantages when used in a rifle barrel. It could be cut into cleaner rifling and it was more resistant to wear so that the actual barrel life was considerably longer than a similar one made by the Damascus method. In addition, the 1880s saw the gradual introduction of nitro powders which tended to be more corrosive than the black powder. Steel barrels were observed to resist this corrosion better than the older Damascus and they also proved, in the following years, to be able to withstand the higher chamber pressures associated with these new propellants.

Even though the double rifle had advanced thus far in strength and elegance, it still could not compete with the single-barrel rifle in terms of accuracy. A .500 double express rifle of 1880 developed a velocity of around 2000 fps with a 350 grain bullet, but at best it would be expected to achieve a 6-in group at a hundred yards. While this was considered adequate for tiger shooting, it would not satisfy shooters who required either greater precision at the existing ranges or those who demanded longer range. For these, the single barrel was still the first choice. In South Africa, for instance, the Boers respected a rifle which would have a dependable trajectory to around 800 yards and there are numerous accounts of these settlers shooting game at ranges up to 500 yards. Among such people the Westley Richards falling-block rifle firing a 500 grain bullet and the .577 Martini-Henry rifle were considered to be the best.

In Britain, three single shot rifles stood out as the favourites. By far the simplest was the single barrel 'drop-down' action rifle built to the same design and often to the same quality as the double. Improvements in barrel locking and rifling ensured that these weapons performed well and produced far tighter groups than did their double counterparts.

Then there was the Martini action single shot rifle. In this design the breech-block was hinged at the rear of the action and when the opening lever behind the trigger guard was pushed downwards, the breech face dropped to expose the chamber. This 'falling block' ensured that the cartridge was easily loaded and firmly positioned when the gun was closed. As a service rifle the Martini-Henry proved to be strongly made and reliable, and the action was readily adapted for use in any calibre rifle. Its one disadvantage was that it could not be cleaned from the breech-end without dismantling the rifle. But rifles in this configuration had many devoted followers, and such is its strength and reliability that Martini-actioned target rifles are still made; there is even a 12-bore shotgun, the Greener 'GP'.

By far the most popular, and possibly the most accurate, single-shot rifle produced in Britain during this period was built to the Farquharson falling block design which was patented in 1872. Again operated by an under-lever, placed this time forward of the trigger guard, the breech-block slid downwards to expose the chamber. When closed, the block was locked in place and the very design of the action produced a uniformity of ballistics which could never be attained with a double rifle. Though substantially modified, single-shot hunting rifles based on the Farquharson action have recently been introduced and have borne out the original rifle's reputation for accuracy.

If Britain led the field in the development of the double rifle, then the United States certainly came to dominate the development of the repeating rifle. In Britain the stimulus had been the increasing number of sporting hunters throughout an expanding Empire; in the United States the chief catalyst in the rapid development of the rifle was the struggle for military superiority during the American Civil War.

As a young nation pushing westwards into unsettled territory, the United States had already developed firearms which had gained international respect. The flintlock Kentucky rifle and later the percussion Plains rifle had set a foundation on which the American arms manufacturers were to flourish during the latter half of the nineteenth century.

Even as early as 1840 experiments with ways in which to increase the firepower of a rifle had produced the Colt revolving carbine. Based on a revolving cylinder which contained a number of pre-loaded chambers, the colt carbine saw action against American Indians but never really proved a success. In its earliest forms there was a great deal of gas leakage between the chamber and the barrel; and while this did not really matter in a pistol held at arm's length, in a rifle this happened closer to the shooter's face. Add to this the tendency to multiple discharge – the flash from the cylinder being fired igniting other loaded cylinders – and it is easy to understand why the action was regarded with suspicion.

Up to 1850 muzzle-loading percussion hunting rifles were still produced to the Kentucky and Plains designs; but spurred on perhaps by the development of breech-loading firearms in Europe and by the increasing tension between the North and South, the pace at which new types of firearms developed increased rapidly over the next decade. In 1855 an experimental rifle was produced by Messrs Smith and Wesson which was the forebear of a long and distinguished line. Designed on an experimental rimfire cartridge of .50 calibre, the rifle's magazine was a tube slung beneath the barrel and the reloading mechanism was activated by throwing a combined hand-lever and trigger guard forward. Returning to its normal position closed the action with a fresh round in the chamber. The lever action rifle had arrived.

In the following year, the Volcanic Repeating Arms Co. marketed the Volcanic carbine in .38 calibre. Based on the same principle, the ammunition took the form of 'self-powered' bullets. These were bullets whose base was hollowed out to take a charge of fulminate mixture. Though the rifle was of good design, the ammunition was its downfall. The average velocity obtained was only about 500 fps which severely limited the effective range and in addition the sensitivity of the fulminate mixture often caused the ammunition to explode while it was being fed into or out of the magazine. By 1860 the production of these rifles had stopped.

At the same time, a variety of rimfire metal-cased cartridges were being developed and in 1860 the Henry rifle using .44 rimfire ammunition was introduced. Unlike the Volcanic, this lever-action 15-shot rifle produced 1200 fps in its semi-pointed bullet, and both rifle and ammunition were readily accepted by a nation preparing for civil war. In the same year the Colt .44 revolving carbine also appeared. Now a much improved solid-framed rifle, the adoption of metallic ammunition meant that a cure had been found for the previous shortcomings of this design, and this rifle, like the Henry, was to see action in the Civil War.

One other pre-war development was to have far-reaching effects. A small rimfire saloon target round was produced to a Flobert design. Like the Volcanic ammunition, the only propellant was the fulminate cap, but unlike it the small round known as the bulleted cap was designed for a pistol and it was successfully developed. Early trials during 1857 showed that the empty case was difficult to extract and this was cured by lengthening the case and increasing the powder charge – in this way the .22 rimfire came into being. From these early experiments has grown the world's most popular rifle calibre.

At the start of the American Civil War in 1861 both sides were still equipped with muzzle-loading percussion rifles, the standard rifle on the Union side for example, was a .58 calibre long-barrelled rifle from the Springfield armoury, although both sides experimented with, and adopted, a wide variety of other firearms. One that did emerge which later evolved into a sporting weapon was the Sharps Carbine. Built in .54 calibre with a 22in barrel, this again was a single-shot muzzle-loading percussion rifle in its original form, and from it came the term used to describe an accurate rifle-shooter – 'Sharpshooter'. Spencer carbines were held in similar esteem.

If the Americans began their Civil War armed predominantly with muzzle-loading rifles, they emerged looking to the rapid development of effective breech-loading repeating rifles. After the war, the US cavalry set about re-arming with breech-loading rifles and the 1871 Springfield carbine was chosen. This weapon, modelled on the style of the Sharps and Spencer carbines, was issued in 45–70 calibre and featured a 'trapdoor' loading system for its single shot. Though the cartridge was powerful enough, when faced with Indians armed with Winchester lever action rifles, their slow reloading rate was a decided handicap. This single-shot carbine design did, however, produce the sporting rifle popularly known as the 'Buffalo' gun in the more powerful calibres, and the Sharps model '74 in 44–77 calibre epitomises the style. (American gunmakers avoided the confusion of calibres that blighted the English gunmakers of the period by citing the bore diameter then the powder charge: thus the 45–70 was a .45in diameter bullet driven by 70 grains of powder.)

Winchester had taken over the production of lever action rifles with their .44 rimfire model 66 immediately after the war, and the transition to centrefire was made in the famous Winchester '73 in that year. An 1888 catalogue of the Great Western Gun Works lists the model 73 in .22 rimfire, .32, 38–40 and 44–40 calibres. At the same time the newer model 86 lever action is offered in no less than thirteen different calibres. The Winchester lever-action as a weapon for self-defence, for survival, or as a sporting rifle totally dominated North America.

In 1885 one other important development took place in that Colt finally abandoned the revolving principle in a rifle and produced the Colt Sporting Carbine – the first pump action rifle. Like other repeaters, the magazine was in the form of a tube beneath the barrel, but reloading was accomplished by sliding the fore-end to the rear and then pushing it forward again. The rearward movement unlocked the bolt and ejected the spent case, and pushing the fore-end forward fed a new round into the chamber and closed the action. This principle was quickly copied and by 1890 a number of arms manufacturers were making pump action rifles.

By the turn of the century the 'American rifle' was well established as a short-barrelled repeating weapon built either as a lever or pump action. Unlike the British rifles, they were a product of a rapidly expanding demand that could not be met other than by mass production. The single-shot buffalo guns satisfied the need for an accurate long-range rifle and the repeaters were sufficiently accurate up to about 150 yards to provide an adequate woodland or brush hunting rifle. Compared to the British calibres, all the American cartridges came into the medium-power bracket, yet they were perfectly adequate for any game the hunter was likely to encounter. The one major development left was to produce an automatic-loading rifle, and this Remington achieved in the first decade of this century. Their Model 8 self-loading rifle, based on the long-recoil system devised by John M. Browning, opened a new avenue which other American rifle-makers, with all their experience in producing repeating rifles, were quick to explore.

In Europe, progress in the development of new rifles was less spectacular, and here the accent was far more on military weapons than those used for sporting purposes. The European powers, jostling for military advantage in the wake of industrial revolutions, finally discarded their percussion rifled muskets in the late 1850s. From then on there is a history of trials and shooting tests in each country to evaluate the military potential of each new design as it came along. Along the way what were originally military calibres and actions permeated through to the sporting rifle scene and names like Krag and Metford still occasionally appear in a sporting context. Two military rifle actions designed during this period stand out above all others in their influence on sporting rifles. Both are bolt-action repeating mechanisms which originated in successful military weapons; both are fed from a clip-type magazine; and although both appeared in the last years of the nineteenth century, they are still made in an unmodified form for sporting rifles today.

The influence on the sporting rifle exerted by the German Mauser and the Austrian Mannlicher rifles cannot by overstated. To the British gunmakers goes the credit of creating beautiful and fearsomely powerful double rifles for big game; to the USA goes the acknowledgement that they have led the world in the design and production of high fire-power repeating and self-loading rifles; but to Mauser and Mannlicher goes the credit for combining simplicity of operation with accuracy which approached 'target-rifle quality' in practically any calibre.

By the first decade of this century the sporting rifle had developed accuracy, ease of loading, a variety of styles and a range of calibres that would have been unthinkable a mere sixty years earlier. The sporting rifle, as we know it today, had arrived.

2. CALIBRES, BULLETS AND SIGHTS

THE beginning of this century up to the outbreak of the Second World War was a period of gradual transition and development in sporting-rifle ballistics. Although the 'smokeless' nitro powders were first introduced in the late nineteenth century, it took some time to develop powders that were equal to, let alone better than, the best quality black powders of the day. So different were the two types of propellant that it was a very difficult task to replace a black-powder cartridge with one containing nitro powder in the same calibre and achieve comparable performance. In the early days the new nitro powders were less reliable, produced lower velocities and were more susceptible to changes in temperature than the black powder they replaced. In later years many of the smokeless powders generated far higher chamber pressures and constituted a very real danger if used in a weapon not designed for nitro powder. Thus, rather than replace black powder with nitro in the existing calibres, a whole new generation of rifles came into existence, designed for the new propellants and exploiting the advantages that these possessed. This was not a rapid revolution but a slow and gradual process as the old black-powder rifles were gently phased out and one by one the modern nitro calibres were introduced.

By the 1930s three distinct 'families' of rifles existed. Slowly dying out were the centrefire black-powder and cordite express rifles, and their place was being taken by a range of new 'high velocity' nitro-powered calibres, the best of which are still going strong today. The third group which first developed in the early percussion days as rook-and-rabbit rifles was also slowly declining.

By the mid 1930s, legislative pressure was bringing about the rook rifle's demise. Many country people in Britain lamented their loss as, in their final form, they were delightful little weapons. A typical rook rifle had a short octagonal single barrel which was shallow rifled with a slow twist. Most were built with a drop-down action in a variety of hammer, semi-hammerless and hammerless designs, and the sights were usually a simple blade fore-sight and non-adjustable 'V' backsight. Nevertheless, they were extremely accurate within a short range and they admirably fulfilled the role for which they were built. The qualities needed for rook-and-rabbit shooting required a light, handy

Rook rifles were simple weapons which were nevertheless excellent for vermin control at restricted ranges.

rifle which would fire a bullet at low or moderate velocity, and which was accurate up to about seventy yards. Beyond this range the bullet velocity would fall away rapidly so as to minimise the danger of a long ricochet and a wide fallout area. This was particularly important in a small and densely populated country like Britain. The ballistics of these rook rifles made them far safer than the weapon that was to replace them as the small-game and vermin calibre after the Second World War. While the .22 Long Rifle rimfire will carry up to one mile, the rook rifle would barely reach half this distance. Rook rifle calibres, now long forgotten, ranged from the .380 long, through .360, .320 long, .300 rook and down to .255. All were centrefire cartridges of low power, minimum recoil and 'quiet' report. Rifles were usually of a sound and well-made quality, often coming from high quality gunmakers that specialised in these little weapons, and some were even made in 'best' grade with fine engraving and figured woodwork. Holland and Holland, Purdey, and Rigby were noted almost as much for their rook rifles as they were for their other firearms. Sadly, most of those that survived are now relegated to wall-hangers or have been bored out to .410 shotguns. Even overseas, where they had served well as 'pot fillers' on hunting expeditions, the lack of ammunition for these calibres after 1945 meant that they were quickly abandoned in favour of the .22 rimfire.

A 1938 catalogue for Manton and Co. of Calcutta highlights the fact that the black-powder rifle calibres lingered on in both India and Africa for a long time after the nitro rifles had superseded them. By way of comparison, the .577 black-powder express cartridge drove a 570 grain bullet and produced around 3700 ft/lb energy while the .577 nitro, on the other hand, drove a 750 grain

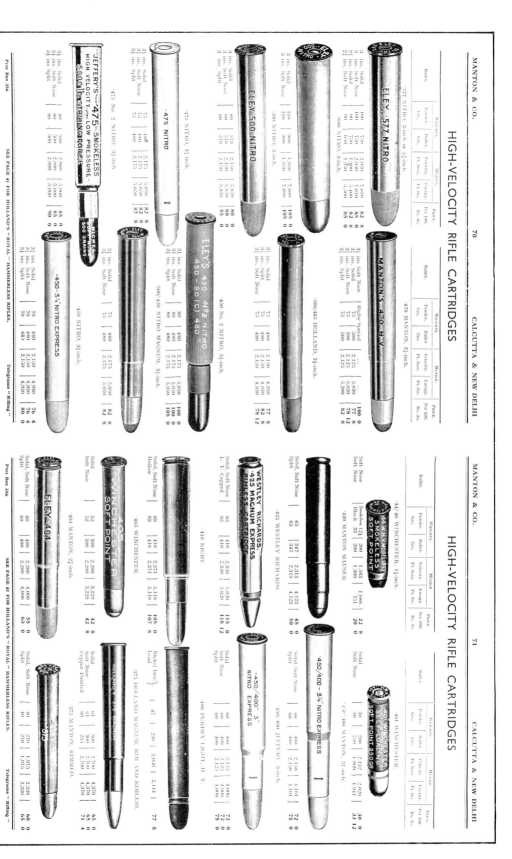

The 1938 catalogue of Manton in Calcutta listed ammunition for eighteen 'heavy' calibres, each generating over 4000 ft/lb muzzle energy.

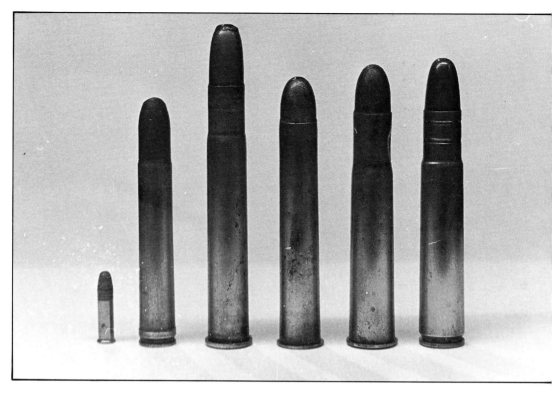

Four examples of the older British 'heavies' with two modern calibres for comparison. (*left to right*) .22 LR and .458 Winchester Magnum (both modern); .475 nitro, .500, .577/500, .505.

bullet and produced over 7000 ft/lb energy. Even so there was still a steady demand for a whole range of black-powder or their equivalent low pressure 'light nitro' cartridges for calibres ranging from the .577 BP Express down to the little .300 Sherwood. Many sportsmen preferred these calibres to the new nitro rifles because they generated safer breech pressures, were generally lighter in recoil and were just as effective if used within their limitations. Those in the .577 down to the .500/450 Magnum were considered suitable for medium-to-large and dangerous game, and were often termed the 'heavy' black-powder rifles. Calibres ranging from the .500/450 express to the .450/400 express were deemed suitable for large deer or other medium game and the .360 express and .300 Sherwood for progressively smaller gazelles and deer species. Again, the Second World War curtailed production of the ammunition for these rifles and by about 1950 they were all obsolete except for those in the hands of enthusiasts and collectors.

Any rifle ammunition list of the period between the wars points to the fact that these were the 'Golden Years' for the British heavy-calibre rifle. Eley's list, for example, contains sixteen separate rifle calibres upwards of .400.

These weapons, utilising the far more powerful nitro powders produce muzzle energies which, by modern standards, are phenomenal. The lightest of this group is the Purdey .400 Light High Velocity round designed for deer and generating just over 2000 ft/lb from a 230 grain bullet. Calibres increase through the .450/400 Nitro Express, .404 Jeffrey and .416 Rigby on to the .500, .577 and finally the mighty .600 Nitro. This fearsome round threw a 900 grain bullet at 7600 ft/lb energy – more than enough to stop the charge of anything large, thick-skinned and angry. Declining game stocks, through over-exploitation and, more importantly, loss of habitat to agriculture, curtailed the hunting of these large creatures and it is only recently that the newly emergent African nations have opened their countries to hunting safaris. By allowing foreign sportsmen to cull their surplus game stocks they benefit in two ways – the game is managed, and they gain valuable foreign currency in the process. This trend has been highlighted by the fact that many riflemakers in Britain are now producing heavy rifles in a variety of these calibres again.

The post-war conversion of Britain's Empire to the Commonwealth of independent nations drastically reduced the overseas sporting opportunities that were available. As a consequence many of the 'medium' rifle calibres also fell into disuse and were abandoned. The death-knell really sounded when Eley ceased the production of metallic rifle cartridges in the early 1950s. In these circumstances it is hardly surprising that the .369 Purdey, .333 Jeffrey, the .318 Accelerated Express and the .280 Ross are but an echo of a bygone era, and their place has been taken by American calibres that have come to dominate the sporting rifle world in the last thirty years.

Present-day rifle calibres can be classified by grouping them under their method of ignition: those using rimfire ammunition and those working on the centrefire system.

RIMFIRE CALIBRES

As the term implies, in a rimfire rifle, the firing pin strikes the edge of the base of the metallic cartridge in order to fire the round. In order to ensure ignition, regardless of the way the round enters the rifle's chamber, the percussion compound takes up the entire rim space within the cartridge. When struck by the firing pin the entire compound ignites and ensures a good clean burn of the main powder charge. The system dates from the earliest days of the breech-loading rifle and there was once a wide range of rimfire calibres. Only one of these old calibres is still with us, and it has recently been joined by another modern development.

The .22 rimfire is now well over one hundred years old. Originally developed as the .22 Short (S) for small pistols, its versatility has been extended by the introduction over the years of the Long (L) and then the Long Rifle (LR) cartridge. At one time it was extended to an Extra Long case but this was discontinued before the last war. Originally a black-powder calibre, the modern nitro ammunition uses minute quantities of very fast burning powder. Even so the high velocity Long-Rifle rounds generate up to 25,000lb breech-pressure when fired.

Of all the rifle calibres, the .22 rimfire is the most widespread and popular.

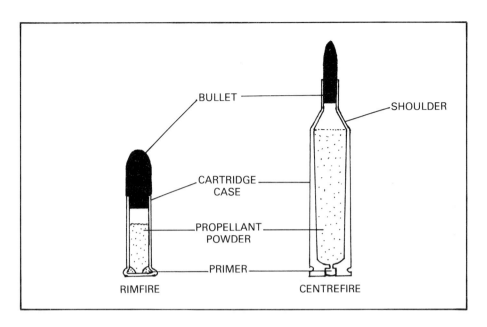

Cross-sections of rimfire and centrefire rifle cartridges.

The inexpensive ammunition, superb accuracy out to about seventy five yards, practically non-existent recoil and mild report have made this the rifle calibre for everyman. Despite being of very crude design, the rimfire cartridge has been extensively researched and developed by the ammunition manufacturers so that today's .22 rimfire target rifle shooter can aspire to put ten bullets through the same hole on a target, and know that his ammunition is capable of doing so. The sporting .22 rimfire can be a 'knock-about' rifle for use against rabbits and other vermin, or it can take on a more serious role when stalking hares or controlling foxes.

Although the .22 rimfire is the lowest powered of all 'powder' rifles, it is also one of the most potentially dangerous. The solid lead bullets driven at moderate velocity do not break up or even distort badly when glancing off a rock or similar surface. The .22 is therefore more prone to ricochet than any other calibre. There is, in addition, a tendency for the novice shooter to underestimate the power in these tiny bullets. Accidents with a .22 rimfire have caused the deaths of many people, and the Long Rifle round has been known to have killed deer, moose and even a grizzly bear.

For hunting small game and vermin, the high speed .22 Short with a hollow-point bullet is useful up to fifty yards and the Long Rifle hollow-point can stretch the range up to one hundred yards in the right conditions. Two recent developments have widened the range of velocities available. On the slow side, the new subsonic hunting rounds have been designed for use in rifles with a sound moderator, and the resulting report is actually quieter than an air rifle. At ranges up to about sixty yards this can take a great toll of a rabbit warren on a summer's evening. On the other side, the newly introduced 'hyper velocity' ammunition pushes the muzzle velocities up to 1500 fps and this has extended

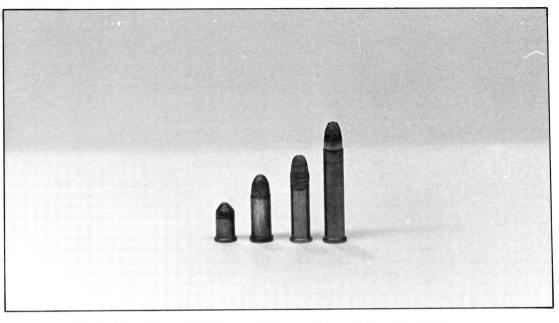

The rimfires. (*left to right*) BB cap, .22 Short, .22 Long Rifle (LR), .22 Magnum.

the range out to, at best, about 120 yards. These bullets are, however, more susceptible to wind so some of this advantage is lost.

All in all, the .22 rimfire is the only calibre which is truly ubiquitous, and it is likely to remain so as long as sporting rifles exist.

A new calibre which improves on the power of the .22 LR is the .22 Winchester Magnum rimfire. This drives a similar weight bullet (40 grains) at about 2000 fps and it is rapidly gaining a strong following among those sporting shooters who require more power and increased range than is offered by the standard .22 LR, yet cannot justify the use of one of the centrefire .22 calibres. An increasing number of rifles are being made in .22 Magnum rimfire and this calibre appears to have a bright future.

CENTREFIRE CALIBRES

Compared to the two available rimfire calibres, there are nearly one hundred different centrefire rifle calibres available today. However, it is possible to group these sporting-rifle calibres into five broad categories, although they could in no way be considered as hard and fast groups. The sporting-rifle scene is in a constant state of flux: old established calibres, some developed early this century, fall by the wayside as new cartridges supersede their ballistics; others, which had hitherto been slowly declining, may suddenly be given a new lease of life by the creation of new ammunition loads which update them to compete with more modern cartridges. The five groupings below refer more to the suitability of the particular calibres for a certain type of shooting rather than to the dimensions of the rifle-bore diameter, though there is a strong correlation between the two.

The high velocity centrefire .22 calibres and similar, therefore, form the first group, which often goes under the Americanism 'varmint' calibres. As the bore diameter increases to .240 we come to the deer rifles and these range up to some cartridges above .300. Beyond this group there is a third family of more powerful calibres useful for medium game and long-range shooting and these come into my 'medium' magnum category. The fourth family of calibres refers chiefly to heavy and dangerous game shooting and a small family of present heavy rifle calibres are just an echo of those existing shortly after the Second World War. The smallest of these heavy calibres is the .358 Norma Magnum and the largest is the .458 Winchester. Finally, there is a group of calibres which were designed for short-range deer shooting in North America using lever-actioned rifles. The cartridges of this group are short and they have the base rims and almost parallel cases that are required for efficient functioning in these traditional American repeaters. Though only of moderate velocity, their bullets are far less sensitive to foliage and twigs than their higher velocity brethren in the other groups.

In all, there are about thirty-six calibres in the above five sub-divisions, which of course means that many have been omitted. In most circumstances these have been omitted because they are becoming obsolete as rifles are not now being produced in the calibre.

Yet again a problem arises as a significant number of rifle manufacturers will chamber a rifle for a customer's specific requirements. If a customer particularly likes the .30–40 Krag, for example, there is a long list of makers who would produce one for him.

.22 high velocity varmint calibres

The high velocity small-bore centrefire rifles have been developed over the years so that now this first group fills a rather specialised role. Despite the variety of calibres that are at present available in this category they all possess a number of common characteristics. Generally they all fire light bullets of around 50 grains at very high velocity. Such is the rate of spin given to the bullets by the appropriate rifles in this group that accuracy is often very good out to around 250 yards. The rifles are generally used for shooting inedible species such as fox, coyote or similar, although, in the countries that allow it, they are often also the favoured calibres for shooting small deer species such as roe. Apart from one exception, they all fall into the general calibre of .22.

The smallest calibre in this group is also one of the fastest. The .17 Remington drives a tiny 25 grain bullet at a muzzle velocity of around 4000 fps. Zeroed at 250 yards the trajectory is so flat that the bullet rises less than three inches above the line of sight in the interim. In addition, the small cartridge produces very little recoil and it has a low noise level. To set against these attributes, however, is the fact that such a light bullet is very susceptible

The most popular .22 centrefires. (*left to right*) .22 LR (for comparison); .22 Hornet, .222 Remington, .22–250 Remington, .220 Swift.

to crosswind deflection and is therefore less reliable than some of the heavier .22s. The .17 Remington has never been a really popular calibre for this reason, although it has a strong following in Australia where many believe it is the ideal fox-shooting calibre.

Next comes the least powerful of the family, yet a calibre which ranks among the most popular in its class. The .22 Hornet first appeared in 1930 and has developed an enviable reputation for its accuracy and reliability. Its 45 grain bullet leaves the rifle at only 2600 fps – quite sedate for this group of calibres – yet it is accepted as an efficient killer of foxes and similar-sized animals out to around 175 yards. Like the .17 Remington, however, its bullet expands far too rapidly for it to be considered for use against small deer. In many parts of Europe and in North America though, the .22 Hornet is a favoured weapon for shooting a variety of game birds: the capercaillie in Czechoslovakia and wild turkey in North America are both considered to be prime quarry species for the Hornet user. Like the .17 again, its low noise level and practically non-existent recoil have certainly contributed to its popularity, and a variety of rifles and combination rifle/shotguns are chambered for this round.

Although standard rifles are no longer made for the .22 Savage High Power (also called the $5.6 \times 52R$), it is another pre-war cartridge which continues to retain a number of devotees. Slightly larger than the Hornet, an increased powder charge drives a 71 grain bullet at a muzzle velocity of around 2800 fps. This gives comparable performance with the Hornet with the added advantage of a less explosive bullet which can, in countries that allow it, be used on small deer. However, despite its long history, the .22 Savage High Power is losing ground to more recently introduced calibres and is likely to continue on this downward trend.

Another cartridge which is called after the European system of calibre naming is the 5.6 × 50 Magnum. (European calibres are described by the metric measurements of the bullet diameter and the cartridge case-length. Thus the 5.6 × 50 Magnum has a 5.6 millimetre (.22in) diameter bullet and a 50 millimetre case-length. Additionally, there are often letters behind the last number which denotes whether the case is rimmed or rimless.) The 5.6 × 50 Magnum drives a 50 grain bullet at around 3000 fps which makes its performance about average for this group of varmint calibres. Very few manufacturers produce rifles in this calibre and it is a predominantly 'European' round which is little used in Britain, America or elsewhere.

One pre-war calibre which has survived due to its amazing qualities as a long-range weapon is the .220 Swift. As its name implies, this is a very high velocity round with a 50 grain bullet being driven out at around 4100 fps; in fact, it is at present the fastest of all the commercial sporting calibres. It has all the qualities necessary for shooting accurately out to around 300 yards and the bullet is heavier and therefore less sensitive to wind than the .17 Remington. Although the .220 Swift now has a serious competitor with similar ballistics in the .22–250 Remington, a number of rifles have recently been introduced chambered for the Swift which is an indication of the following this calibre has developed.

The two remaining calibres are by far the most popular in this category. Both have been introduced since the Second World War and both achieved popularity very rapidly. The .222 Remington is the milder of the two, generating a ballistic performance which is significantly better than the Hornet and rendering the old .218 Bee and .219 Zipper obsolete. A low noise and light recoiling cartridge, the accuracy of the .222 Remington is highlighted by the fact that it was quickly adopted by bench-rest target shooters as a standard by which other calibres are judged. In countries that allow it, the .222 Remington has become a favourite calibre for roe deer and there are a large number of rifles, from a wide variety of countries, chambered for this round.

The final calibre in this group is the modern .22–250 Remington. Unlike other rounds, this .22–250 evolved from a variety of experimental 'wildcat' rifles in America. In 1965 Remington adopted the calibre and standardised ammunition, thereby creating a cartridge which drives a 50 grain bullet at around 3800 fps. In many parts of the world this calibre is looked upon as excellent for long-range fox shooting and for shooting game up to roe deer size. In this country it ranks with the .22 Hornet and .222 Remington in the top three of the group, and many vermin controllers and gamekeepers will vouch for its ability to shoot with reliable accuracy up to 300 yards.

One of the problems associated with these high velocity centrefire .22 calibres lies in the selection of the correct design of bullet. Lightly constructed bullets travelling at these high velocities tend to break up so quickly that their effect on small animals is almost explosive. As a consequence they are not for use against small edible game such a rabbit or hare as there would be an unacceptable amount of carcass damage. On deer up to the size of roe, on the other hand, these light bullets have been known to break up so quickly when striking a shoulder blade, for instance, that they fail to penetrate and only cause a horrible surface wound. For these animals a heavier constructed bullet which would be less prone to break up cures the problem. Even so, this tendency for the rapid break-up of the bullet makes these calibres considerably safer in use because ricochets are practically unheard of. In a densely populated country like Britain, the high power .22s used in vermin control pose far less of a danger than the rimfire .22s because they use light and fragile bullets at high velocity.

Deer-stalking calibres

This group of rifle calibres shows a jump in bore diameter from the .22s up to .24in. Within the bore diameter range from .24 to around .30 there is a group of calibres which has come to be accepted as the standard for deer-stalking rifles. Compared to the first category, bullet weights are higher, ranging from around 100 grains to 180 grains, and the muzzle velocities are generally lower, ranging between about 2800 and 3200 fps.

For all practical purposes the two smallest of these calibres, the .243 Winchester and the 6mm Remington, can be grouped together. The latter started life as the .244 Remington varmint calibre using bullets of 75 or 90 grains. In order to compete with this, Winchester produced the .243 in a range of bullet weights up to 100 grains, thus extending the use of the calibre into the realms of the deer stalker. The .243 became by far the more popular of the two and Remington were forced to rename the .244 and produce 100 grain bullet loads to compete with Winchester's calibre. The resulting 6mm Remington has never caught up on the headstart the .243 had gained even though it is slightly more powerful, and nowadays the .243 is far more widely used.

Both .243 and 6mm are widely regarded as dual purpose calibres in that they make fine long-range varmint rifles using the 80 grain bullet. Accuracy out to beyond 250 yards is good and they are less sensitive to wind than the lighter bullets of the centrefire .22s. In addition, loaded with the 100 bullet, they produce muzzle velocities of around 3000 fps which makes them sufficiently powerful for any deer species up to red. In parts of lowland Britain where the woodland stalker may encounter anything from a small roe buck to a large red stag, these calibres are ideal. Powerful enough for the large deer, the 100 grain bullets also minimise meat shredding and carcass damage in the smaller species. While some people consider them to be on the light side and would prefer to rely on a heavier calibre rifle for the large deer species, the .243 remains the first choice of many seasoned professional highland stalkers and deer managers. Most hunting rifle-makers produce models in both .243 Winchester and 6mm Remington.

Moving up the scale of calibres is a lesser known cartridge yet one which is considered to be one of the finest for deer shooting. The .25–06 was produced by necking down the old American .30–06 calibre to fire a .25 diameter bullet.

Popular deer calibres in Britain. (*left to right*) .22 LR (for comparison); .243 Winchester, .308 Winchester, 7 × 57 (.275), .270 Winchester; .30–06.

The resulting range of bullet weights, from 87 grains to 120 grains, that are commercially loaded for this calibre has produced a rifle which is capable of both long distance varminting and taking on woodland elk and similar sized animals at closer range. Although the cartridge was first designed around 1920, it was only in 1969 that Remington adopted the calibre much in the same way that they had with the .22–250. Since its adoption the ballistics have been standardised and maximum use has been made of the large capacity shell to produce velocities as high as 3450 fps for the light bullets and around 3000 fps for the heaviest.

Another necked down .30–06 design has produced what is probably the most widely used of all the deer rifle calibres. The .270 Winchester was introduced in 1925. Though it rapidly became popular in the USA, it took a long time before it really gained acceptance this side of the Atlantic. From this size upwards we are getting beyond the varminting calibres and into the deer and heavier category. Bullet weights range from 100 to 150 grains and over the years this variety has allowed the .270 Winchester to dominate the deer-stalking scene. In North America it is considered by many to be capable of taking any type of game that exists on that continent, up to moose and brown bear size. In Europe it is a favoured red deer calibre and is gaining popularity in Scandinavia as an effective round for elk. A muzzle velocity of over 3000 fps with a 130 grain bullet has also caused it to become popular as a flat shooting and reliable long range gazelle cartridge in the tropics. Like the .243 Winchester and 6mm Remington, practically all rifle-makers produce rifles chambered for the .270 Winchester and it is likely to continue to dominate this group of stalking calibres.

Two European calibres which have achieved a fair degree of popularity are the 7 × 57 and the 7 × 64. Both have a history which stem from the adaptation of a military calibre for sporting use and both generate somewhat lower velocities but drive a heavier bullet than most of the deer calibres already mentioned.

A great many sporting rifles chambered for the 7 × 57 Mauser are converted military rifles of some vintage. These actions tend to be weaker than that of the modern sporting rifle and therefore commercially-produced ammunition is loaded to generate lower pressures. A 150 grain bullet is consequently driven at about 2700 fps, yet this is no handicap at the sort of ranges that are normal in British and European deer shooting, and the 175 grain loading provides enough shock for the wild boar. One of the great advantages of the 7 × 57 is its low recoil compared with similar high velocity calibres and this has made it a favourite in many European countries where it is appreciated as a 'sweet shooting' round.

The 7 × 64 is a longer-cased cartridge with consequently more powder capacity and is capable of higher velocities. Again popular in Europe, this calibre drives a 150 grain bullet at around 2900 fps and compares favourably with the .270 Winchester. Even so, its popularity has not spread much beyond the European mainland where it is a respected round capable of doing anything that a .270 Winchester can do.

Finally in this group are three military calibres of about .30in bore diameter which have been successfully developed for sporting purposes. The British .303 was for many years the standard calibre for our armed forces and even before the last war it had gained an excellent reputation in Britain and many Commonwealth countries as a very good deer-stalking round. When the .303 was finally dropped as a military cartridge the flood of 'sporterised' service rifles into Canada and Australia ensured that its popularity as a sporting rifle calibre continued for many years. However, few sporting rifles are produced in .303 and the calibre is slowly declining as it is being superseded by more modern ballistics. Even so, a 150 grain .303 bullet leaves the rifle at 2700 fps and this makes it a fine deer-stalking round.

Probably the best respected of all hunting rifle calibres, and one by which others have been judged, is the .30–06 Springfield. This American services calibre began life in 1906 (hence its name – .30in calibre 1906 Springfield) and was quickly adapted for sporting use. Since then it has become to the centrefire rifle what the .22 LR is to the rimfire. Ammunition is available in a range of bullet weights from 130–200 grains and with this selection the .30–06 rifle will handle practically any game with the exception of the Indian and African 'heavies'. As a deer calibre it can be somewhat overpowered but careful loading by most commercial ammunition makers has controlled this tendency. Even so it is not a calibre for roe deer or small antelope. Despite the long history of the

.30–06, it is still in the forefront of hunting calibres and there is a steady demand for sporting rifles chambered for this round.

The sporting version of the NATO 7.62 rifle calibre is the final one in this group. Named the .308 Winchester, this cartridge has the short brass case which is also necked down to produce the .243 Winchester. With a bullet weight range from 130 to 180 grains, it lacks some of the .30–06's versatility yet it scores in that the shorter overall cartridge length makes for a more compact action and a handier rifle. As a consequence its popularity has been growing rapidly since its introduction. With its smaller powder capacity, the velocities produced by the .308 Winchester are lower than the comparable .30–06 loads. In all normal deer-stalking situations, however, this is of little consequence and the .308's lower velocities actually enable it to be used on the smaller deer and antelope species without the shredding one would expect with the more powerful calibre. As an additional bonus the recoil is less noticeable and this has encouraged the adoption of the .308 for target as well as for sporting use. It is questionable whether the .308 will ever supplant the .30–06, but it is nevertheless becoming one of the more popular all-purpose hunting calibres, and a wide range of sporting rifles are produced to accommodate this round.

There are, of course, many other calibres in this category which have been omitted here. The .257 Roberts, for instance, is one which has been steadily sliding into obscurity even though a new loading from Winchester has done much to bring the calibre up to date. There may be a resurgence of interest in the .257 in the future, but I feel it will be only of minor significance, after all it has to compete with the .25–06.

None of the calibres in this deer-stalking group develop high pressure or what has come to be termed magnum velocities and muzzle energy, yet they are all perfectly well suited to the variety of rifle sport that is available in Britain, Europe, and Australasia. In addition they can be handy, general purpose, light-medium rifles for those lucky enough to be able to hunt in the tropical regions of the world.

Medium magnum calibres

So far, I have described rifles that are of major interest to sporting rifle users in Britain and Europe. In this part of the world the accepted maximum range for shooting at deer, mouflon and similar-sized animals is about 200 yards, with the average actual range probably half this. Even in the open expanses of the Scottish Highlands shots at greater than the stated range of 200 yards would be considered both unsporting and unacceptable. The risk of wounding and losing a beast increases proportionally with distance, and in an area where visibility often deteriorates rapidly and the topography is treacherous, the long range shooting possible in other parts of the world is just not a practical proposition.

Though this group of calibres are often used very successfully as deer rifles, their advantage lies in the fact that they are far better suited to the sort of extended ranges that are impractical in Britain. This group is therefore less applicable to rifle sport in Britain and more relevant to those areas of the world which make accurate shooting at ranges up to 400 yards a necessity. These areas include parts of the Great Plains and Western Mountains of North America, the African Veldt and Indian Plateau, parts of the Australian Outback and other mountainous areas which make close approach difficult and therefore demand a long-range rifle. In terms of bore diameter, these medium magnums go from about .240 up to .340 and they are all notable for their flat trajectory, resistance to wind deflection, fairly definite recoil and sharp report.

One rifle-maker which pioneered the development of these medium magnums is Holland and Holland of London, and their most recently designed calibre, the .244 H & H Magnum, is the smallest in this category. There is, in fact, no more powerful rifle in the .240 class, and as a long-range deer cartridge it will kill reliably up to 400 yards. Designed by David Lloyd, the .244 Holland and Holland Magnum was introduced in the post-war years and has become a respected and rather exclusive calibre in the rifle-shooting world. A few hand-built rifles are made for this cartridge each year and ammunition is available from only a few sources, yet the .244 Magnum has gained an enviable reputation for its long-range capabilities and its tremendous knock-down potential at closer ranges.

The same can be said of its older and more powerful brother, the .275 Holland and Holland Magnum. This calibre, which was developed in the period before the First World War, quickly gained a great deal of popularity throughout the English-speaking world and it was the foremost light-medium rifle in Africa and Asia. Powerful enough for any deer species, the .275 Holland and Holland Magnum also proved capable of being an effective antidote for the larger and more dangerous animals found in those regions. The small number of rifles that are built in this calibre and the limited availability of its ammunition has caused this calibre to be eclipsed by powerful American calibres, yet the .275 Magnum still has an exclusive following in various parts of the world.

In 1920 Holland and Holland produced their 'Super 30', which was the first ever calibre to drive a 150 grain bullet at over 3000 fps. Compared with the .30–06, velocity was significantly higher and the increased bullet energy gave it a terrific knock-down potential. It was also a very accurate cartridge and was extensively used in competition before the last war. Adopted by the Americans, the calibre was renamed the .300 H & H Magnum, and it proved to be the catalyst which caused the development of the American medium magnum calibres. Many of these more recently developed magnums are more powerful than the .300 H & H Magnum, yet this calibre still remains the one by which others are judged. Even so, rifles built for this ageing calibre are still available from a number of makers and the .300 H & H will continue to satisfy a small demand for a stable and accurate calibre which has a decided edge over the .30–06.

In 1962 Remington announced their 7mm Remington Magnum, and it took the shooting world by storm. This cartridge has a short-belted case which, if correctly loaded, matches the striking power of a .30–06 together with the trajectory of the .270 Winchester. For a long-range Plains rifle the 125 grain bullet develops very high velocity at around 3400 fps and the 175 grain bullets still exceed 3000 fps. With such versatility the calibre is proving to be very popular in many parts of the world where a flat shooting load is required for use against long-range targets. Not as heavy as the .300 H & H Magnum, the 7mm Remington Magnum has a far larger following within the sporting rifle world.

A year after the appearance of Remington's 7mm Magnum, Winchester introduced their .300 Winchester Magnum as a direct competitor to the .300 H & H Magnum. More powerful than the older cartridge, the new calibre appeared to make the .300 H & H Magnum obsolete, yet the noticeably increased recoil failed to convert many from the old calibre, particularly in countries where loyalties lay with the British calibre. In America though, the .300 Winchester Magnum has proved to be adequate for all their game including the moose and even the large bears, and its use is spreading to Africa where it is considered a good calibre for the largest antelope and other hoofed game.

Two European calibres also fall into this category. The 6.5 × 68 fills the space between the .244 H & H Magnum and the .275 H & H Magnum, and it has become popular with European sportsmen who hunt in the tropics. It is lighter than the 8 × 68 and like rifles with similar specifications, it makes a good long-range deer round.

The 8 × 68, as its designation implies, fires a heavier bullet at somewhat lower velocities, yet the muzzle energy is still high enough to produce a good knock-down potential. Though its use in Europe is very limited, it has become a reasonably well-known round in parts of Africa where it fulfills the same role as the other .300 magnum calibres, and a number of European rifle-makers now produce weapons for this and the 6.5 × 68 calibre.

Finally in this group there is the .338 Winchester Magnum. A post-war cartridge, it has been hailed by many to be the leading candidate for the title of 'all-round' rifle. It will kill large deer at long range, often producing less carcass damage than a .270 bullet, yet with its heavier loads it will tackle Alaskan brown bear and bison with confidence. In addition, the heavier bullets, reaching in this calibre up to 275 grains, are less prone to deflection by wind, grass and brushwood which has won it much support from woodland hunters of larger and heavier game. The .338 Winchester Magnum is becoming increasingly popular with moose and elk hunters and has recently developed a following in Scandinavian countries.

Heavy-game calibres

These rifles are known as 'heavy rifles'. This term does not refer to the actual bore diameter (two of the group are really medium-bore rifles) but to the type of game that these calibres are capable of stopping. They are all extremely

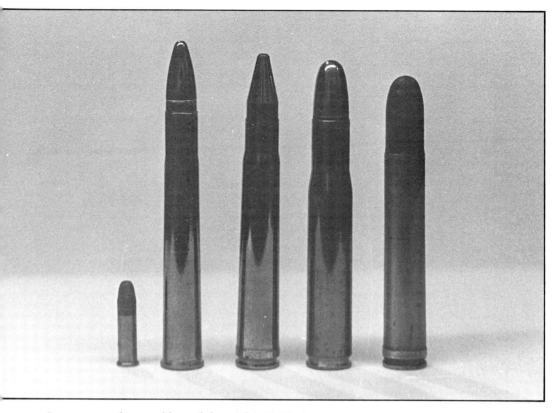

Contemporary heavy calibres. (*left to right*) .22 LR (for comparison); 9.3 × 74, .375 H & H Magnum, .404 Jeffrey, .458 Winchester Magnum.

powerful cartridges developing muzzle energies of over 4000 ft/lb, and using bullets of 250 grains and heavier. African hunters are even more specific in their definition of a heavy rifle as one with a bore diameter exceeding .450.

The smallest rifle in this group is also one of the newest. The .358 Norma Magnum was first introduced in 1959 and has slowly become accepted as a powerful medium–heavy rifle in the big-game hunting areas of the world. In Alaska it has become a popular moose calibre and in Africa it is considered to be a good choice for hoofed big game. It is certainly also sufficiently powerful to cope with dangerous soft-skinned big game but in many countries there are regulations which enforce a lower bore diameter limit of .375 or .400 for such species. With a 250 grain bullet being driven along at around 2800 fps this calibre produces 4322 ft/lb energy which definitely justifies its place in this group of 'heavies'.

The .375 Holland and Holland Magnum has become the 'maid of all work' for the big-game hunter wherever there are large and dangerous animals. First developed in 1912, it still has no equal as an all-round calibre in Africa and Alaska. It will cope with any American game with ease, and in Africa it has sufficient power to be used effectively against both elephant and cape buffalo. It is a true high velocity cartridge driving a big 270 or 300 grain bullet on a flat trajectory; and despite this power it still has almost varmint calibre accuracy. The hunting folklore that has grown around this calibre often has a sound basis in truth. It is one of the very few calibres which will deliver any of its original loadings to the same point of impact, and there was no need to re-zero the rifle when bullets of different weight were used. A muzzle energy of over two tons delivers a terrific knock-down blow to any large game, and in addition you are made very aware through your shoulder that you have fired a big cartridge! The recoil of the .375 H & H Magnum, particularly in the lighter rifles, can be ferocious. Firing off the first round in this calibre leaves one with, among other things, a great sense of achievement. A fair number of rifles are still made in the .375 Magnum, and ammunition is easily available in all the big-game hunting regions of the world. Despite more modern calibres, it is unlikely that the .375 will ever be replaced as the general purpose big-game rifle.

The only other heavy calibre which is at present readily available in both rifle and ammunition is the cartridge introduced in 1956 by Winchester and called the .458 Winchester Magnum. As American hunters expanded their sphere of interest towards Africa after the last war, there developed from them a demand for an American rifle designed to supersede the older British heavy rifles. The .458 Magnum has succeeded in doing this. Its 500 grain bullet has won its spurs as a stopper of angry elephant and bison and there is a steadily increasing demand for rifles made in this calibre as more African countries open their borders to overseas hunters. Unlike the .375 Magnum it is not a long-range accurate round, but up to about 150 yards it is both sufficiently accurate and develops enough energy to cope with anything on four legs. If anything, its recoil is even heavier than the .375 Magnum, but as one African hunter put it, that is the last thing one worries about when faced with a charging bison! The .458 Winchester Magnum is at present the dominant heavy African calibre and it is likely to remain so despite a recent rebirth of interest in some of the older British Nitro Express 'heavies'.

For bolt action magazine rifles calibres such as the .416 Rigby, the .425 Westley Richards and, to a lesser extent, the .404 Jeffrey, now compete with the .458, and even a small number of rifles have recently been built in .505 Gibbs! All that has been said of the .458 is also true of these powerful rimless cartridges, though the .404 is somewhat weaker than others.

What is even more surprising is the number of double rifles that have recently been built for the heavy 'rimmed' cartridges. With the re-introduction of cartridge brass and ammunition from both European and American sources, calibres such as the 450/400, .470, .500, .577, and the enormous .600 Nitro Express have been recalled from obsolescence and are again seeing use on the African continent. Rifles for these heavy British calibres are, however, hand built rather than being mass produced so the lead taken by the .458 is unlikely to be lost.

The final calibre in this group was developed by the European hunters of tropical heavy game and the long, tapered cartridge which was evolved was called the 9.3 × 74R. Often used in continental double rifles, this calibre does not reach the muzzle energies of others in this class, yet with bullet weights from 232 to 286 grains they are excellent for heavy hoofed animals. As a consequence it has become popular as a knock-down calibre for Scandinavian elk in addition to its use in tropical big-game areas. However, it does not have the versatility of the .375 Magnum, and it is this calibre which has remained the undisputed leader of this category.

Lever-action calibres

The cartridges for this final group of calibres are easily recognised because the bullets have flat noses, and with only one exception, the brass case is only slightly necked down. The traditional American lever-action rifle with its tubular magazine demanded this kind of cartridge in order to prevent the bullet points of one round firing off the one in front of it as it is jolted around in the magazine. With two exceptions these are essentially low-powered calibres which fire comparatively heavy bullets at low velocity.

Taken as two similar calibres, the 25–20 and the 32–20 conform to these general characteristics. The former drives an 86 grain bullet at 1400 fps and the latter a 100 grain bullet at only 1200 fps. At first sight these figures may seem to render them useless as sporting rifle calibres, yet in America they are still popular for short-range use against edible game. The 32–20 in particular is a favoured turkey calibre.

Moving up the scale of low-powered rounds, the immortal 44–40 is still surviving and the 45–70 has recently experienced a strong revival. Again these throw out heavy bullets at low velocity, the 200 grains of the 44–40 leaves the barrel at less than 1200 fps, and the ponderous 405 grain bullet of the 45–70 has a muzzle velocity of just over 1300 fps. Despite these rather unimpressive figures, all the calibres in this group possess some common characteristics which in certain circumstances make them a better choice than any of the high velocity rounds detailed in the other categories.

Compared with the 'high power' rifles, all these rifles have a light recoil and lower noise level. They are sufficiently accurate up to about one hundred yards to make small-game hunting possible, and the low velocity heavy bullets dissipate most of their low energy on striking the target. In this way the meat shredding often seen from the high velocity bullets does not occur and the bullet often gives the impression of having a good knock-down potential on game up to the size of wild turkey. They are generally far too underpowered for use against even the smallest deer species. Before the more powerful calibres were evolved, these killed many deer (and probably wounded many more).

There are two exceptions in this low-powered family which have evolved as favourite North American woodland deer calibres. Used in light and handy short-barrelled repeating rifles, the 30–30 has been a long-time favourite of the deer hunter. In this calibre a 150 grain bullet has a velocity of nearly 2400 fps and nearly 2000 ft/lb energy. However, it is neither a sufficiently accurate round for small game nor does it have a trajectory which would allow ranges over about 110 yards. The 30–30 is primarily a close range deer cartridge and in this function it performs well.

The second exception is the .444 Marlin which is the most powerful of the group and has a 240 grain bullet developing 2300 fps and 2900 ft/lb energy. Again, it is not accurate enough for small targets and is, like the 30–30, primarily a deer calibre. With the extra power made possible by its long, tapered brass case, the range of the .444 can be extended out to 150 yards while still retaining a hefty blow. Introduced only in 1964, the .444 Marlin is capable of taking on any North American species at ranges of under one hundred yards, but its use is limited by the fact that few rifles are chambered for this round.

In North America this group of calibres has become known as 'brush busters' – because their bullets are far less prone to break-up than the more fragile high velocity rounds. This fact alone has contributed to their use against the variety of game that is hunted in the forests of America and historical tradition also helps to keep them popular. In Britain and much of Europe, on the other hand, the high density of human population has resulted in the higher velocity rifles being more popular as they are far less prone to ricochet than these lever-action calibres. The brush busting rifles in their variety of calibres are as characteristic of North American hunting as the heavy double rifle used to be of Africa.

THE BULLET

The bullet is that part of the cartridge which is fired out of the rifle's barrel with the intention of striking the target. Very often the entire full rifle cartridge is referred to as the bullet and this is quite wrong as it is only one part of the entire round.

When used against live quarry, the bullet's only function is to kill the bird or animal in question as quickly and humanely as possible. To do this two conditions must be met. Firstly, the bullet must enter and disrupt a major life-support part of the creature (this is usually taken to be the heart, lungs, brain or neck vertebrae) and therefore it must be placed accurately by the shooter. Secondly, the bullet must be of the appropriate construction so that it can enter these vital areas and cause sufficient disruption to bring about instantaneous death.

Until the end of the muzzle-loading days, the only bullet in common use was the lead ball which was rammed down on top of the powder charge. Since those days, ballistic knowledge, propellant powders, and metallurgy skills have all made tremendous advances, particularly in the past thirty years or so. As the powders became more efficient the problems of stripping the lead ball (see page 16) were only really overcome when the jacketed bullet was created. In such a bullet the lead is surrounded by a protective jacket of harder metal which is sufficiently strong to take on the spin of the rifling even when this is as tight as one turn in nine inches and the bullet is being driven out at very high velocity. Variations in the thickness of this jacket, which is usually made of gilding metal (a mixture of around 90% copper and 10% zinc, sometimes with small

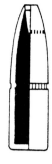

Pointed soft-point (PSP). Lead core exposed at the tip. Spitzer shape allows good penetration and thin metal jacket provides rapid expansion. The most widely used deer bullet.

Hollow-point (HP). Cavity in the bullet's nose gives rapid expansion. This is the most effective hunting bullet for the .22 rimfire calibres.

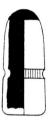

Round nose. Nose shape gives greatest shocking power at close range. Soft point gives good expansion. Not a long-range bullet but good for driven boar.

Full metal jacket (FMJ). Lead core encased (except base). Designed for maximum penetration – a bullet for big and dangerous game.

Main Hunting Bullet Designs.

quantities of tin) are used to produce a variety of bullets for the various shapes and sizes of rifle quarry.

For sporting rifles, the only all-lead bullets are now used in .22 rimfire ammunition, and even with these there is usually a thin coating of grease or copper to reduce the intense friction generated when the bullet is fired. Without this coating the surface of the lead bullet would partially melt, even at these low velocities, and accuracy would suffer as a consequence – as would the internal bore of the barrel.

The .22 rimfire bullets come in a variety of weights to suit the case length and powder charge, but they generally tend to take the form of solid lead for target shooting and small game, and hollow-point for rabbit to fox-sized game. The solid in this instance causing sufficient shock to small game to ensure a clean kill, yet it prevents excessive meat damage as it is reluctant to expand rapidly. The hollow-point bullet, on the other hand, expands rapidly and creates a far higher degree of shock as it dissipates its energy. In this way it is better suited to the larger .22 rimfire quarry species where the increased meat damage is tolerable and the additional shock is necessary to kill instantly.

The variety in the type of game animals that are hunted with high velocity rifles has given rise to four main types of jacketed bullets. Each type has been designed to administer the maximum shock to its intended quarry and each is unsporting and even dangerous to use outside its limits.

Varmint bullets

Varmint bullets are designed for use against small quarry animals such as foxes, up to the maximum accurate range of the various high velocity .22 calibres. In order to be effective against such small and lightly built animals the bullet has to expand instantly on contact, otherwise it would pass through the animal before becoming effective. The varmint bullet is designed to do just this. It has a core of soft lead and a thin jacket which under high rates of spin and velocity become very fragile. The frictional heat generated when such a bullet is pushed up the barrel on discharge makes it possible for these bullets to become fragile 'bottles' of molten lead. Certainly their effect on small animal species can be accurately described as explosive, and these lightly constructed bullets are of little use against edible game. Neither are they suitable for larger game such as the various-sized species of deer and antelope. For these animals the varmint bullet expands far too rapidly, often before the body cavity has been penetrated, and the unfortunate animal receives a terrible surface wound which causes a lingering and painful death.

Deer bullets

The deer bullet is one where expansion is controlled to a greater extent so that the body cavity of the animal is penetrated before maximum disruption occurs. To do this the bullet-makers have evolved four different designs of deer bullet. One of the most popular and widely used has a jacket which becomes progressively thinner and therefore weaker towards the point, where the lead is often exposed. There are also various hollow-point bullets in which the front end of the bullet collapses in contact with the animal and final expansion only occurs on deeper penetration. Wedge points also achieve the same end by using a plastic or bronze plug to fill a cavity in the front end of the bullet. This drives a wedge into the bullet to ensure rapid expansion only after the initial contact. Finally, controlled expansion can also be achieved by exposing more lead at the front end of the bullet. This causes a progressive deformation of the bullet as it strikes its target – the soft lead expanding rapidly on initial contact and the jacketed and therefore reinforced rear portion of the bullet expanding later. With all these deer bullets, expansion is still quite rapid. After all, with the possible exception of elk and moose most other species of deer are thin-skinned and comparatively light-boned animals.

Thin-skinned game bullets

Heavy game can be divided, for bullet design purposes, into thin-skinned and thick-skinned animals. Thin-skinned species in this category include moose and other large hoofed species together with the big cats and the larger bears. For these the deer bullet would be far too sensitive and an altogether more heavily constructed bullet is required. These heavier bullets are still designed to expand, but only after breaking through tough sinew and bone. Delayed expansion is therefore a necessary design virtue and this is usually achieved by increasing the thickness and strength of the jacket. The delay in expansion caused by this strengthening would allow such a bullet to pass clean through a lighter animal like a deer yet it is designed to dissipate all its energy within the chest cavity of, say, a lion or elk. Heavy calibre rifle cartridges are usually marketed with soft-point bullets which provide the delayed expansion necessary for these soft-skinned species.

Thick-skinned game bullets

Thick-skinned big game is the term used for rhino, elephant, African and Asian bison and other similar species. For these, the emphasis in bullet design must be for the deepest penetration without the risk of the bullet expanding. There is a preference for bullets that will break through thick bones and immobilise a potentially very dangerous animal and it was for this purpose that the fully jacketed bullet was designed. In these bullets the lead core is entirely enclosed with a strong metal casing and, when used in the heavy calibres, the resulting penetration is phenomenal. Full metal cased bullets in a .458 Winchester Magnum are designed to penetrate six inches of bone to reach the elephant's brain, and such a bullet would break both shoulders of an African bison before dissipating its energy. For any other game they are far too heavy and a 'solid' from a .375 Magnum has been recorded as passing through three large antelope before finally coming to rest. Though they can cause terrific wounds, when they pass clean through an animal they fail to dissipate much of their energy as internal shock and are therefore less efficient, and a lighter bullet designed specifically for the lighter animal should be used.

Bullet shape

If bullet construction is the most important factor in the effectiveness of the projectile, its shape also has a bearing on its trajectory and other ballistic characteristics. The most efficient-shaped bullet is one with a sharp point, and this is often known as a 'spitzer'. These hold their trajectory for longer distances and, in consequence, most of the long-range calibres use spitzer bullets. They are, however, more sensitive to wind and intervening foliage and as such are more prone to deflection than round-nosed bullets. It is therefore no coincidence that most of the medium and short-range calibres are of the rounded bullet form. Tubular magazine rifle calibres usually have flat-nosed bullets, even less efficient than the rounded type, but very necessary if magazine explosions are to be avoided.

Most bullets have square-cut bases but a number of ammunition manu-facturers market a tapered base bullet, often referred to as a boat tail. These are marginally better at holding their velocity and only show markedly improved ballistics over the conventional base bullet when the velocity drops to subsonic levels. This usually happens at ranges well beyond the accurate

(*left*) Many modern rifles are equipped with a simple leaf rear-sight . . .
. . . which folds flat to allow the use of a scope sight. (*right*)

trajectory of the round so the difference between a boat tail and conventional bullet is negligible for all sporting purposes.

Ideally, a bullet should be constructed so that its expansion at close range, when it is travelling at high velocity, is not markedly different from its expansion at lower velocities and longer ranges. Up until the 1950s this was an unattainable quality yet the advances made in ballistic science since then have produced a wide variety of bullet shapes and constructions which do have this consistency of performance at short and long ranges. In all but very few instances a wounded animal cannot be blamed on a poor bullet and it is far more likely to be 'shooter error', either in aiming or in bullet choice. Careful selection of the right bullet for the species is now possible and is essential if the shooter wishes to make quick and clean kills.

THE SIGHTS

The sights of a rifle are simply the various contrivances which help the shooter point the weapon in the right direction, and there are three basic types. These are open sights, aperture or 'peep sights', and telescopic sights.

The majority of rifles made today are equipped at the factory with open sights. These are the traditional sights of the hunting rifle, in which the shooter lines up the muzzle or fore-sight with the notch of the rear-sight and places this alignment on the target. In doing this the open sight system highlights its major design fault – it demands that the human eye focus on three separate objects, two of them reasonably close and the third, the target, at some distance. In fact, this entails rapid re-focusing of the shooter's eye on the three objects in turn. Despite this drawback there are definite advantages in using this system in certain situations, and open sights are second in popularity to telescopic sights.

Open sights really come into their own in situations where aiming is verging on the instinctive point and shoot. Thus a woodland hunter who anticipates

Target rifle shooters can demonstrate just how accurate aperture sights can be.

that most of his shooting will be at ranges of under fifty yards will find open sights perfectly adequate. The same is true of the person who is likely to encounter large and dangerous game at close quarters, for example, the European wild boar or the African bison. He will find that a telescope is a decided handicap and would naturally prefer the subconscious aiming of the quick 'snap' with open sights at close ranges.

At any distance over about fifty yards, however, the open sights fail to do justice to the accuracy of most modern rifles. The fore-sight bead can actually obliterate a six-inch circle on a hundred yard target, yet the rifle itself may be capable of producing a 1-in group. Of the three types of sighting systems, open sights are the most imprecise.

The aperture or 'peep' sight is a considerable improvement upon open sights, and in the hands of the target shooter can produce a fantastic standard of accuracy. In this system the shooter looks through a small aperture and lines up the fore-sight with the target. The peep sight is therefore mounted at the rear of the rifle's action (and they are therefore sometimes called receiver sights) so that the actual aperture is close to the shooter's eye. The eye now only has to focus from the fore-sight to the target and therefore alignment is much more precise. Although it is generally recognised to be an excellent system, two factors have probably led to it being far less popular among sporting rifle users than it should be. Firstly, the small aperture that is usually supplied with the sight cuts down on the light transmission to the eye so it is not an easy sight to use in the poor light of evenings or winter days. In addition, the fact that the aperture device is so close to the eye prevents its use in any rifle where the recoil is even moderate.

Most devotees of the aperture sight would claim that it is sufficiently precise for use up to ranges around one hundred yards and for this reason constitutes a good hunting sight. It is, however, slower to use properly than open sights and less efficient than a telescopic sight in low light conditions. Like the open sight the actual accuracy of the aperture system, in the hands of the average rifle user, is far below the accuracy potential of most modern rifles.

As if to match the post-war development of the efficient and accurate bullet, there has also been great progress in the optical sciences resulting in the production of low cost and good quality telescopic sights. So persuasive have the qualities of the modern telescopic sight been that it is now considered to be the 'normal' sight for the great majority of hunting situations and the open and peep sight user is looked upon with some suspicion.

Before the Second World War the reverse was true. At that time most of the criticisms levelled at telescopic sights were true. The majority of the telescopic sights at that time were not of the sealed tube type and any change in temperature or humidity caused them to fog up and rendered them useless. In addition they encountered problems in withstanding the battering the scope suffered each time the rifle recoiled, and they tended to shake loose. Many of the pre-war scopes were mounted in a haphazard way so that with the slightest rough treatment they went off their aiming point, i.e they lost their zero. The optical quality of the majority of these scopes left much to be desired and the generally small front objective lenses caused them to perform badly in poor lighting conditions. With all these problems 'iron sights' were understandably more popular and the scope was even viewed as being unsporting by some factions of the rifle-shooting world.

After the war things changed rapidly. The USA came to the forefront of scope technology in developing progressively improved optics. Firms like Weaver and Redfield brought mass production to the industry and made the first reasonably priced but reliable telescopic sights available to a much wider section of the sporting public. Further advances came from Japan, who began producing comparable sights in the wake of its rapid rise to world domination in camera making, and it is from these two countries that the great volume of sporting telescopic sights originate.

Germany, who led the field before the war, did not appear to cash in on the telescopic sight revolution and today it seems content to produce comparatively low quantities of the very best sights. Firms like Zeiss, and Schmidt and Bender, are recognised as producing the Rolls-Royces of the telescopic sight market.

Even the lower priced scopes of today have features which before 1939 were only found in the very best models. Nowadays scopes are nitrogen filled and sealed to prevent condensation; the sighting reticule, in any of a variety of crosswire or post designs, is adjustable for elevation and windage (side to side movement); and throughout the adjustments the sighting point stays central in the field of vision. Models are available in a wide variety of magnifications to suit different shooting distances, and objective lenses come in different sizes to allow for their use in a wide range of lighting conditions.

The widespread adoption of this type of sight in sporting rifle shooting has given rise to a new vocabulary which can cause much confusion to the uninitiated and some of these terms are explained below. All scopes are described by their degree of magnification and the diameter of the objective lens. Thus, one of the most popular types of scope, the 4 × 40, magnifies the image four times and has a 40mm diameter front lens. These figures will also give an indication of the ability of the scope to perform its function in poor lighting. If we divide the object lens diameter by the magnification we arrive at a number which is often called the 'luminosity' or 'twilight' factor. The larger the object lens the more light it will collect, and dividing this by the magnification indicates roughly how much of this light reaches the eye through the scope. A 4 × 40, with its factor of 10, is therefore more efficient at collecting and transmitting light than a 6 × 30 scope with a factor of 5, and will thus function better as a 'dawn and dusk' sight.

Another term that is often used as an indication of a telescope's performance is its 'exit pupil'. In low light conditions the pupil of the human eye dilates to about 7mm diameter. The light transmitted through a scope comes to a focus in a small circular area known as the exit pupil. If the diameter of this is less than 7mm then the human eye receives less light than it is capable of handling. If the scope's exit pupil is more than 7mm, then the dilated human eye cannot use all the transmitted light. In both cases the scope, even though it may have a very high twilight factor, is not performing efficiently with respect to the optimum amount of light the eye can accept.

The term 'eye relief' refers to the distance the eye must be behind the rear lens in order to see the whole field of view. This becomes important when a scope is selected for use on a heavy-recoiling rifle. A sight with a relatively short eye relief exposes the shooter to the danger of being hit on the forehead by the rear edge of the scope when he fires the rifle. The result is often a neat crescent-shaped cut over the eye – the rifle shooter's 'third eyebrow'!

The reticule or reticle is the device within the telescope which forms the aiming point of the sight. Perhaps the most well-known is the simple fine crosswire or crosshair reticule, but in poor light these fine wires become difficult to see. This has led to the adoption of a variation which is now probably the most widely used of all reticules. Known variously as the 'Dual X', the '30–30', or the '4 Post', it retains the fine crosswires in the centre but the lines are thickened considerably away towards the edge of the field of view. Even when light fails and the fine crosswires disappear, the thick wires remain visible and the target can still be centred using them. Other reticules exist but the single vertical post and the post and crosswires types are popular in Europe. A new addition is the 'electronic dot', in which a small battery-powered device lights up a small red dot in the centre of the sight picture.

With the variety of reticules available, selecting one for your own needs depends to a great extent on your personal preferences. Each has its own attributes and there is not really much to choose between them.

55

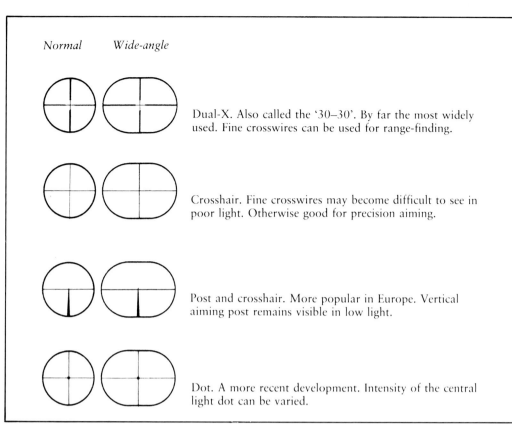

Normal   *Wide-angle*

Dual-X. Also called the '30–30'. By far the most widely used. Fine crosswires can be used for range-finding.

Crosshair. Fine crosswires may become difficult to see in poor light. Otherwise good for precision aiming.

Post and crosshair. More popular in Europe. Vertical aiming post remains visible in low light.

Dot. A more recent development. Intensity of the central light dot can be varied.

Popular Telescopic Sight Reticules.

With the wide variety of telescopic sights available for today's sporting rifle user a suitable model can be found to fit practically any hunting environment. The general purpose scopes come in the 4 × 32 to 6 × 40 range and these are perfectly adequate for the majority of sporting rifle shooting at ranges up to about 120 yards. For the long-range fox-shooter, a more powerful scope is required and the specialist varmint scopes with up to twenty times magnification will provide a precise aiming point out to about 300 yards.

For close-range woodland deer shooting, on the other hand, various low-power scopes are available in the 1½ to 2½ times range. These give a wide field of view, a bright sighting image and are considered by many woodland stalkers to be far better than iron sights because the eye does not have to shift focus from reticule to target.

The way a telescope is mounted on a rifle is more or less standardised today and modern rifles are either ready grooved to receive scope mounts or mounting blocks are supplied as standard accessories. Thus with today's efficient telescopic sight mounted solidly on a modern rifle, the average sporting rifle shooter has equipment which is capable of an accuracy which only a few decades ago was impossible except in target shooting.

Nowadays it cannot be denied that the telescopic sight will allow far more precise aiming than the other two types of sight, and this means that more game should be hit properly and killed cleanly than before. Unfortunately, this is not always the case as many inexperienced or unsporting shooters misuse the telescope. Rather than seeing it as a device which allows more precise aiming over normal ranges, the addition of a telescope seems to give some people the idea that they can extend their range. These long shots are more affected by wind so the advantage of a telescope is lost, and more importantly, animals which should never even have been shot at are wounded. This has tended to give the telescopic sight a bad name, but it should be remembered that it is the user and not the equipment that is to blame.

Finally I must refute one popularly held misconception about telescopic sights. It is often said that a telescopic sight leads to inaccurate shooting as it exaggerates aiming error. This is totally untrue. What does happen is that a telescope actually brings to light poor aiming. Imagine, for instance, a shooter firing at a hundred yard target with open sights. Having settled the rifle sights onto the bull, a slight movement may cause the actual point of aim to shift three or four inches from the aiming point, yet the movement will be so slight that the shooter may not even notice it. The same shooter using a moderate-powered scope to take the same shot will actually see the crosshairs move off the bull even though he would probably be unaware of any body movement. A shooter unaccustomed to a scope would probably conclude that the scope was too sensitive, whereas in effect it is merely showing precisely how the aiming point has shifted. Moreover, I have heard it said that a small movement of the point of aim viewed through a scope is in reality a large movement at the target. This again is nonsense. In a properly zeroed rifle, if the scope's crosshairs move three inches to the left of the one hundred yard bull, then the bullet will also land three inches to the left, not a multiple of the error.

The choice of sporting calibres, the various designs of bullet, and the variety of sighting devices, make today's sporting rifle a far more precise, accurate, and effective weapon than it has ever been. The high velocities generated by most of the centrefire calibres have, quite paradoxically, made the sporting rifle a safer weapon because of the tendency of the bullet to break up rather than ricochet. In addition, any velocities over about 2500 fps induce a phenomenon known as 'hydraulic shock' in animal tissue and this, in turn, helps the rifle shooter achieve the desired instant and painless kill in the majority of pursued game.

When the sporting rifle user makes up his mind as to what rifle calibre and bullet type will best suit his needs, and he has decided the type of aiming method to use, all that is left is the selection of a particular rifle style, and this is dealt with in chapter 3.

3. THE SPORTING RIFLE TODAY

IN the years following the Second World War observers of the sporting rifle scene witnessed the decline of one era and the dawn of another.

Britain, drained of her wealth and resources by the war effort, was also losing much of her 'prime hunting' territories as her colonial Empire rapidly changed to a Commonwealth of self-administering and independent countries. The wartime scale of arms production had been cut back rapidly to the pre-war level of sporting rifle production and this was reduced still further by two factors.

Firstly, the overseas opportunities for the British 'white hunter' were far more restricted than during the pre-war years. The newly emergent Commonwealth nations grappled with the problems of resource exploitation and wildlife management and the very fact that they were independent also meant that a sporting rifle market existing in these countries did not feel the same degree of allegiance to the British gunmakers. These became areas where competition between British and American rifle-makers was fierce.

Secondly, in Britain the ever increasing legal restrictions on the use of rifled firearms saw the final death of the rook rifle and a great curtailment of .22 rifle shooting. At the same time deer stalking was also rather restricted and exclusive and the cumulative effect of all this was that the British rifle-makers produced fewer and fewer weapons as the home demand was stifled and the overseas market became dominated by American rifles. Perhaps the final blow came when Kynoch ceased production of metallic ammunition in the late 1950s which effectively rendered all but a very few British calibres obsolete. Even so, the rifle-making industry in this country has refused to die, and the British-made sporting rifle still enjoys a respected reputation in all parts of the shooting world.

If the sporting rifle production in Britain declined in the post-war years, the rifle-makers in Europe experienced a remarkable re-birth. The firearms makers of Austria, Belgium, Finland and Germany, for example, had been devastated by the Allied bombing offensives and other wartime destruction, but strangely this was an advantage in the post-war years. Whereas many of the British rifle-makers were producing weapons of the highest quality by time-honoured methods and craftsmen's skills, their European counterparts went through a process of re-tooling the workshops and incorporating more modern techniques into the manufacture of sporting rifles. In this way many of the continental rifle-makers flourished to compete successfully, not only with the British, but also in many parts of the world, with the American giants in this field. Although employing many modern machines, the European rifle-makers have not been wooed over to the concept of total mass production, and the rifles they produce illustrate the quality that can be achieved when traditional craftsmanship is blended with modern high-technology production methods.

After the end of the war the USA finally abandoned her isolationist way of thinking and began to play her part as a dominant world power. The rifle-makers in the New World, when scaling down from wartime output to the post-war production of sporting rifles were not faced with the drastic cut in output that the British makers encountered. Bolstered by the firmly held belief in the right to bear arms, a right which is dear to the people of the United States, there was still a healthy home market for the sporting rifle manufacturers to meet. The mass production techniques which had been developed during the war complemented the Americans' traditional willingness to adopt new manufacturing methods and the rifle-making firms of North America quickly incorporated the new ideas into their sporting rifle production. New styles of rifles appeared as well as a whole new generation of rifle calibres. The post-war 'mild' American cartridge was far less an imitation of an established British calibre and more a reflection of the new-found confidence in American design and development skills. As the USA took on a more outward-looking international role, so the newly affluent American sportsman began looking further afield for rifle shooting opportunities.

On the overseas market the American calibres had subdued the popularity of the European metric rounds and had almost completely supplanted the British-developed rifle in most prime hunting areas of the world. At the same time the American-made rifle was gaining a more respectable image in the eyes of the majority of European and British rifle shooters. So powerful has the influence of the American sporting rifle become that on a world scale the most widely used centrefire weapon is the American-made rifle chambered for an American-designed calibre.

Nowadays there is such a wide range of qualities and designs of rifles produced in Britain, Europe and North America that it is easiest to describe the contemporary sporting rifle market in terms of area of manufacture.

BRITISH SPORTING RIFLES

To most people interested in sporting weapons, the term 'British Sporting Rifle' would conjure up an image of a medium or heavy calibre double-barrelled weapon. A minority would see a bolt actioned sporting rifle from names that are respected throughout the shooting world for the accuracy and low price of their rifles. The British output of sporting rifles breaks down neatly into two distinct categories with one exception: the London gunmakers, the Midlands rifle-makers and a small group of custom rifle-makers.

The custom-built rifle, either a double or bolt action repeater, is available from a small number of prestigious gunmaking firms in London or an equally small number of provincial rifle-makers. These firms cater for the middle to upper range of the sporting rifle market. The quality of workmanship and the degree of skill and artistry is unquestionable in such weapons and they confer a great deal of pride and pleasure in their ownership and use.

At the other end of the market, the bolt actioned repeating rifles that were until recently produced in the English Midlands have also won a good reputation for dependability and accuracy. Indeed, there are few areas in the world where one would not come across a British-made sporting rifle.

London gunmakers

The double rifle is nowadays almost exclusively the product of the London gunmakers. These firms, despite the worldwide financial recession, are buoyed by their prestige in the gunmaking field and they still build rifles of the very highest quality for those who desire only the best and can afford to pay for it. A rifle can still be ordered from such companies as Purdey, Holland and Holland, and Rigby, and the final weapon, which may take up to three years to build, will be generally acclaimed as the ultimate in prestige rifles. These London gunmakers whose reputations have arisen from the production of high quality hand-built weapons since the early nineteenth century, are anxious to maintain this esteem and would never consider economising to produce a poorer quality rifle or shotgun. As a consequence, a rifle made by one of these firms will be very expensive, yet the cost is justifiable when one considers the actual amount of time that has been spent on the production of the weapon by highly skilled craftsmen.

The very design of a double rifle makes it a difficult weapon to build, and it is one which demands gunsmithing skills that are rarely found nowadays. Even though it is built on the same lines as a double-barrel shotgun, there are a number of additional difficulties which make the production of an accurate double rifle a far greater task. Practically all double rifles are now built to the sidelock pattern. Not only does this allow greater strength to be built into the weapon than if a boxlock mechanism were used, but it also provides more scope for the artistic flair of the engraver in the decoration of the lock plates. There are three basic stages in the production of a sidelock double rifle: barrelling, actioning and stocking.

As the starting point of the production of barrels, gunmakers usually purchase rough steel rods from the steel manufacturers. Where, as is usual, the rifle has both barrels side by side, these rods also have a 'lump' of metal on the end which is used to form the method of locking the rifle closed. The first task of the barrel maker is to reduce these rods to the desired length. They are then rough bored to the eventual calibre of the rifle. The design of the barrels is worked out in great detail beforehand so that the external dimensions can be reduced or 'struck' down initially by machine and finally by hand. Great care is taken to make certain that the point of balance in the finished rifle is in exactly the right place, and the barrel is shaped accordingly. After the approximate dimensions (both external and internal) have been achieved using boring lathes and other machine tools, the hand work starts by working up to the eventual internal configuration of the bore with precisely cut rifling and accurate chambers. Here, in the workshops of the best London gunmakers, a great deal of time is spent in careful and painstaking hard work, and the finished product is a barrel made to finer tolerances than would be possible using a machine.

Remember too, that in the case of a double rifle both barrels at this stage will have to be the exact match of each other in terms of weight, barrel thickness, rifling accuracy and chamber dimensions. They are now carefully polished and prepared for brazing together, and this is where the difficulties associated with this type of rifle design begin to emerge. It is a fairly straightforward task to align a pair of shotgun barrels so that they shoot to the same point of aim at forty yards. To get a rifle to group both barrels together at one hundred yards is infinitely more difficult. In order to get this right the barreller needs to know whereabouts in the world the purchaser intends to use the rifle. Tropical temperatures affect the ballistics of most modern nitro powders and a rifle that shoots both barrels to the same point in Britain will not do so in the tropics. When the final alignment calculations have been made, the barrels are then brazed together and the top and bottom ribs soldered in place. The loop (the hook which fixes the fore-end under the barrel) is usually brazed on and shaped up, and the lumps are filed down close to their final dimensions. Extractors are shaped and the barrels are submitted to provisional proof which highlights any flaws in the metal and construction. When this test has been passed the barrels are ready for actioning.

Like the shotgun, the sidelock action of a modern rifle is usually of the 'bar action' type. In this style, the mechanism for cocking the internal hammers which fire the weapon are housed behind the metal plates on either side and slightly behind the breech. The bar action rifle takes its name from the fact that the main springs are housed in the part of the sidelock which extends into the bar of the action – that part which lies under the barrels.

The term actioning is self explanatory. The forgings are received from the gunmaker's suppliers and from these the action is cut, filed and shaped, so that the mechanisms which lock the barrels, cock the internal hammers (called tumblers nowadays), fire the weapon, and work the safety device, all work smoothly. A great amount of time is spent in careful and highly specialised work as the 'actioner' achieves this, and all working surfaces would, in a best London gunmakers' workshop, be shaped and tested by the 'sooting' process. Time consuming though it is, this method is still recognised as the best way of ensuring that different parts of the action fit together perfectly. Basically the method is to coat each surface with soot from a paraffin lamp. When both parts, for example the barrels and action, are brought together, this soot is rubbed off the 'highspots' which are then carefully filed down to ensure a

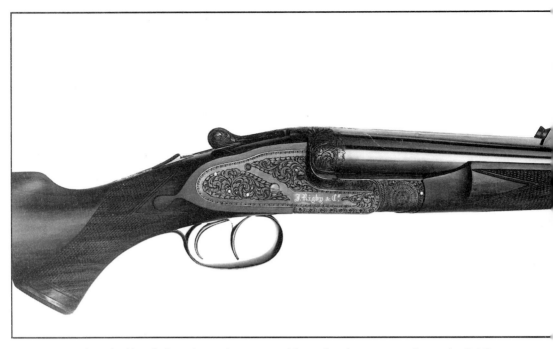

A modern double rifle by John Rigby in .470 calibre. The ultimate in quality and reliability.
(*John Rigby & Co (Gunmakers) Ltd*)

perfect eventual fit. If skilfully carried out, such meticulous attention to detail gives a final tolerance of one soot grain – but it may have taken months to achieve.

With the mechanism functioning correctly and the barrels and action fitting to the gunmaker's satisfaction, everything is submitted to final proof in order to test all the components at higher than normal pressures. After the proof charges have been fired, the assembly is carefully inspected for signs of weakness, and if none are detected, both the barrels and action are stamped with the appropriate proof marks. The rifle is now ready for stocking and finishing.

In 'best grade' double rifles, the customer can select the particular piece of walnut from which the stock and fore-end for his rifle are made. Before a walnut block can be used it must be matured and seasoned for at least five years and it is carefully weighed periodically to detect the degree of weight loss from its drying-out. It is only when the weight has stabilised that it is considered ready for use. After roughly cutting to shape, the action end is worked on very carefully so that the fit between wood and metal is precise. In addition, just enough wood is cut out to allow the locks to function – excessive removal of wood would weaken the timber. Like the meticulous actioning, precisely fitting the stock to the action is a laborious and painstaking process. Any undetected 'high spots' in the wood to metal fit focuses the force of the recoil in one place and the uneven stresses which result can warp or crack the stock. When all fitting work is completed the stock is cut, filed and finally sanded to the correct dimensions for the individual customer. At this stage it may be weighted and hollowed to adjust the final balance of the weapon.

The rifle, after the stocking has been completed, can now be put together and fired, but it still has to go through the final part of its manufacture, the 'finishing'. Nowadays, double-barrel rifles are invariably weapons of the highest quality, and those London firms that still produce them to order would seek to produce not only a 'best' rifle, but also a weapon which embodies a high degree of artistic skill.

Thus, while the barrels are blacked and polished, the stock is finely chequered and the action mechanisms are given their final 'tuning'. At the same time the lock plates come to the attention of the engraver. Here the artistry of the skilled engraver is given full rein and men like Ken Hunt have achieved world renown for the beauty of their work. Depending on the customer's taste and wishes, decoration of the lock plates can vary from fine scroll engraving to relief-carved big-game animals with varying degrees of gold inlay.

When a double rifle leaves Purdey, Holland and Holland, or Rigby, it has received thousands of hours of careful attention throughout its building, and has been thoroughly tested and inspected so that it can be relied upon to function and shoot reliably under conditions which would probably incapacitate lesser weapons. It will also be an artistic delight, and a London-made double rifle is still considered by the majority of sporting rifle users as the ultimate in prestige weaponry. Other weapons may be more accurate or shoot further, but none commands the respect of a Rigby or Purdey 'Double Express' or a Holland 'Royal'.

Midlands rifle production

The London gunmakers may cater for the very exclusive top end of the sporting rifle market but the factories that until recently produced rifles in the English Midlands played an equally important role in the lower-priced range of sporting rifles. Far from being labelled as cheap and nasty, such makers as Parker Hale and BSA achieved an enviable worldwide reputation for being able to produce really low cost rifles which perform well and possess excellent accuracy.

Like the London rifle, these Midlands produced rifles all conformed to a general style. All were bolt action magazine-fed repeating rifles. Using an English-made rifle barrel and a European-made bolt action, the resulting rifles combined the best of both worlds. The Mauser type bolt action possesses great strength and is noted for its consistent operation. The forged barrels produced by Parker Hale gained a good reputation for their accuracy potential. In combining the two, these rifle makers produced sporting rifles

A Rigby bolt action stalking rifle in the 'Classic' British style. Calibre .275 (7 × 57). (*John Rigby & Co (Gunmakers) Ltd*)

that were as accurate and reliable as any other of similar design, yet they were generally lower priced than their competitors.

While the London built double-barrel rifle is nowadays generally built in the heavier calibre, the mass produced bolt action repeater made in the Midlands tended to be made in the 'deer' calibres. Even so, within the general style of rifle each manufacturer developed a range of weapons to suit the varying requirements and tastes of rifle shooters throughout the world.

The classic English style magazine rifle, developed pre-1939 before satisfactory telescopic sights were available, still retains the standard stock, and such is the demand for this conservative style that in the 1980s Parker Hale introduced a rifle to this design, the M81 Classic. Even so, there was less drop at the comb of the stock in this new rifle so that a scope could still be used. Apart from this, its matt oil rubbed woodwork, plain chequering and absence of line spacers and rosewood embellishment make it a modern echo of the golden age of British overseas hunting. Very recently Parker Hale ceased all rifle making in this country and its machinery was moved to the United States where production has been resumed.

Parker Hale also produce a range of standard rifles of varying grades, together with a heavy barrel varminter and an African rifle – the former chambered for four calibres from .22–250 to .25–06, and the latter designed for either .375 H & H Magnum or .458 Winchester Magnum. The Midland Gun Company produced their Midland Model 2100 in nine different calibres. This rifle uses a Springfield bolt action yet its Parker Hale barrel ensures that it is still an accurate and businesslike weapon.

No mention of the Midlands rifle-making trade would be complete without the name of Westley-Richards. Rivalling Holland in their development of such calibres as the .425 and the .318 Accelerated Express, nowadays they build best quality double rifles in a variety of heavy calibres and they also produce a wide variety of excellent bolt action magazine rifles.

In Britain, where the gun industry has a long history and a traditional outlook, the two main styles of sporting rifle now produced have 'traditional' styling. The double rifle and the bolt action magazine rifle are the styles on which the British gun trade built its reputation and the great gunmakers would be very reluctant to abandon these in favour of other designs. As far as I know,

The Model 1200 Super Clip rifle made by Parker Hale is styled on American lines, with a roll-over cheekpiece, contrasting fore-end tip and grip cap, and white line spacers. (*Parker Hale Ltd*)

The Midland 2100 is probably the lowest priced centrefire rifle available today, yet it lives up to Parker Hale's reputation for accuracy and strength. (*Parker Hale Ltd*)

no self-loading, lever actioned or pump actioned centrefire sporting rifles have been produced in Britain except on a very experimental basis.

Custom rifle-makers

The decline of the .22 rimfire market in Britain and fierce competition from abroad saw the eventual abandonment of .22 rimfire sporting rifle production in the 1960s. Prior to this, firms such as BSA produced simple rimfire rifles which, though crude compared to those made in Europe or the USA, were superbly accurate. As a twelve-year-old I could confidently shoot pigeon and rabbits at any range up to a hundred yards with open sights on a simple BSA 'Sportsman' rifle, yet in terms of sales these weapons could never compete with the more stylish and modern designs coming from Anschutz, Brno, Winchester or Savage. The decline of production in the .22 rimfire rifle left Britain as a country which produced only centrefire rifles for the export market. The only domestic demand came from the small group of deer stalkers, but it is this group which has shown a healthy and encouraging growth during the post-war years. Perhaps as a response to this group a third, albeit small, group of rifle-makers exists which cater more specifically for the stalking market. These small firms of custom rifle-makers are scattered around Britain. Although the London makers also produce bolt action magazine rifles (Rigby are particularly famous) such names as Proctor, Armstrong, and especially David Lloyd, are gaining much recognition within the deer-stalking market of temperate countries and the antelope hunters in the tropics.

Generally, these rifles are built on Mauser and, more recently, Sako bolt actions and are sighted and zeroed to the customer's requirements. The David Lloyd rifle, on the other hand, is rather different. In most rifles the telescopic sight is added as an accessory. This usually means that the scope mount is the weak link in the rifle's overall performance and it is sensitive to rough handling, which may knock it out of zero. To solve this problem the Lloyd rifle is really a telescopic sight around which a rifle has been built. Fundamentally different in its design to a normal bolt action rifle, the scope and action are first built as one solid unit after which the barrel is aligned and the rifle bedded in the stock. In this way the weapon retains its zero under any of the rigorous conditions encountered while stalking deer on open ground. Apart from the standard calibres, the Lloyd rifle is also produced in .244 H & H Magnum, the 7 × 66 Von Hofe, and the .264 Winchester Magnum for long-range deer and antelope shooting. This rifle is slowly gaining much esteem in other parts of the world as a virtually indestructible and very accurate bolt actioned sporting weapon.

Like the London doubles, the custom bolt action rifles are built only to order and are not usually available 'off the shelf'. Building such a weapon is time consuming and therefore costly, though the price is still well below that of a London-built double rifle.

EUROPEAN SPORTING RIFLES

The sporting rifle production of Britain is directed to the top and lower end of the market whereas the European sporting rifle-makers direct their products towards the middle of the range. As with the evolution of the 'English' style of rifle, the long tradition of gunmaking in many parts of Europe has resulted in a number of European weapon styles which owe their design more to shooting on the mainland of Europe than to any expansion into the tropics. Again, as in Britain, the dominant mass-produced rifle is a bolt action magazine rifle, and it is from Europe that the best bolt designs originated. Though copied and 'improved' by rifle manufacturers throughout the world, the basic actions designed by Mauser and Mannlicher have never been bettered and very few centrefire bolt action rifles are made with bolts that differ markedly from either of these two types.

(*opposite*) Built on a different principle to conventional bolt actioned rifles, the David Lloyd rifle is virtually indestructible. (*David Lloyd*)

In addition to the bolt action, two other styles of rifle have a small but loyal group of adherents within European sporting rifle circles: the double barrel rifle and the 'drilling'. They both developed in response to the sort of driven game shooting that is practised throughout Europe.

The double-barrel rifle has always had minor support and the European double is more often an over and under than a side by side. These weapons, accurate at the short ranges for which they were designed and chambered for the more powerful continental calibres, are considered by many European hunters to be ideal for shooting driven boar at close quarters. It is this sort of driven shoot which has evolved perhaps the strangest and yet most undeniably European style of weapon. In the large forested areas of Europe a sportsman on a driven shoot may be faced with anything from a snipe to a stag. In order to cope with this sort of variety he would have to have had at least one shotgun and possibly two rifles, but the German arms manufacturers solved the problem by building a whole variety of combination shotgun/rifles. These weapons, often called 'drillings', can be built with up to four barrels. They are usually chambered as a double-barrel shotgun with two separate rifle calibres – one a small bore .22 rimfire or Hornet and the other a more substantial calibre. Thus armed, a sportsman would have a selection of cartridges, all loaded into the one weapon, that could cope adequately with any game likely to be driven to him.

In terms of production volume, the European output of shotguns is centred in Spain and Italy. These countries have dominated the shotgun market for the last twenty-five years. Production of sporting rifles, on the other hand, is concentrated in the more northern areas of Europe, particularly in the Scandinavian and Germanic countries. But two other areas make a significant contribution to the sporting rifle market. To the east, the only ex-communist bloc country to really impress the West with the quality of their sporting weapons is the Czech Republic, and on the west coast, the variety of rifles to come out of Belgium adds another dimension to the present-day European output of sporting rifles.

Scandinavian rifle-makers

The bolt action rifle is the dominant sporting weapon to be produced in the Scandinavian region although such companies as Valmet produce a few combination rifle/shotguns. Earlier this century, names like Schultz and Larsen and Krag and Jorgensen brought Scandinavian weapons to the attention of the sporting public and this was reinforced by Husquvarna before the last war. In the post-war years, however, the power base of the Scandinavian rifle-making industry has shifted from Norway and Sweden to Finland, and it is from this country that the bulk of production now comes. Two companies dominate the output from Finland, and the rifles from the Sako and Tikka works, two recently amalgamated companies, are now known throughout the sporting rifle world.

Sako produce a range of rifles which highlights the fact that they are now geared for exporting their weapons to all parts of the world, and their four

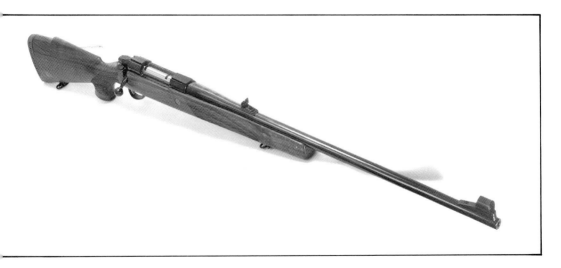

A front-end view of the Sako Deluxe bolt action centrefire rifle. One of a range of medium priced, yet high quality rifles from Finland. (*Gunmark Ltd*)

basic models are each directed to a particular market. Their smallest rifle, the Finnscout, is their .22 rimfire and Hornet weapon – designed specifically for these calibres they are light and very accurate. Moving up the scale there is the varmint rifle made in the centrefire .22 calibres and called, appropriately enough, the Vixen. Like many rifles made for this purpose, the model is available in a variety of barrel weights and is designed solely for use with a telescopic sight. The other two models, the Forester and Finbear cater for the deer stalker and heavier-game hunter in turn, with the former available in standard calibres up to .308 and the latter generally chambered for magnum rounds from .264 Winchester Magnum to .375 H & H Magnum.

Tikka offer a similar range of weapons made to two basic designs. Within these designs they present a range of calibres, stocks and barrel weights to cater for most shooting requirements. In general terms the rifles produced by both Sako and Tikka are well made and very accurate. The amount of time spent in ensuring that they are well finished and that they operate smoothly does mean that they are priced slightly above average for their type, yet this has evidently been of little consequence because both Sako and Tikka rifles have become well-known and popular weapons on the world market. They have established the Finnish-made sporting rifle as a well made weapon that is the equal of any similar design from other countries.

German/Austrian manufacturers

The history of sporting rifle manufacture in the German-speaking countries of Europe goes back a long way. The variety of game that existed in the forested lands of Bavaria and along the northern border of the Alpine mountains gave rise to the production of heavy multi-calibre weapons of the drilling type. Even today a fair number of these are still produced and there is a steady demand for them both in their traditional hunting areas and from other parts of the world where similar conditions and shooting methods exist. Strictly speaking, a drilling is a double-barrel side by side shotgun with one rifle barrel hung underneath – and each design has its own specific name. A double side by side rifle is a 'doppelbüchsdrilling', an over and under rifle is a 'bockdrilling', and a double shotgun with two different rifled barrels is a 'Vierling'.

All these weapons are built on a drop down action with usually a top lever opening, much the same as a normal double rifle or shotgun. The safety catch is usually of the Greener pattern 'side safe' with the button on the side of the action, and the barrel selector is on the top strap where one normally finds the safety catch on a conventional double. For the sport for which they were designed, close range shooting of driven game, they are excellent weapons which offer a great deal of versatility. For instance, a shooter could load one shotgun barrel with No. 6 shot for pheasant, black game or similar, the other shotgun barrel with a Bremmeke slug for wild boar, the .22 rimfire barrel with a hollow-point round for hare and the 7×57 barrel with a deer round. All that remains is the selection of the appropriate barrel for each target! However, though effective for close-up shooting, the formidable problems in aligning the barrels correctly during construction means that they cannot really be considered as sufficiently accurate for ranges beyond one hundred yards. Building a multi-barrelled shotgun/rifle is a complicated and very time-consuming process. The same care and attention is lavished upon these weapons as is seen in the workshops of the London gunmakers, and the price of these drillings is therefore high. Like the London rifles, these German weapons are usually only made to order and to personal specifications. Foremost among the makers of these combination firearms are such firms as Ferlach, Saur, and Krieghoff, and their products bear the evidence of high quality and skilled workmanship which reflects the centuries of skilled gunmaking tradition.

These multi-barrelled weapons only make up a small proportion of the total output of sporting rifles and it is for two designs of bolt actions that Germany and Austria are justly famous throughout the world. Stemming originally from a military rifle, the Mauser 1898 pattern bolt action was quickly adapted to sporting use where its simplicity and strength were exploited. Though the British Lee-Enfield bolt action was considered quicker to operate, the design lacked the Mauser's strength and it was the Mauser which was used for any cartridge which generated high pressures. After the First World War it was the Mauser action which was accepted as the dominant design for the magazine-fed sporting rifle.

The Mauser factory still dominates the sporting rifle output of Germany. Nowadays, they offer a wide range of centrefire rifles in the variety of different designs the shooting public has come to expect for different sporting purposes. Thus the Mauser model 77 is available in a wide range of calibres and action lengths to encompass any type of rifle sport from varminting to big-game hunting. The Mauser model 66 goes one stage further in having the facility to change barrels, and therefore calibres, on one action

Drilling. Double side by side shotgun with a centrefire rifle barrel underneath.

Doppelbüchsdrilling. The opposite of the drilling. Double side by side centrefire rifle with shotgun barrel underneath.

Vierling. Double side by side shotgun with rimfire and centrefire rifle barrels underneath.

Bockdrilling. Single shotgun, rimfire rifle and centrefire rifle assembled in an over and under form.

Types of European Combination Shotgun/Rifles.

and stock. This greatly increases the versatility of the weapon and can be looked upon as a significant advance in sporting rifle design.

Producing sporting rifles on the same bolt action, Friedrich Heym has gained a reputation for both accurate and stylish rifles. His two basic models, the SR 20 and SR 40, cover the deer stalking and .22 centrefire calibres. They are also available with left-handed actions and bolts. In addition to these models, Heym have also collaborated with Ruger of the USA to build superbly accurate single shot rifles on the falling block action. The Ruger produced action is fitted with Heym barrels and woodwork and the result is an outstandingly accurate and strongly built single shot rifle. This model is offered in nine standard and magnum calibres from 6.5 × 57R to 9.3 × 74R.

Still in Germany, the firm of Heckler and Koch, noted for its importance as a designer and producer of military weapons, also produces a number of self-loading sporting rifles in calibres ranging from .223 to .30–06, but they have very limited appeal at present and the market in this sort of weapon is dominated by the North American manufacturers. Perhaps the most attractive sporting weapon that is produced by Heckler and Koch is their .22 rimfire self-loading rifle which has put the company firmly into the sporting rifle market.

In output of .22 rimfire rifles, the dominant German producer in this calibre is Anschutz. Well known in the target shooting arena, the Anschutz sporting rifles are no less respected in sporting rimfire shooting circles. Although they do produce .22 centrefires, the bulk of the Anschutz factory production is made up of rifles chambered for .22 LR and .22 rimfire magnum. The experience gained in building match-winning target rifles has had a spin-off into their sporting rifle production and these sporting rifles have a fine reputation for accuracy.

Austria is the home of another sporting rifle giant. Like Mauser, the name 'Mannlicher' is well known wherever sporting rifle shooting takes place and rifles from this manufacturer are still prized as hunting weapons. Though widely used before the last war, the original Mannlicher style bolt action lost favour to the Mauser action as the telescopic sight became accepted in post-war shooting circles. Originally the Mannlicher bolt handle was drawn back through a gate in the receiver and this made scope mounting very difficult. Although side mounts were devised they never became as popular as a top mounted scope and the Mauser bolt action, on which a scope could be easily mounted, is now the most favoured. If Mauser now dominates the design of bolt actions, then it is Mannlicher who have exerted a great influence on the style of the modern bolt actioned rifle.

In the deep woods of south central Europe, a long-barrelled rifle can be a positive disadvantage and there evolved an altogether shorter-barrelled weapon. In addition, the uneven terrain and often thick undergrowth called for the barrel to be protected to its muzzle, and thus the full-stocked 'Mannlicher Style' rifle was born. Nowadays this design, which is also called the Stutzen, is riding on a wave of popularity and has been copied by many manufacturers and on all calibres of rifle. Anschutz, for instance, produce their model 1418 .22 rimfire to this format and the BSA CF 2 Stutzen is also a copy in centrefire calibres.

Mannlicher themselves produce a wide variety of rifles based on three calibre groupings. Their model SL and L rifles are built in the lightweight calibres for .222 Remington up to .308 Winchester. These are essentially varmint and deer rifles and, like all the Mannlicher weapons, they are available in full-stocked and half-stocked styles with a variety of barrel weights. Medium calibre rifles come under the letter code 'M' in the variety this maker offers, and the big game rifles come under the letter 'S' (strong) for non-dangerous big game and 'ST' (strong tropical) for African shooting. Like any firm which has a long tradition and high reputation, Mannlicher are keen to maintain their respected place among the rifle-makers of the world, and a great deal of care and

All Mannlicher rifles have a characteristic spiral on the breech-end of their barrels which reflects their method of forging the tube. (*Steyr-Mannlicher*)

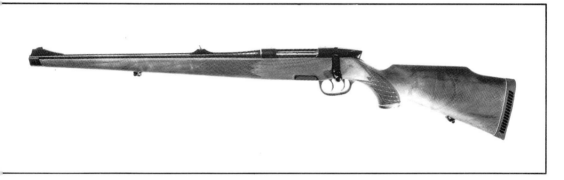

A left-handed full-stocked Mannlicher rifle. (*Steyr-Mannlicher*)

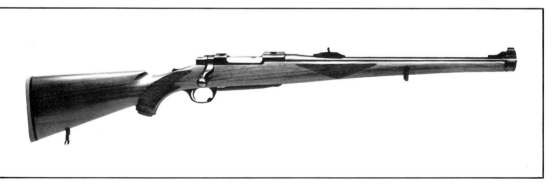

Mannlicher's full-stocked Stutzen design has been copied by manufacturers in many countries. This is a model made by Ruger in North America. (*Sturm-Ruger Corp.*)

The BRNO bolt action .22 rimfire is probably the most popular rimfire hunting rifle in Britain.

attention is put into the production of their rifles. By combining their traditional rifle-making skills with modern production techniques, this firm stays in the forefront of the rifle-makers of Europe.

Two other names have become established on the rifle hunting scene in recent years, and both again stem from the Austrian/German group of rifle manufacturers. Voere rifles are similar in appearance to those produced by Mannlicher and are offered in a range of calibres and stock designs to cover most European hunting situations. Using the Mauser 98 action as their starting point, Voere produce good quality standard rifles and are now breaking into the luxury market with a variety of engraved and silver and gold decorated rifles. Krico also produce a wide variety of rifles and, like the others in this group, they are rapidly gaining a good name for themselves as makers of carefully constructed and accurate weapons. Unlike the other manufacturers, though, they are not concentrating production on either rimfires (like Anschutz) or centrefires (like Voere). The Krico .22 rimfires are beautifully made weapons and their centrefire sporting rifles have all the refinements of the other weapons emanating from Germany and Austria.

Czech rifle production

The arms factories of Brno in the Czech Republic gave the British armed forces the bren-gun before the last war – bren being an abbreviation for Brno and Enfield. It is from these factories that the modern Brno sporting rifles are exported to most sporting areas of the world. With only one exception, a rather unpopular self-loading .22 rimfire, Brno rifles are bolt action designs and have the reputation for being solidly built and accurate.

While lacking the finish of many of the other European rifles, they are nevertheless reliable and good performers. They are also considerably cheaper than their West European counterparts.

The Brno big-game rifles are made on short, medium or long bolt actions according to the length of each cartridge, and calibres range from .243 Winchester up to .404 Jeffrey and .458 Winchester Magnum. One little refinement these weapons have is that there is a concealed aperture sight built into the action and it can be clicked into the upright position to be used instead of the normal open sights. While this would seldom be used in this day of telescopic sights, it does illustrate the degree of thought which goes into the design of these rifles. In 1946 Brno introduced a bolt actioned rifle design specifically for the .22 Hornet cartridge, and though it met with moderate success, production was halted in the late 1950s. However, the demand for this weapon was such that it was brought back into production in the 1960s and since then it has become recognised as one of the best .22 Hornet rifles available. Appropriately named their model Fox, the rifle is now produced in both .222 and .223 Remington.

Their .22 rimfire bolt action rifle has a similar reputation and impresses with its smoothness of operation, strength and accuracy. It looks good, giving the appearance of a true hunting rifle rather than a 'plinker'. Its design and styling have not changed for twenty years and the ZKM452, also called the No.2 rifle, is now established as one of the best .22 rimfire rifles in both Britain and Australia. Nowadays, it is probably the most popular sporting rifle in these two areas and it has certainly helped to earn Brno a reputation as a producer of hard wearing, inexpensive and accurate rifles.

Belgian production

Fabrique Nationale in Belgium produce what is probably the widest variety of different styles of sporting rifles in Europe, and they are all marketed under the 'Browning' trade name. At the top of the range comes their double 'Express' rifle. Unlike the English double, the Browning model is of a boxlock action on an over and under (O/U) rifle. But, like their London-made counterparts, these are really luxury rifles built to special order and personal taste and measurements. Only occasionally is one available off the shelf. A Browning Express rifle is often embellished with beautifully engraved dummy side plates which give it the appearance of a sidelock rifle, and one weapon may take up to two years to complete. Barrelling, actioning and stocking follows the same general processes as described for the London-made rifle, and this is reflected in the eventual price of the weapon. The locking mechanism used in these O/U rifles is not really as strong as the side by side design, so Browning tend to make these rifles in 7 × 65R and 9.3 × 74R calibres for use against hoofed big game on driven shoots of the 'battue' type.

With this sort of 'quick reaction' shooting in mind, Browning also produce Europe's only truly sporting self-loading rifle in deer calibres – the model known as the 'BAR' – Browning Auto-Loading Rifle. This weapon, which evolved from the wartime Browning BAR gas-operated automatic, is designed specifically for battue shooting where quick sighting and fast handling are a priority. Large open sights and an increased drop in the stock help to achieve this, though the weapon will accept a scope if the shooter wants one. A stalking version of this weapon is available which has a straighter stock and more accurate open sights. Calibres range from .243 up to .338 Winchester Magnum.

Browning also produce two models of bolt action centrefire rifles and the only European centrefire lever action rifle. One bolt action, the BBR, is of conventional design on an improved Mauser action, but the FN Sauer is of different design and has a characteristically European-style stock in which the line from comb to heel forms a 'hog's back'. While the FN Sauer is directed towards the European market, the lever action rifle is definitely styled to the taste of the American rifle shooter.

As well as these centrefire rifles, Browning also produce five different rimfire rifles to cater for the demands of most rimfire users. Their simple 'T Bolt' bolt action repeater is an ideal training weapon which is also sufficiently accurate for small-game hunting. At the other end of their rimfire range are the sophisticated BAR and BPR rifles which work on an auto-loading and a pump action, respectively. These are really full-sized hunting rifles and they reflect the quality for which Browning have become famous. The two remaining models, the lever action and the Auto 22, are both long-lived designs which saw service before the last war. The lever action is a scaled-down version of John M. Browning's 1881 design and the Auto 22 was a favourite shooting gallery weapon in the 1930s.

The European rifle-makers have given a great deal to the sporting rifle scene. In terms of rifle mechanisms, the Mauser bolt is probably the most widely used action on centrefire sporting rifles, and in terms of styling we have been given the elegant 'schnabel' fore-end tip and the 'hog's back' stock. However, the most important contribution to the style of sporting rifles is perhaps the Mannlicher or Stutzen stock and this often complements the Mauser action on many of today's rifles. The European manufacturers can call on many centuries of experience in the traditional rifle-making skills, which they have effectively and successfully blended with modern technology, and they have a sound reputation wherever sporting rifles are used or discussed.

AMERICAN MANUFACTURERS

Even though the rifle-makers of Britain and Europe have made important contributions to the sporting rifle scene since the last war it is generally accepted that the American arms manufacturers are now the dominant force in this market. Even though such concerns as Winchester, Remington and Savage had made a tentative foray into the world market during the 1930s, in general they were still producing weapons mainly for their home market. This continued until the decline of the British rifle and the setback in European production due to war damage had left a big gap in the overseas markets. It was this gap that the American rifle manufacturers were quick to fill and in doing so they now have an unassailable lead in the world.

To be fair, many of the pre-war American rifles were not made for the style of hunting practised in Europe, Africa and Asia and they showed up poorly compared to the British and European rifles. The traditional lever action repeating rifle was chambered for cartridges which, though powerful enough for American game, were considered far too underpowered to cope with Old World species. The standard of workmanship too was inferior to the craftsman-built weapons on this side of the Atlantic and anyone seen using an American repeater was viewed with some suspicion in traditional European shooting circles.

The breakthrough and establishment of American influence on the world rifle market came about for two reasons. Before the last war ammunition research had been more actively developed in the USA and this led to the introduction of calibres which, to the British and European sportsman, produced quite startling ballistics. Among the leaders were such rounds as the .250 Savage (sometimes called the 250/3000), the .270 Winchester, and the .22 Hornet. Each produced velocities and trajectories far superior to their competition and gunmakers in Europe were quick to build rifles in these new calibres. Other calibres followed, the .220 Swift was the first to develop standard velocities of over 4000 fps, the .257 Roberts, the .22 Savage High Power, and the 219 Zipper all brought a new respect to their country of origin. At the same time that these calibres were being introduced both Winchester and Remington introduced bolt action repeating rifles with Winchester's model 70 first appearing in the 1930s. These rifles, together with Savage's model 99 lever action, were chambered for the new calibres and were quickly recognised as a serious threat to the established order. They were strongly built, reliable and accurate, and they were also considerably less expensive than similar rifles produced by the established firms in Britain and Europe.

The foothold gained in those pre-war years was readily exploited after the war as each of the already well-known arms manufacturers turned their sights on the overseas market. As a consequence, the present day output from such firms as Remington, Savage, Winchester, Ithaca, Marlin and others, highlights the fact that they are producing weapons for both domestic consumption and overseas trade.

It is for this reason that the USA can now boast a larger output of rifles, a greater volume and variety of ammunition, and a wider choice of rifle style than any other continent, let alone single country. Unlike Europe, therefore, where rifle production can be classified by area, the simplest way to categorise sporting rifle output from the USA is by rifle type: lever action, pump action, auto-loaders, single shot and bolt action.

Lever action rifles

To the majority of people the lever action rifle conjures up images of the

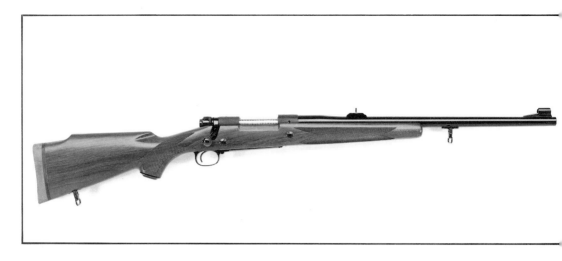

Today the Winchester model 70 is still selling well. This rifle is the model 70 African Magnum available in .375 H & H Magnum and .458 Winchester Magnum. Note that the front sling swivel is mounted on the barrel. This avoids the forward hand being cut by the swivel during the rifle's heavy recoil. (*U.S. Repeating Arms Co.*)

American Wild West and cowboys, and this traditional repeating rifle design has a strong following among modern American hunters. The present Winchester model 94 perpetuates this legendary style and much research has been carried out to improve the power capacity of this design. Initially the lever mechanism's design limited it to handling straight or only slightly necked cartridges. This meant that the earlier models of the rifle were not chambered for the newly developed high velocity calibres and they therefore had limited overseas appeal. Although the 30–30 calibre went some way towards a solution, only recently have new ballistic developments improved the overall power handling of the Winchester. Two new calibres, the .307 Winchester and .356 Winchester, have recently been developed which give the Winchester 94 a comparable performance with the other, more conventional, deer rifles.

Marlin produce the model 444 which is chambered for the most powerful lever action cartridge of their own design, the .444 Marlin. This has adequate power to stop any North American game but both this rifle and the Winchester 94 have only a limited appeal on the overseas market.

The only lever action rifle to gain any overseas recognition, the Savage, was introduced before the First World War and is now chambered for a variety of modern calibres – .243 Winchester, .308 Winchester, and 7mm/08 Remington. Built on a different principle to the Winchester and Marlin actions, the Savage is strongly constructed and can handle higher pressure cartridges with safety. Current variations on the model 99 employ clip or rotary magazines, have straight or pistol grip stocks, and appear to be little changed from earlier models of the same rifle. Even among the more conservative British and European rifle shooting circles it has been recognised as a fine and accurate rifle and its design has certainly stood the test of time.

Lever action rifles chambered for the .22 rimfire are popular in the USA and

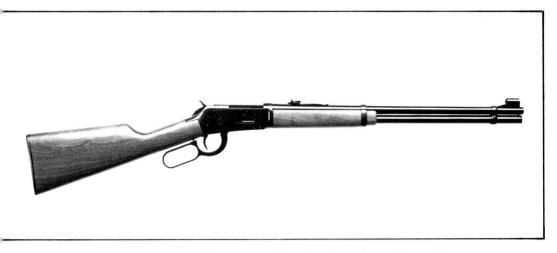

The latest Winchester model 94 lever action rifle – virtually unchanged for nearly a century, it speaks volumes for the reliability of this design. (*U.S. Repeating Arms Co.*)

Marlin produce the most powerful lever action rifle in their .444 calibre. (*Marlin Arms*)

models in this calibre are produced by Ithaca, Marlin, Winchester, and Savage, although the Savage is a single shot rifle. Their main attraction is that they are short, light and quick-handling weapons with sufficient accuracy for plinking or shooting short-range small game.

Pump action rifles

Though just as much an American design as the lever action, the pump action rifle appears to be less popular. Only two companies produce centrefire rifles in this style and it seems that, while the pump shotgun is very popular, the equivalent rifle is slowly going out of favour. Remington produce a pump

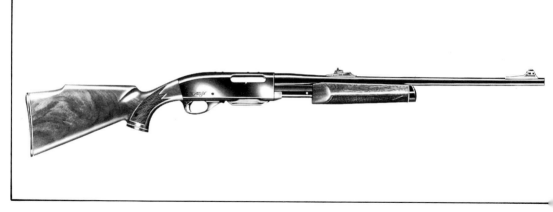

The Remington model 6 pump action has been popular for many years, but this design of rifle is losing ground to other mechanisms. (*Remington Arms Co.*)

action rifle around their well-tried mechanism and the model 6 is available in a variety of medium calibres from 6mm Remington to .308 Winchester. It is a stylish rifle, enhanced by its intricate chequering and straight line stock and it is proving popular among devotees of this style of rifle.

The Savage model 170 looks far more functional and yet it has been in demand for many years. Chambered for either 30–30 or .35 Remington, it appeals to a significant number of American backwoods hunters for use against deer and black bear.

Compared to other rifles, the pump action has the advantage of rapid reloading without disturbing the aim unduly, and it can carry heavier calibres than most lever actions. Although this design is recognised for its merits as a sporting rifle in other parts of the world, recent legislation in Britain has made the centrefire pump-actioned rifle a prohibited weapon for sporting purposes in this country.

Even in .22 rimfire, the selection available has shrunk to one American model, the Remington Fieldmaster model 572, although Browning's newly-introduced pump action .22, the BPR, is also available. With the advantages inherent in the very nature of the pump action repeating rifle we are unlikely to see the total demise of this style of sporting rifle.

Auto-loaders

In the early 1900s, Remington produced the first successful auto-loading rifle – the model 8. Since then they have gained much experience in the design of such weapons and Remington still dominate the centrefire field with their model 4. Like their model 6 pump action, it is a graceful weapon which has a fine reputation for accuracy and lack of recoil. Reloading is by the gas-operated system whereby a small quantity of the propellant gas is used to activate the reloading cycle of ejecting the spent case, rechambering a fresh round, cocking the bolt and locking the whole mechanism ready to fire. Like the model 6, this Remington product comes in a variety of medium-power calibres and is a well-

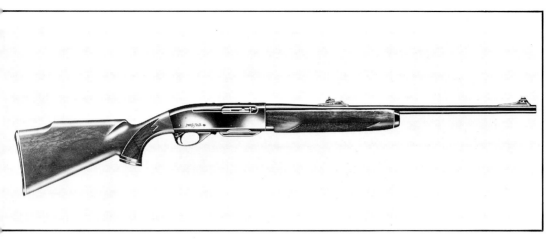

The Remington model 4. This centrefire auto-loader has clean and simple lines.
(*Remington Arms Co.*)

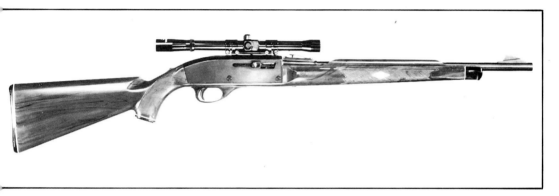

The Remington Nylon 66 was a revolutionary design when it first appeared. The stock and fore-end are made of synthetic materials and the bearing surfaces in the action are of nylon.
(*Remington Arms Co.*)

respected weapon in hunting circles. Other firms have experimented with the centrefire auto-loader but Remington remain well in the lead in this style of rifle. Like the centrefire pump action, legislation has also prohibited the centrefire auto-loader for sporting purposes in Britain while still allowing the use of both mechanisms in .22 rimfire sporting rifles.

The auto-loading .22 rimfire is a fiercely contested field. Here, the Remington 522 Speedmaster and their lightweight Nylon 66 compete with offerings from Harrington and Richardson, Savage, Mossberg, and Marlin. Unlike the centrefires, these tend to operate on the 'blow back' principle where the reloading cycle is recoil operated. Though not as accurate as a well-made bolt action rifle, the auto-loading .22 is a weapon which is just as effective against small game. I once saw my father shoot six bolting rabbits with six rapid shots from his Savage .22 and the whole sequence must have lasted less than five seconds! Overall, the auto-loading .22 rimfire is probably

Perhaps for the top end of the .22 rimfire auto-loader market, the Weatherby mark XXII is a very attractive weapon. (*Roy Weatherby*)

second only to the bolt action in terms of popularity, and the models produced by the American manufacturers are as good as any.

One American manufacturer has produced a short carbine type of rifle and offers it in two calibres. The Ruger auto-loading carbines are available in either .22 LR or .44 Magnum. The former is a drum-fed, ten-shot rifle which is becoming popular in Britain and Australia, and the latter, chambered for what is really a heavy pistol round, is considered to be adequate for small to medium deer at short ranges and therefore comes under the sporting rifle category.

Single-shot rifles

Of the single shot rifles, two significant styles emerge in the centrefire calibres. Harrington and Richardson produce a range of drop down single shot rifles in a variety of calibres from .22 Hornet up to 45–70. These are simple weapons which cannot boast the accuracy or power of other rifle designs yet they are

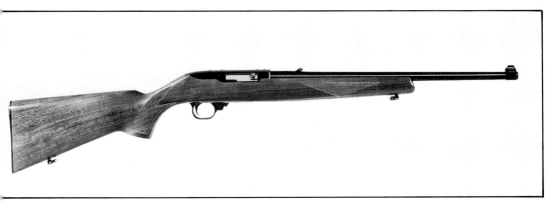

The Ruger model 10/22 features a ten-shot drum magazine in its .22 rimfire version. (*Sturm-Ruger Inc.*)

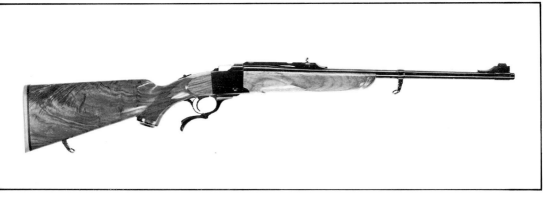

The Ruger No.1 single shot centrefire rifle has established a reputation for strength and great accuracy. (*Sturm-Ruger Inc.*)

rugged and reliable and are often used to initiate the American novice into the world of sporting rifle shooting.

The other type of single shot rifle is in a different league. The Ruger No.1 rifle is based on a modified Farquharson falling block action. As such, it utilises the compactness and great accuracy potential of this old design to produce one of today's most accurate hunting rifles. The barrel length ranges from the standard 22in to 26in in the appropriate calibres and this also helps to give the model an edge on accuracy. Several versions of the Ruger No.1 rifle are made in calibres ranging from the reintroduced .220 Swift up to .458 Winchester Magnum so there is a Ruger falling block for practically all types of rifle hunting. They also make a short-barrelled carbine version in calibres from .22 Hornet to 45–70 to cater for the home market in the USA. Even in the few years since its introduction, the Ruger No.1 single shot rifle has established itself among accurate hunting weapons as one with worldwide appeal.

Single shot .22 rimfire rifles abound. They are made in a great variety of styles, break-open, drop down rifles with bolt actions and lever actions vying

Many American manufacturers build scaled-down single shot .22 rimfire rifles for young shooters. This is Marlin's Little Buckaroo bolt action rifle. (*Marlin Arms Inc.*)

with each other for the bottom end of the rimfire market. These are essentially designed as 'boys' or 'learners' rifles and are intended to help in safety instruction and shooting discipline. As such they are reliable yet inexpensive. Even so, they ought not to be dismissed as unimportant weapons. It is from such firearms that many sporting shooters, myself included, have graduated to bigger and better weapons later in life.

Bolt actions

Compared with the other repeating rifles described, the American bolt action sporting rifle is a latecomer to the scene. Though rifles of this type were adopted for military use early this century, the breakthrough into the world sporting rifle market was only achieved in the 1930s when Winchester started producing its model 70 centrefire bolt action rifle. Competing as it did with the bespoke rifle from the English and European makers, the model 70 undercut their price yet still retained the quality and accuracy for which it is famous.

Nowadays, most of the leading arms manufacturers of North America produce bolt action centrefire rifles which are fed from a clip magazine housed under the action. The majority of them are based on the Mauser pattern bolt but in America there is a wider variation in the design of bolts than we find in Europe. Many of these rifles have now been in production for a number of years and have proved the reliability of their respective designs. The two arms giants of North America, Remington and Winchester, concentrate a large proportion of their production on bolt actioned centrefires. Remington has gained widespread acclaim for their model 700 and the new model 7, and their economy model 788 quickly gathered a strong following in both Europe and Australia where it is seen as an accurate but inexpensive deer rifle. The model 788 is also available in carbine form with an 18½in barrel for shooting in thick brush country. The Winchester model 70 is still available in a variety of styles and calibres and is probably one of the world's most widely used rifles – perhaps even more respected as a sporting rifle than the famous Winchester lever action firearm.

Two other manufacturers are producing bolt action rifles of their own design

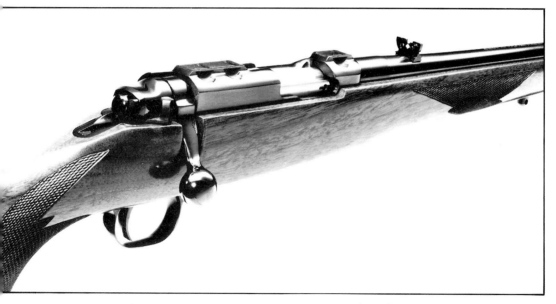

Ruger's new model 77/22 is a high quality bolt action .22 rimfire rifle. (*Sturm-Ruger Inc.*)

which have become popular as hunting weapons. Savage produce their model 110 in both standard and economy grade and they also produce left-handed rifles in the same design. Ruger's bolt actioned centrefire rifles come under the model M77 type with two styles of bolt action and a wide variety of calibres to cater for a very extensive range of sporting rifle shooting requirements. Calibres range from the .17 Remington to .458 Winchester which illustrates the choice available.

Other manufacturers to produce centrefire rifles in this style include Harrington and Richardson with their model 300, Ithaca, who collaborate with BSA to market their CF2 hunting rifles, and Interarms who assemble and market their wide range of Mark X rifles.

Practically all rifle-making firms in North America produce bolt action repeating .22 rimfire rifles and these fall into two styles which depend on their magazine capacity: clip-fed and tubular.

Clip-fed rifles have a magazine capacity of up to ten rounds and these are housed in a clip below the action and in front of the trigger guard. Usually they are sold as five-shot rifles, with a ten-round clip being offered as an optional extra. Remington produce their model 581 to this design and their luxury .22 rimfire, the model 541–S, is also built to this format. Similar weapons come from Mossberg, Ithaca, Hi-Standard, Savage/Stevens, and Harrington and Richardson.

The large capacity .22 bolt action rifle tends to hold between fourteen and eighteen rounds in a tubular magazine slung below the barrel in much the same way as some lever action designs. In all other respects these tubular magazine rimfire rifles are the same as their five-shot, clip-fed counterparts and indeed, most manufacturers offer both designs.

Within the field of sporting shooting with .22 rimfire weapons, it is generally

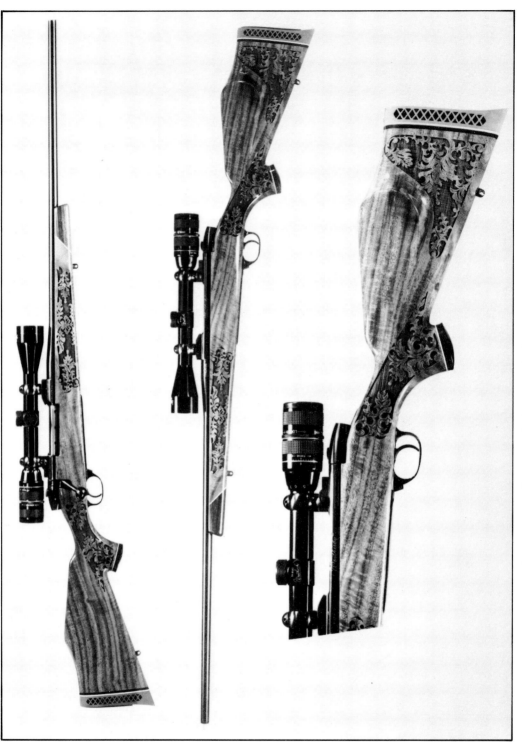

Weatherby Magnum rifles are at the luxury end of the American market and have become the byword in powerful ballistics. *(Roy Weatherby)*

accepted that the bolt action design provides the most consistent chambering, positive ignition, and stable ballistics of all the repeating rifle designs. Where it loses on rate of fire it gains in consistent accuracy, and the bolt action is therefore the most popular choice of the largest section of the small-game hunting rimfire users. One other factor that may also be taken into account is that the bolt actioned rimfire rifle tends to be simpler to make, and therefore less expensive, than other repeating or auto-loading designs. But the budget-conscious hunter will find that a bolt action is still a very accurate rifle. My own .22 bolt action rifle cost me less than the scope sight I put on it, yet without the scope I could not do justice to the rifle's accuracy.

Weatherby rifles

No description of present day American rifle production would be complete without mention of the works of Roy Weatherby in California. Unlike the good quality yet mass produced rifle that comes from the arms manufacturing giants of the USA, Weatherby resembles more the low output, bespoke rifle-makers of London and Europe. Inspired initially by the pre-war ballistics of the English Magnums produced by Holland and Holland, Roy Weatherby set about designing a whole new family of calibres which conformed to magnum specifications. These included a higher than normal velocity and much increased energy for a given bullet weight which in turn produced a weapon which gave better knock-down power at extended ranges. The Weatherby Magnums thus evolved, and he now produces rifles in a range of calibres from the .22 Varmintmaster up to the mighty .460 Weatherby Magnum. These are luxury rifles. Using the inherent strength of the bolt action, finely-bored barrels, and custom stocks, they are recognised as being precision instruments as well as potent weapons. The .460 Weatherby Magnum is, in fact, the only calibre to develop a greater energy than the old .600 Nitro Express – it is advertised as driving a 500 grain bullet out with a muzzle energy of over 9000 ft/lb.

All the Weatherby calibres generate greater chamber pressures and therefore develop increased recoil. This has given rise to the term 'Weatherby Eye', the black eye and cut on the forehead which is the result of being hit by the back end of a telescopic sight under heavy recoil. Certainly Weatherby's .460 Magnum is acknowledged as the most ferocious calibre in modern-day usage.

This account of sporting rifle production is by no means complete; there are other rifle-makers in a variety of locations producing a limited number of weapons for a limited local market; and these small concerns will continue to operate as long as sporting rifle shooting exists. But each area does seem to produce a characteristic style of rifle to meet the various demands of the sporting rifle market. If a prospective buyer first decides the style and calibre of rifle that would suit his or her needs, a firearm can be found that will exactly fill the requirements. The selection of rifles available on the world market indicates that sporting rifle shooting is in a healthy state indeed!

weapons for a limited local market; and these small concerns will continue to operate as long as sporting rifle shooting exists. But each area does seem to produce a characteristic style of rifle to meet the various demands of the sporting rifle market. If a prospective buyer first decides the style and calibre of rifle that would suit his or her needs, a firearm can be found that will exactly fill the requirements. The selection of rifles available on the world market indicates that sporting rifle shooting is in a healthy state indeed!

PART TWO

THE SPORT

4. .22 Rimfire Sport in Britain

RIFLE shooting in the British Isles is more restricted than shotgun sport for two main reasons. Most of our large animals – wild boar, wolf, lynx, brown bear – had become extinct before rifles were developed. Even in the mountainous areas of Scotland there were no remote tracts of wilderness and forest to harbour these species such as those in central Europe and Scandinavia, and in those unenlightened times most people followed a policy of ruthless extermination. Having lost these creatures and with the deer numbers still declining, it is hardly surprising that during the nineteenth and early twentieth centuries Britain looked to her Empire for the best of her rifle shooting. Secondly, during the last two centuries the population of Britain increased dramatically and the countryside, far from remaining empty, began to acquire a density of population which would make the indiscriminate use of rifles a serious threat to human safety. As a consequence a series of Firearms Acts have served to restrict rifle shooting to very definite limits. As the law stands at present, a sportsman wishing to use a sporting rifle must prove to the appropriate authorities that he has cause to own and use such a weapon. The onus is on him to declare the purpose for which the rifle is needed and the ground on which he has authority to use it.

Despite these two factors, there are still many opportunities for sporting rifle shooting in Britain and there has been, for several reasons, a recent reversal of the immediate post-war decline in rifle sports. Sporting rifle shooting today can be divided into three main categories: deer stalking, vermin control and small-game hunting. These can, in turn, be identified by the variety of rifle calibres used.

Deer stalking is at present an expanding sport and rifles for the British deer species range from the .243 Winchester, up to the .30–06 and the .308 Winchester, in England and Wales. There is also a small demand for varmint shooting (mainly fox control) and calibres most often used for this sport fall into the .22 centrefire family. However, by far the most widely used sporting rifle calibre in Britain is the .22 rimfire. In Britain there are probably over one hundred rimfire rifles in use for every one centrefire sporting rifle and, despite legislative pressure and restrictions, the .22 rimfire is a very popular weapon.

In East Anglia many coypu are shot using .22 rimfires. (*Alan Savory*)

After 1960, when Eley finally ceased production of ammunition in the rook-and-rabbit calibres, the .22 rimfire came to totally dominate the field vacated by the rook rifle's demise. Nowadays it is the prime calibre for use against small-game and vermin species. Within its limits of accuracy it is accepted as a suitable calibre for shooting quarry species up to the size of a fox, and a variety of ammunition is available to cater for this range of target size. Unlike shotgun shooting, the variety of sport available to the user of a .22 rimfire cannot be categorised in terms of the habitat or environment in which the shooting takes place. Compared to the coastal wildfowler, the moorland grouse shooter, or the lowland driven pheasant specialist, the sportsman armed with a .22 rimfire rifle will find his quarry species in a far wider variety of habitats than his shotgun shooting counterpart. It is therefore simpler to classify the sport and quarry available to the user of this calibre under species headings rather than by environment. The sport that is relevant to the .22 rifle user thus divides neatly into the pursuit of ground-game species, and the control of both furred and winged vermin.

GROUND GAME

The rabbit is by far the most popular and most common target for the rimfire shooter. Despite its frequent classification in the British Isles as a vermin species, I think this creature falls into the small-game group on the grounds that the hunter often takes rabbits for the pot or for sale. In this book, the term vermin is confined to inedible species such as rat, fox, feral mink and others.

The rabbit was introduced to Britain from France in the twelfth century and initially it was closely protected as a semi-domesticated animal. From those early days it has spread and colonised all of lowland Britain. By the early 1950s practically all land up to about 1200 ft had a thriving and healthy rabbit population. In the early 1950s the rabbit population was estimated at over sixty million, but 99% of these were killed by the spread of myxomatosis in 1954. Not only did this dreadful disease almost wipe out our rabbits, but the side-effects of this population crash saw the rapid decline of the rabbit's natural predators. Birds of prey, and buzzards in particular, have never recovered from this episode. The chalk downlands of southern England, for centuries cropped closely by rabbits, were quickly colonised by weed species that the rabbit had hitherto controlled. In some areas the whole landscape changed within a few years of the rabbit's departure.

Thankfully, the rabbit is a survivor, and in the last twenty years the population has been steadily increasing again. Although there are still sporadic outbreaks of myxomatosis in different parts of the country, it is now proving to be less lethal and there is some evidence to suggest that rabbits may have developed an immunity to it.

Rabbits are very social animals. From the salt marshes and sand dunes of the coast to the fringes of the high moorland, colonies of rabbits live in warrens which take the form of a number of burrows dug haphazardly into the ground. These warrens are made up of a series of interconnecting passages with emergency exits. Life within the colony is controlled by a 'pecking order'. The rabbit breeds prolifically if an adequate supply of food is available and the disturbance level is low. Though the young are born blind and without fur, they grow to full size in nine months and are capable of breeding at only three or four months. In a good year one buck and doe are capable of producing over one hundred offspring – though this does not happen often.

Rabbits are mainly nocturnal animals but the hunter will find them active at dawn and dusk also. During the day they may lie up either underground or in thick cover and daylight rabbit hunting is dominated by shotgun shooting and ferreting. The hours of twilight, however, belong to the rifle shooter and his sport can extend into the hours of darkness by using powerful lamps to seek out and light up the quarry. For the .22 rifle user, there are three usual ways of hunting rabbits and the choice of method depends largely on the terrain, the season, and the equipment the sportsman has at his disposal.

Sitting up

I have spent many pleasant hours sitting up in some cover on a warm summer evening waiting for rabbits to emerge from a nearby warren. This method of ambush requires patience, low noise ammunition, and an accurate rifle. In such a situation many of the high velocity rounds make too much noise and cause alarm which quickly spreads underground. Sitting downwind helps to overcome this problem, but the shooter must try to be sure of a clean kill with every shot. A wounded rabbit kicking back down a burrow to die underground

is not only upsetting on ethical grounds, but it also puts the others down for a long time. In order to be sure of clean and instant kills, head shots are recommended so ranges should not exceed eighty or so yards.

Stalking

If adequate cover is available, or the ground is undulating, rabbits can also be stalked. In this method individual animals can be spied at distance and approached to within an accurate range of the rifle. This sort of shooting requires stealth and a degree of fieldcraft if the quarry is not to be alarmed. Remember that rabbits are very wary creatures with very sensitive hearing, keen sight and a good sense of smell. Rabbit stalking does not usually result in many rabbits killed, yet the excitement of the silent and concealed approach can make it every bit as enjoyable as any other form of rifle hunting.

Lamping

Lamping rabbits at night can take the form of hunting open country on foot during the hours of darkness, armed with a rifle and a powerful spotlight. Alternatively, the headlights of a vehicle such as a tractor or Land Rover can be used for these nocturnal forays. When lit up by the beam from spotlight or headlight, rabbits often become confused and remain motionless for a few seconds. This allows time for an accurate shot, usually at ranges below fifty yards, and often many rabbits can be killed in this way. Two words of caution however. When using a rifle at night the shooter must be absolutely certain that there is a safe backdrop so that no dangerous richochets occur. In the excitement it can be all too easy to become disorientated and the whereabouts of public roads or even houses adjacent to the lamping field can become uncertain. It cannot be stressed too strongly that the utmost care must be taken while lamping rabbits with any sort of firearm.

When using a vehicle's headlights, there is also a dangerous tendency for the shooter to use the vehicle as a mobile shooting platform. The back of a pick-up truck or the open roof of a car might seem attractive but it is not to be recommended for two reasons. Firstly, the engine's vibrations certainly make for less accurate shooting, and secondly, if the vehicle is moving the slightest lurch on uneven ground could send the bullet in an unwanted direction. Far better when using the headlights of a van or tractor for the shooter to walk alongside and use a stick to steady his shot. In this way the risks can be minimised.

As rabbit numbers gradually recover, so the methods of control continue to expand. Nowadays it is recognised that the shotgun is a noisy and inefficient method, and a sportsman armed with an accurate rifle and using 'quiet' ammunition will enjoy better sport and be more effective than his shotgun-using counterpart.

(*opposite*) Rabbits are the prime quarry for the .22 rimfire user.

The brown hare, an 'opportunist' quarry for the .22 rimfire user, is a deceptively large animal. (*Mark Newman-Wren*)

Hares

The two native species of hare make up the remainder of the ground-game category. The brown hare is the larger and more common of the two species and the blue or mountain hare is confined to the higher ground in the Scottish Highlands.

The brown hare is a deceptively large animal, with full-grown adults sometimes reaching 14lb. Unlike the rabbit they live above ground throughout the year and shelter in small hollows in open fields or in grass tussocks in more enclosed country. Though essentially an animal of open ground and farmland, the reduction in rabbit numbers following the myxomatosis epidemic saw the hare colonise woodland as well. Since the early 1970s however, changes in farming methods and the modern emphasis on grain monoculture have resulted in hare numbers declining rapidly in many parts of Britain and, in such areas, sportsmen and conservationists have called for a moratorium on hare shooting. In other parts of the country the hare is traditionally controlled by an organised hare shoot shortly after the end of the pheasant season. As such it is recognised as a legitimate quarry species for the shotgun shooter and it is viewed as a dual-purpose animal much in the same way as the rabbit. Where they occur in reasonable numbers they undoubtedly cause a significant amount of crop damage and are therefore seen as vermin. On the other hand, they are also a traditional game animal, covered by the country's game laws and hunted not only with gun and rifle, but also by beagle packs and coursing dogs.

Even in areas where the hare population is stable, this animal can only be considered as an incidental quarry species for the rifle shooter. Like the rabbit, it is a chiefly nocturnal feeder so that dawn and dusk are the best times to hunt

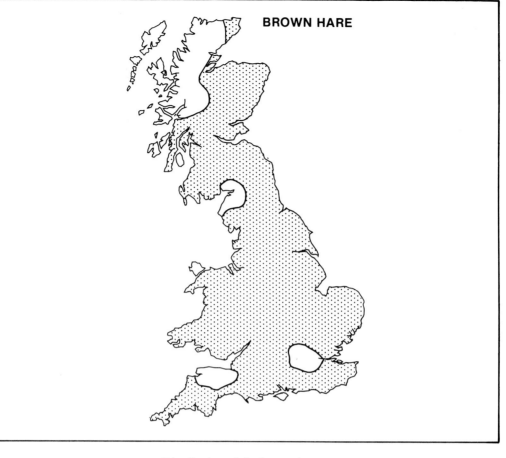

Distribution of the brown hare.

the hare. Despite being covered by our game laws, hare shooting at night is legal though they rarely occur in sufficient numbers to warrant lamping, so hare shooting with a rifle usually takes the form of stalking. During the spring and early summer, before the arable crops have grown to conceal them, hare shooting can take on the sort of open ground stalking that is reminiscent of deer stalking in Scotland and a corresponding degree of luck and skill are needed if the hare is to be approached close enough for a fatal shot.

As hares are quite large animals, a high velocity hollow-point bullet is needed to make an instantaneous kill. It seems to be normal practice to chest-shoot hares rather than go for neck or head shots, and the reason for this may lie in the fact that a hollow-point has sufficient time to expand in the hare's chest cavity and so give an instant kill and sufficient knock-down blow. Even when a heart-shot animal runs on, it will only travel a few yards before collapsing and there is little chance of the animal disappearing down the nearest burrow as would a rabbit.

A sportsman armed with a .22 rimfire rifle will rarely set out specifically to shoot hares in this country. What is more likely to happen is that the odd hare

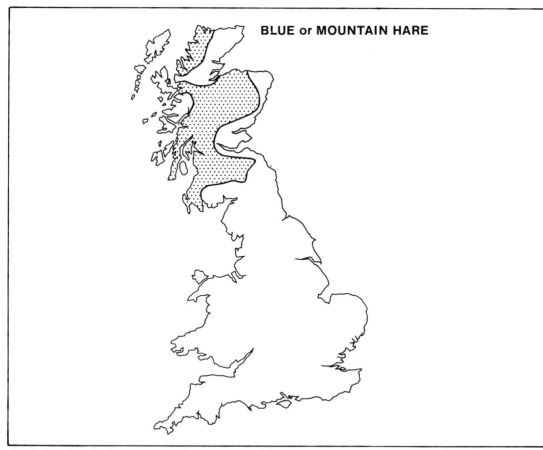

BLUE or MOUNTAIN HARE

Distribution of the blue or mountain hare – they are usually confined to the high ground in the areas shown.

will be taken while the shooter is out after rabbit or vermin, and the hare is therefore usually looked upon as 'opportunist' quarry.

The blue or mountain hare is a species confined to the Highlands of Scotland and to Ireland. As such it is not considered to be an important quarry species on a national scale, yet many are killed by rifle shooters in their respective areas. It is an animal only of high ground where, unlike the brown hare, it takes on a white coat in winter. This helps to conceal it from foxes, eagles and other predators in the upland environment it shares with the red grouse and the ptarmigan. Like the brown hare though, it sometimes figures in the bags of shotgun users – often shot during grouse or ptarmigan drives – and it is only regarded as an opportunist species for a rifle shooter out after vermin such as foxes or hooded crows.

Though slightly smaller than its lowland relation, the mountain hare is still large enough to require the use of a high velocity hollow-point bullet for a humane kill. In upland areas where rifle sport seems to be confined to using centrefire rifles and stalking red deer, the blue hare can add a touch of variety to the overall shooting scene.

VERMIN

Rabbit and hare can be, and often are, classified as vermin where they cause damage to farm crops, and the game laws of this country reflect this. However, the identity of true vermin species is far better defined. Rats and grey squirrels constitute the smaller mammals in this category while foxes define the upper limit of the .22 rimfire's capabilities. In addition there are a number of bird species which are also looked upon as legitimate targets for the .22 user, and these include woodpigeons, magpies, jays, and carrion crows. I have omitted rooks from this list as there is some evidence to suggest that this species is more of a benefit than was previously assumed. However, an over-population of rooks in an area would certainly need some control. In certain parts of the country other species may be added – the wild mink in parts of the south-west and South Wales for instance. So a sportsman armed with a .22 rimfire will usually be called upon to be a controller of vermin rather than a game shooter. Nevertheless, there are far greater opportunities to use a .22 rimfire in this country than one would imagine considering the degree of restriction the authorities place on the use of such weapons. With the shotgun shooting scene now largely consisting of the do-it-yourself syndicate shoots, there is now a greater opportunity for vermin control using rifles than in the days of the large estates which supported their own teams of full-time keepers. With this increase in opportunities for rifle shooting the optimists among us may look for a growth in sporting .22 rifle ownership in the next decade or so.

Brown rat

The brown rat is one of Britain's most common animals. Brown rats are found throughout the British Isles and although they live successfully in the countryside they are most often associated with man's activities and his dwellings. They can do a great deal of damage around farms where they can contaminate stored grain and other produce, and they are also active predators in that they will kill poultry and take eggs. In more built-up areas rats can pose a health hazard and each year there are still instances of human deaths from rat-transmitted disease.

Because of this habit of living close to man, farmyards and rubbish tips are places where a rat population can be controlled by shooting. Another method of control is poisoning, but very often this is impractical due to the risk of the poison being consumed by domestic pets and livestock. In addition, a great deal of fun can be had from 'ratting' with a small terrier and a low-powered shotgun such as a 9mm or a .410 loaded with a 2in cartridge. There are places, however, when even these low-powered shotguns are too indiscriminate or noisy and this is where a powerful air rifle or a .22 rimfire can be used to good effect.

Ammunition for a .22 rimfire used for ratting needs to be in the low-power category as rats are usually encountered at short range and there is often a danger of ricochet. When shooting in large barns an air rifle would be a more suitable and wiser choice but a .22 rimfire loaded with bulleted caps could also be used. Open sights are preferable to a scope at these short ranges but care must still be exercised to avoid ricochets within these buildings. When shooting over more open rubbish tips or disused quarries the ranges tend to be longer and rats are often killed at distances up to sixty yards. For this sort of shooting a .22 Short hollow-point is a good choice as it has reliable accuracy at these distances and the hollow point minimises the chance of the bullet carrying too far. Like all rifle shooting in an island as small and as densely populated as Britain, a great deal of care needs to be taken to ensure that each shot has a safe backstop for the bullet. Even a round as small as a .22 Short can carry for perhaps half a mile and within this radius there may be houses, roads, footpaths, and other places where humans or livestock may be exposed to risk. If the sportsman bears this in mind, and takes the appropriate precautions, rat shooting can be an enjoyable way of whiling away the long summer evenings. As a teenager I spent many hours overlooking a local farmer's rubbish tip on warm summer evenings, armed with an air rifle for close range shots and a single shot .22 which I used to good effect out to beyond fifty yards. My best sortie accounted for thirty-eight rats and the farmer was delighted.

Grey squirrel

A relative of the brown rat, the grey squirrel is another animal which inflicts a considerable amount of damage on our countryside and wildlife. As a species the grey squirrel is a native of North America and was only introduced into this country earlier this century. Since then it has spread rapidly to colonise most of the woodlands of lowland Britain and its habits have made it an enemy of the forester, farmer, and conservationist alike. In young timber plantations its habit of bark stripping has caused the Forestry Commission and the Ministry of Agriculture to wage a constant campaign to control its numbers, and until recently a bounty was payable for squirrel tails. In the spring a large portion of its diet is made up from eggs and fledgling birds and this has not endeared the species to the ornithologist and conservationist.

In addition, a great deal of debate has arisen because the grey squirrel's rapid expansion coincided with the population crash of our own smaller, native, red squirrel. The latter species is now confined to the forested areas of central and northern Scotland and North Wales and all its previous territories are now occupied by the foreign grey. Whether the grey squirrel's expansion caused the red's decline, or whether it simply filled an ecological niche left by an already declining species is still a subject of much debate. The net result is that, where a small population of red squirrels once lived, a larger colony of the heavier grey squirrels now has a far more damaging effect on the environment.

Control of the grey squirrel population by shooting takes place during early spring, late autumn, and in the winter when the deciduous woodlands are bare of their leaf canopy. At these times the squirrel's dreys can be identified and the animals ambushed as they go about their territory. Air rifles and shotguns are

Grey squirrels can be effectively controlled by the .22 rimfire user. (*J. Walton*)

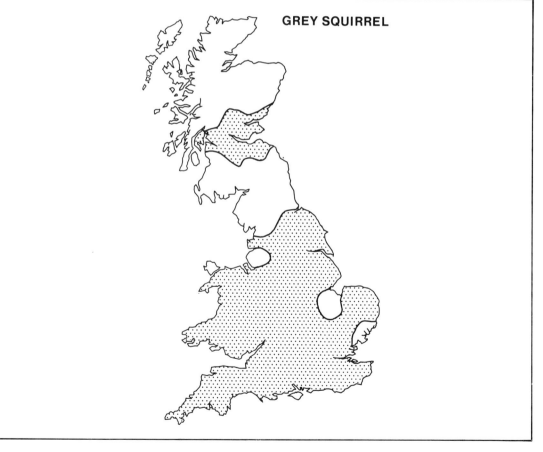

GREY SQUIRREL

Distribution of the grey squirrel.

most often used for squirrel shooting but there are some drawbacks in using these weapons. In terms of safety however, both weapons are preferable to a .22 rimfire because squirrel shooting almost invariably involves taking high angle shots in woodland. The carrying power of both the air rifle and the shotgun pellet is considerably less than a rifle bullet and this in turn means that there is practically no 'fallout' area for the air weapon and shotgun. On the other hand, the air rifle has a very limited range and is often less accurate than a .22 rimfire, and during the winter months using a shotgun for shooting squirrels may cause unwelcome disturbance to the game birds in the woods. There are times when squirrels may often be found foraging on the ground in winter and early spring. Providing there is a safe backdrop to the shot the .22 rimfire can be considered to be the ideal weapon. As in rat shooting, the rimfire .22 causes far less disturbance than a shotgun while it effectively has double the range of an air rifle. The .22 Short hollow-point bullets are probably best for squirrel shooting as they are sufficiently accurate up to about sixty yards. Only on rare occasions will any shots be taken at ranges beyond the capability of .22 Short ammunition and for these a standard Long Rifle hollow-point round can be substituted.

Endless patience and the ability to move very quietly are two qualities needed to be an effective squirrel controller. The grey squirrel has keen senses and will be quick to detect your presence. Once alerted it will rush off into the branches thus giving the shooter very little opportunity for a steady or safe shot. Considering the amount of damage done to trees and wildlife that can be attributed to squirrels, the squirrel shooter is performing a valuable service from which he can gain some satisfaction and also derive a great deal of enjoyment.

Fox

The fox is usually regarded as the largest of the rimfire quarry in this country, indeed many centrefire enthusiasts would maintain that a rimfire is too underpowered for fox control. Nevertheless, with the advent of the new hyper-velocity ammunition the vast majority of foxes killed in this country will fall to rimfire rifles. There is a widely held belief that the fox population is on the increase throughout Britain and this does seem logical in the light of the increase in the population of one of its main food sources, the rabbit. It is certainly an adaptable animal and it will be found in all environments from the shoreline to the rocky crags of the country's uplands. In recent years much publicity has been given to foxes that have taken to living in densely populated urban areas, and the term 'urban fox' has become widely recognised and understood. This serves to highlight the ability of the fox to adapt to a wider variety of environments than most wild animals, and indeed, they seem to thrive in the most unlikely places.

Lacking any natural predator other than the golden eagle, the fox has traditionally been controlled by hunting with hound packs. It has been introduced into many other parts of the world and nowadays there are large fox populations in such places as Australia and New Zealand. In Britain, the fox is considered primarily a hunted species – one that is pursued by hounds. There are, however, many parts of Britain where hound packs do not operate and it is in these areas that other control methods may be necessary.

The trapping and snaring of foxes is a skill which every good gamekeeper soon acquires, and foxes are also killed on the occasional shotgun 'fox drive' at the end of the game-shooting season. Fox shooting with a rifle forms a small but effective part of the overall picture and the .22 rimfire is considered to be the smallest suitable calibre for this.

A fully-grown fox is a strong animal in comparison with other rimfire quarry and so requires a high energy bullet in order to administer an instantaneous kill. For this purpose a .22 Long Rifle high velocity hollow-point bullet is considered ideal and the new hyper velocity rounds are attracting much attention. A fox will not move far if it is chest shot with either of these rounds.

Apart from the opportunist shot at a fox while out after other species, fox shooting usually takes the form of sitting up in the evening or during the night to await their arrival at a chosen spot. In late summer when the cubs are fully grown, sitting at dusk in some hide overlooking a fox's earth can be very rewarding, and intercepting them on a known and well-frequented trail can also lead to success. Here ranges need not be long and the average shot can be taken at under fifty yards. There will be occasions though, when a longer shot is required, and the shooter needs to be able to place a bullet accurately up to about one hundred yards.

The advent of low priced but reliable telescopic sights has extended the ability of the fox shooter to operate in poor light and some of the new large aperture scopes have created the sport of 'moonlighting'. As the term implies, the nights near to a full moon can see the land illuminated to such an extent that these sights can be used to very good effect. Nowadays, therefore, sitting up for foxes can take place not only during the summer twilight, but at all times of the year when the night sky is clear and the moon nearly full.

Recently there has been a growth in the demand for fox pelts and many hunters seek some cash return from their shooting. This is where the rimfire .22 rifle has a definite advantage over the more potent centrefire rifles. The rimfire will generally inflict far less skin damage than one of the larger calibres and the pelts will therefore be more marketable. On the other hand, ranges are restricted to about one hundred yards or less, although it is only in open country shooting that this may be a disadvantage. Unlike many other forms of rifle sport, fox shooting is largely a waiting and watching procedure but actually being out in the countryside when most other humans are ensconced in front of the television or in bed has a charm and magic of its own.

Winged vermin

In many parts of the world shooting game birds with a rifle is an accepted sport. In North America, for instance, the turkey and the various species of open country and forest grouse are all accepted as legitimate rifle quarry. In

The jay is an elusive species which is often difficult to intercept. (*R. V. Collier*)

some parts of Europe the ptarmigan and capercaillie are regarded in a similar light, yet within the shooting traditions of Britain it would be practically unthinkable to shoot pheasant, grouse, or partridge with a rifle. Winged vermin are a different matter, and the .22 rimfire can be an effective weapon to use against such species. In general, the one problem with bird shooting lies in the fact that the shots must only be taken where there is a safe backdrop and this may limit the opportunities available. However, providing the conditions described when shooting grey squirrels are adhered to, a great many head of feathered vermin can be accounted for with a rifle.

Jays are birds of mixed and deciduous woodland, sharing their habitat with the grey squirrel. They are shy and retiring birds who generally give away their presence by their harsh call. Nevertheless, they take great toll on the young and eggs of other birds and as such their numbers need to be controlled. They are usually very wary of humans and the best method of hunting jays is to ambush them in late winter and early spring. As is usual for this form of shooting the sportsman needs to be well hidden, for the jay is a very observant bird, and with the general lack of ground cover available at this time of year effective concealment can pose a problem.

During the autumn, family parties of jays work through the woodland stopping here and there to pick up an item of food before passing on. When engaged in this behaviour they pose difficult targets as they are rarely still for more than a second or so. A scope-sighted rifle is ideal for this form of shooting as they are a little quicker to use than open-sighted weapons.

Magpies often frequent farmyards where they can do much damage in the poultry rearing pens. (*J.B. and S. Bottomley/Arden London*)

Magpies are birds of hedgerow and farmland and their habits of nest robbing have not endeared them to the gamekeeper and farmer. Most magpies are shot when an opportunity arises, though it is possible to go out specifically to shoot this species. Like jays, magpies are wary and observant birds and success depends largely on the shooter's stealth and patience in outwitting his quarry. Unlike jays, though, the magpie spends much of its time on the ground and a fair number can be accounted for as they seek food on freshly sown fields. When shooting against a suitable backdrop the Long Rifle rounds can be used and the effective hunting range extended.

The carrion crow in England and Wales and the hooded crow in Scotland and Ireland are the largest of the avian vermin to be of interest to the .22 rimfire shooter. These are birds with a wide-ranging appetite and they have been observed to kill very young lambs. Like the other species they are wary of any hint of human presence so hunting methods are similar to those described for jays and magpies. Crows are, however, solitary creatures and more often than not the shooter will set out to kill a particular bird or pair of birds. Because they are dwellers of more open country, shooting these birds demands an ability to place a bullet accurately at greater ranges and the .22 rimfire may be extended to the limit of its range – somewhere around 120 yards depending on the rifle and the person behind it! Usually a deliberately aimed shot is taken and a well-adjusted telescopic sight helps to attain the accuracy that is demanded in this form of shooting.

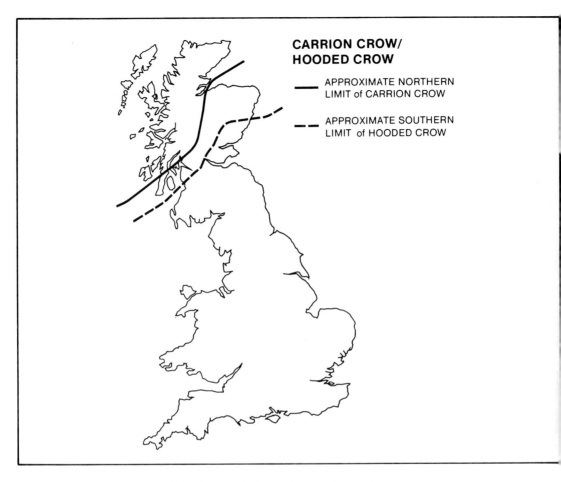

**CARRION CROW/
HOODED CROW**

—— APPROXIMATE NORTHERN
LIMIT of CARRION CROW

‒ ‒ APPROXIMATE SOUTHERN
LIMIT of HOODED CROW

Distribution of the carrion crow/hooded crow.

Finally, there is the woodpigeon. It is probably true to say that more pigeons are shot by shotgun users than any other bird species in Britain, and they may even come second only to the rabbit as a quarry species for both the air rifle and the .22 rimfire user.

Shooting roosting pigeons with an air rifle is a sport that can take place from late autumn to spring. During these months large numbers of birds fly in to roost in a favoured patch of woodland, and the lack of foliage works to the shooter's advantage in that he can easily find his quarry as it sits in the upper branches. This does not mean that shooting is easy. A bird that perches on a branch that is swaying around in an autumn gale is a very testing target for the air rifle user. At this time the roosting birds can also be stalked for there is often enough undergrowth or intervening tree trunks to allow for a concealed approach. The same safety precautions need to be observed in roost shooting as in any other form of woodland shooting against the sky, and this is a factor which cannot be stressed too strongly. Shooting pigeons with an air rifle in autumn and winter does have the advantage of creating far less disturbance

The woodpigeon is probably second only to the rabbit as .22 rimfire quarry.
(*Dennis Green*)

than using a shotgun. However, during the game season most sportsmen would be anxious not to disturb patches of woodland and holding coverts unduly as the pigeons will often share their woods with a good number of pheasant.

Decoying pigeons onto their feeding fields is a method that can be used by the rifle shooter. Again he must be placed so that there is a safe backdrop for the bullet, but once this is obtained he may enjoy very good sport. Bags will invariably be smaller than a shotgun user as the sportsman armed with a rifle needs to wait for an incoming pigeon to land before firing. Even so an effective pattern of decoys helps to dispel a pigeon's natural wariness and to exploit the gregarious nature of the species. Ranges should not be extended beyond fifty yards and the .22 Short rounds are ideal – the high velocity Long Rifle ammunition can create too much meat spoilage to be worthwile. It must be remembered that a pigeon is a culinary delicacy as well as an agricultural pest, so it is sought by the pot hunter as well as the vermin controller. My own best day of shooting pigeon over decoys with a rimfire rifle accounted for twenty-six birds, and of those only two were too damaged for the pot.

AMMUNITION

In a densely populated country like the British Isles, the main limiting factor to rifle shooting may be the potential carrying power of stray bullets and ricochets and the sportsman must be constantly aware of this. Nevertheless, many of these risks can be minimised by the correct choice of ammunition to match the style of shooting, the anticipated ranges at which shots will be fired, and the environment in which the shooting takes place. A wisely selected bullet type, accurately zeroed in a rifle, will go a long way towards preventing much unwanted lead flying about the countryside.

There is a greater variety of ammunition available for the .22 rimfire than for any other calibre. Though it is essentially quite a 'primitive' round, ammunition manufacturers have invested millions of pounds in development and research and what we have today is reliable and accurate ammunition in a variety of bullet styles and weights to cater for all the rimfire shooter's needs.

For sportsmen using a .22 rimfire against live quarry these needs are twofold. Firstly, the ballistics of the bullet fired at an animal must show sufficient velocity and energy to kill the creature instantaneously when it is struck in a vital organ. This power requirement, of course, varies with the size of the animal concerned and a greater velocity and striking energy would be required for a fox than for a grey squirrel. These variations are usually achieved by altering the bullet weight and charge of propellant powder which in turn produces a variety of velocities and striking energies.

Secondly, the bullet must be so constructed to administer the greatest shock to the animal, and for this it needs to deform and 'mushroom' on impact. In addition, these bullets are fired at velocities well below the smallest centrefire calibres and therefore they do not break up readily. The .22 rimfire is often regarded as the calibre most prone to ricochet and when shooting in a populated rural area the bullet must be designed to minimise the risk of it 'bouncing' around.

Generally, there are two types of .22 rimfire bullet used for sporting purposes: the solid and the hollow-point. The solid lead bullet, often coated with a bright alloy or wax to protect the barrel from lead fouling, has the advantage of retaining its velocity and energy to greater distances. As such its accuracy is usually better than a comparable hollow-point and it is no surprise that practically all target ammunition is loaded with 'solids'. Because it sheds its velocity less quickly it is also less prone to wind deflection which may be an important consideration when shooting in an exposed location.

Ballistically, the solid is therefore superior to a hollow-point, but in terms of shooting live targets it is far less efficient. For example, a solid bullet will often pass straight through the rib cage of a rabbit without deforming at all. It therefore does not expend its energy within the animal and the knock-down power is wasted. In some instances this lack of deformation does have an advantage in that it causes less meat spoilage than a hollow-point, but if humane killing of the quarry is to be important, the latter bullet design is preferable.

In terms of safety the hollow-point is again the better choice. Its rapid deformation on hitting any object means that it at once sheds much of its energy and velocity, and a deformed bullet does not travel very far. The solid, on the other hand, being far less prone to deformation is far more likely to 'bounce' a fair distance.

For all-round sporting shooting with a .22 rimfire the hollow-point is the more effective and the safer of the two designs. Despite its tendency to be blown about by crosswinds, the two criteria of humane killing power and safety make it, in my opinion, a better choice than a solid bullet design.

Having decided on bullet design, the next considerations are the length, weight and velocity of the cartridge. For all practical purposes the .22 Long is an obsolete round. Conceived initially to increase the velocity of the Short bullet, its performance now falls well below the .22 Long Rifle. Choice of cartridge length is therefore between the .22 Long Rifle and the .22 Short. For use against the smaller quarry species, the .22 Short hollow-point is an effective round; the Remington high velocity Short, for example, is loaded with a 27 grain HP bullet and has a muzzle velocity of over 1100 fps. Within fifty yards this will deal with animals up to the size of a full-grown rabbit and by restricting shooting to that range the effects of wind deflection can be kept to a minimum, even on such a light bullet. At a distance of one hundred yards the striking energy is still nearly 50 ft/lb, though this falls away rapidly beyond this distance as the little bullet loses momentum. This in turn makes the .22 Short rather safer to use in a moderately populated countryside than the .22 LR round.

For many years, the .22 Long Rifle has been considered the best rimfire hunting round and the cartridge is now available in a great variety of types. In recent years there has been a growth in the use of sound moderators or silencers on .22 rimfire sporting rifles. When fitted, these reduce the report to a quiet 'plop' which is in fact less noisy than most sporting air rifles. To a person sitting up for rabbits the advantages of using a silenced rifle are obvious, but in order to achieve this noise reduction a low velocity round must be used.

As a general principle, when a bullet accelerates beyond the speed of sound the resulting 'sonic boom' greatly increases the volume of the rifle's report. The silencer is very inefficient at muffling this supersonic noise as it is designed to absorb the lower frequency noises of the primer detonation and exhaust gases. In order to gain maximum benefit from a silenced rifle, therefore, a range of subsonic .22 LR ammunition is available. Though generating only around 1000 fps muzzle velocity, the fact that they do not have to cope with supersonic turbulence means that they are slower to lose speed. This has the effect of producing a flatter trajectory than would first be imagined and such rounds as the Winchester 'Hushpower' and others are very effective.

Moving up the scale of velocity is the standard .22 high velocity round. This type of ammunition generally produces a muzzle velocity of around 1300 fps with a 36 grain hollow-point bullet and these form the mainstay of the sporting rimfire shooter's ammunition. Each manufacturer adds his own minor variations to bullet shape and its lubrication surface, but the performance of the .22 LR HV round from most makers seems to be practically identical. With a down-range velocity of around 1000 fps at one hundred yards, and a striking energy of over 80 ft/lb, these bullets are effective on all .22 rimfire quarry species at this distance, and in a good rifle this can even be extended by another ten to twenty yards.

In the late 1970s Remington produced a .22 rimfire round which was the first real departure from the other well-established designs. Their Yellow Jacket ammunition was the first of a new generation of 'hyper velocity' rounds. Winchester soon followed suit with their Expediter ammunition and there have been more recent additions by other manufacturers.

These new rounds generate velocities of over 1500 fps, by using a rapid burning powder to drive a lighter bullet of around 32 grains. At ranges of up to one hundred yards they do produce startling effects on small game, but beyond that distance the lighter bullet sheds its velocity more rapidly than the normal .22 LR HV and at 120 yards the older kind of bullet actually delivers more striking energy. In addition, there have been reports of the hot powder in these hyper velocity loads causing more barrel erosion in the first few inches beyond the breech. Though this will only occur perhaps after thousands of rounds have passed through the rifle, it may be a point worth considering when selecting ammunition. It cannot be denied, though, that these hyper velocity bullets do deliver more knock-down power at average rimfire ranges, and this would make them a good choice for shooting hares and foxes up to about ninety yards.

Recently there has been a growth in the popularity of the .22 Magnum rimfire calibre and it is now seen as a useful rifle for small game at ranges up to about 150 yards. First developed by Winchester in the late 1960s, the rimfire Magnum fires a 40 grain bullet at a velocity of around 2000 fps, and as such it has been hailed as the calibre that bridges the gap between the standard .22 rimfires and the .22 centrefires. The ammunition for this calibre is not interchangeable with the standard .22 rimfire and it is altogether a more powerful round. Certainly at close range it is too potent for small game up to the size of rabbit, and at one hundred yards it still retains the equivalent of the .22 LR's muzzle energy. With this sort of performance, game-shooting range stretches from around fifty yards out to about 140 yards, though if edible game is being hunted the closer ranges require a head shot. In the more open country of northern England, Scotland, and North Wales, the .22 rimfire Magnum may be a preferable choice of calibre.

There is a wide variety of sport available to the user of the .22 rimfire rifle in Britain. Within this variety, the shooter can take on the clearly defined role of vermin controller and fulfill an important function while enjoying the sport. The skills of fieldcraft and the accuracy demanded of such a sportsman form an excellent schooling before the shooter graduates to centrefire rifle sport. Experience gained in stalking rabbits with a .22 rimfire can be very valuable when the sportsman first turns his attention to the roe deer of Britain's woodlands, and it is probably true to say that anyone who cannot become an accurate .22 rimfire shooter will never hope to be good with a larger calibre rifle.

Shooting with a .22 rimfire is, however, a sport in its own right. Despite the current restrictions on rifle ownership there are probably more opportunities nowadays for using the .22 than at any other time since the early 1950s. The revolution which has so radically changed the sporting shotgun scene has produced more openings for the use of a rimfire than hitherto existed under the more exclusive 'estate' system. Many game and rough shooters find themselves in a position which allows far more flexibility in the ways in which vermin is controlled on their own shoots. These people quickly learn that the .22 rifle is a very useful tool for the part-time or amateur keeper.

In addition, the steady recovery of the country's rabbit population since the myxomatosis epidemic has also increased the potential opportunities for rifle shooting. In some parts of the country where rabbit numbers have increased rapidly there has also been a corresponding increase in the population of foxes and other predatory vermin. Here again the rimfire rifle can be called in to provide an effective control measure. The .22 rimfire shooting scene in Britain is an area that could see a growth of popularity in the next few years. It is an inexpensive sport which can be taken up by any safe and careful shooter and it can provide a very valuable schooling for the novice in many aspects of fieldcraft and shooting safety.

5. The .22 Centrefires

SINCE the passing of the 1963 Deer Act, the use of .22 centrefire rifles has shown a marked decline in England and Wales. This Act prohibited the use of rifles below a calibre of .240in for deer shooting and a large number of deer stalkers south of the Scottish border were forced to swap their Hornets, Swifts, and .22–250s for larger calibre rifles when the Act came into force.

Since 1963 these high-powered .22s have become very much the 'betwixt and between' weapons. They do, however, have a role to play as long-range vermin rifles in many parts of the country. Compared with the rimfire .22, these centrefire calibres are very much more powerful. As a general rule they all drive bullets of around 50 grains at far higher velocities along much flatter trajectories and consequently produce greatly increased striking energies. Within these general characteristics, though, they vary in power from the mild .22 Hornet up to the very 'hot' .22–250.

In Britain, and indeed throughout the rifle-shooting world, three calibres have come to dominate the .22 centrefire family and these reflect the power variation within the group. Though many other calibres are available from many rifle manufacturers, the .22 Hornet, the .222 Remington, and the .22–250 Remington, are by far the most popular.

As the lowest powered cartridge in this family, the .22 Hornet takes over where the .22 rimfire Magnum falls off. At one time, loaded with its 45 grain soft-point bullet, the Hornet was the favoured calibre of many an experienced woodland roe stalker, and in steady hands it was an effective weapon against these small deer at ranges normal in dense woodlands. In other countries the .22 Hornet continues to be used for shooting the smaller species of deer and its popularity is perhaps due to the fact that the cartridge has a very mild report and practically no recoil. Rifles are built specifically for this calibre and those produced by Brno and Anschutz are among the most popular.

In this country, the popularity of the Hornet dropped rapidly after its use against deer was prohibited, and despite the fact that it is a delight to use, its ballistics did not set it very far apart from the Magnum rimfire which may also have contributed to its decline. It is far too powerful to be used against rabbits at ranges below 150 yards, and beyond this distance it appears to be rather too prone to wind deflection to be considered really accurate. For shooting non-edible vermin, and foxes in particular, the .22 Hornet has a number of advantages over both the rimfires and its larger and more powerful brethren. This calibre has been demonstrated to be sufficiently accurate and potent for shooting foxes out to a range of around 170 yards. As such it is a better choice than either of the rimfire calibres if the serious fox shooter intends to take fairly regular shots at these ranges.

The Hornet produces muzzle velocities of around 2600 fps and as a consequence its bullet is far more likely to break up on hitting the ground, a twig, or other obstacle, than any rimfire round. This does, paradoxically, make it a safer weapon to use than the lower powered rimfires as it is less prone to ricochet. This safety factor, which is common to all high velocity centrefire calibres, only applies when soft-point or hollow-point sporting ammunition is used as these bullets are designed for rapid expansion on impact.

Compared with the more powerful .22 centrefires, the Hornet is markedly quieter and this can be a decided advantage when fox shooting is carried out in the more populous rural areas or where the presence of deer or game birds demands a minimum of disturbance.

The .222 Remington is a further step up the power ladder, and since its introduction in the post-war years it has become perhaps the most popular of all the .22 centrefire calibres. Driving a 50 grain bullet at just over 3000 fps it is a good deal more powerful than the Hornet yet it is still a 'low noise' and mild cartridge. Throughout Europe it has become a firm favourite for the roe stalker and many are still used in Scotland for this purpose. After its introduction this calibre quickly earned a high reputation for precise shooting and it is now ranked as one of the world's most accurate rounds. For this reason it has extended the fox shooter's range out to about 230 yards at which distance the bullet's velocity is still around 2000 fps. With this sort of performance the trajectory is markedly flatter than that of the Hornet and its accuracy is more reliable at greater distances.

Many people consider that the .22–250 Remington is the ultimate varmint calibre. Adopted and standardised by Remington in recent years the cartridge is based on the old .250/3000 Savage, necked down to .22in. As such it has a large powder capacity and even factory loads drive a 50 grain bullet along at around 3800 fps. Though slower than the .220 Swift, it nevertheless has a very flat trajectory and the round possesses excellent accuracy out to beyond 300 yards. A fox-shooting friend owns a Ruger No. 1 .22–250 rifle on which he has mounted an 8 × 56 Schmidt and Bender scope. With this outfit I have seen him kill foxes with almost monotonous regularity at ranges up to 350 yards.

The .22–250 is by far the most powerful of the .22 non-magnum calibres and was considered by some experienced shooters to be suitable for use against deer up to the size of fallow and even red hinds and the small Highland stags. However, even in Scotland this calibre is now restricted by its bullet weight to roe deer. In terms of effective ballistics, there is really nothing to choose between the .22–250 and a .243 – anything one can do the other can do equally well. The smaller calibre has the edge on long-range accuracy while the latter scores on down-range striking energy.

A heavy-barrelled Ruger .22–250 with a Schmidt & Bender 8 × 56 scope – the ultimate in long-range, fox-shooting weaponry.

'Squeaking' for foxes in the early morning or late evening often attracts the younger animals, such as this young dog fox. (*John Marchington/Arden London*)

In England and Wales the .22 centrefire calibres are identified as belonging to the world of the serious vermin controller, and the fox shooter in particular. Among this group of rifle users we find a fair proportion of gamekeepers who, along with other experts in predator control, have developed two main tactics for fox shooting: passive shooting and night lamping.

Passive shooting involves sitting up in the early morning or late evening overlooking an area that foxes are known to frequent. This could be near their earths, where they can be intercepted at fairly close quarters, but usually these centrefire .22s are used where the terrain prevents close approach. In areas of chalk downland in southern and eastern England, and on the fringes of the open moorland of Wales, northern England, and Scotland, these calibres really come into their own. Where the average range exceeds one hundred yards, the .22 LR ceases to be an effective and humane tool for fox control, and the .22 WRF Magnum falls by the wayside at around 130 yards, so the only really satisfactory rifles for shooting at greater distances are those in the .22 centrefire category. This is the closest we come in this country to the American style of varmint hunting and the rifles selected by some of our fox shooters seem to reflect this similarity. In some parts of the country attempts are made to draw the quarry closer to the shooter, either by calling or baiting a chosen point. A fox can be called from quite a distance by imitating the cry of a rabbit or hare in distress, and a number of proprietory fox calls are available on the market. Many experienced shooters, well versed in the lore of the countryside, can produce the same effect by using the back of the hand or by blowing across a blade of grass.

I know of one hill keeper who takes a great number of foxes from an otherwise impossible area by the careful placing of a dead sheep or other suitable bait on a chosen spot on a known fox's circuit. Lying in wait at a convenient distance he has been known to shoot three or four per sortie.

Another contrasting style of fox shooting has developed rapidly in the last decade. Ever since rifle shooting began, attempts have been made to extend rifle sport into the hours of darkness by the use of artificial light. These attempts met with only very limited success until the development of compact and portable quartz-halogen lamps, and this has led to a minor revolution in fox control. Nowadays it is estimated that more foxes are shot at night using night lamping techniques than are shot during the day. This tends to be a more active two-man sport in which the shooter and the lamper slowly cover their area of land in search of a fox using the high intensity narrow beam of light to sweep the hedgerows, woodside margins, and other likely spots. Here care must be taken to identify the eye glow that is picked out by the light, as the shooter may encounter other animals like deer, badger, hares, and even domestic cats out on their nightly prowl. Once a fox is located the shot must be taken quickly as it is easy for the animal to slip out of the beam and vanish.

Although this may appear to be a rather uncertain method of controlling fox numbers a great many animals are accounted for in this way. Like any form of rifle shooting at night, the shooter must be constantly aware of the direction and backdrop of each shot so as to avoid the risk of endangering the other livestock and human inhabitants of the countryside. It is sometimes quite alarming to see how many people enjoy late evening strolls through the countryside during the summer months, and a shooter out in what would normally be called unsociable hours may encounter the bluebell picker, the overnight camper, and the courting couple in the course of his shooting foray.

Rifle shooters in North America developed a particular style of rifle for their long-range varmint shooting and these are available in this country for our fox shooters. As they are essentially long-range weapons for use against small targets the use of a telescopic sight is considered essential. At ranges above the 120 yard mark open iron sights are ineffective and this led to the rifle being built without any iron sights on the barrel. In addition, the barrel itself is of the heavy target type to provide even greater accuracy, and the way in which this is inletted into the stock is given considerable attention. These varmint style rifles are built heavy and this is further enhanced by using a full pistol grip stock with a high Monte Carlo raised comb with roll-over cheekpiece. With the addition of a solidly mounted high-power telescopic sight these rifles take on the distinctive appearance of the American-designed weapon. They were never really intended to be very portable or quick-pointing and were designed rather for deliberately aimed shots taken from a stable rest. With some sort of support they are extremely accurate up to the limitations of each particular calibre and cartridge. In Britain many of the situations where the centrefire .22 rifle is used requires the shooter to carry the rifle for some distance and most shots need to be taken quickly. In such circumstances the American varmint style of rifle is less than ideal.

A centrefire rifle is the obvious choice for the serious fox controller.

It is the standard style of rifle that is more popular with the British rifle shooter and bolt actioned rifles in the three main calibres of this .22 centrefire family predominate in this rather restricted branch of rifle sport. Considering the shooting ranges involved, the followers of this style of sport tend to use telescopic sights of more powerful magnification than normal, and 6× up to about 15× seems to be the popular range. Zoom telescopes are also considered useful for fox shooting, and some people use the low-power setting to pick up and identify the target and then increase the magnification to make a more accurately-placed shot possible. It is, however, a lazy and dangerous habit to use the rifle's scope rather than binoculars for the initial identification of a potential target. That movement that caught your eye may be a stray farm animal or, worse still, a human being, and to point a loaded rifle at an unidentified object is inexcusable.

Quality of the optics can be quite critical for this style of shooting. The shot is taken, more often than not, in poor lighting conditions and at remote targets, so the better the quality of the scope the better the light transmission and consequent image quality.

Although the Deer Act severely restricted the use of the .22 centrefire calibres in England and Wales to the type of vermin control described, in Scotland the situation is quite different. Despite pressure from some authorities to bring deer calibre restrictions in Scotland into line with the rest of Britain, the Deer Act (Scotland) of 1985 still allows the use of some high velocity .22 cartridges for roe deer. As a consequence the .222 Remington is likely to remain very popular among the roe shooters of Scotland. Nowadays, the little .22 Hornet is considered too underpowered for deer and as a result it has slowly declined in popularity as the more powerful and versatile .222 Remington has gained

recognition for the excellent calibre it has proved itself to be.
are also used by a few experienced stalkers for their red deer stalking. Nowadays, the little .22 Hornet is generally thought to be too underpowered for deer shooting except in circumstances where shots are only taken at close range. As a result the Hornet has slowly declined in popularity as the more powerful and versatile .222 Remington has gained recognition for the excellent calibre it has proved itself to be.

Since the passing of the 1963 Deer Act for England and Wales, the growth in the deer population may, in the not too distant future, bring about changes in the calibre restrictions the Act imposed. During the post-war years, and in the last two decades in particular, the roe deer population has widened its range to colonise many fresh areas in southern England. Recently, roe have begun to occupy territory north of the River Thames, and its spread westwards has reached into Cornwall. At the same time its other population strongholds in northern England and Scotland have similarly expanded. The smaller muntjac has also extended its territory considerably in recent years. From initial escapes out of Woburn Park at the turn of the century, small pockets of population established themselves in the home counties, and again in the last twenty years there has been a startling population explosion. By the early 1980s their range extended into Wiltshire and Dorset to the south-west, and to the Welsh border in the Midlands. Muntjac have reached the south of Lincolnshire and it is anticipated that Wales will be colonised within the next decade.

For these smaller deer species there are occasions where even a .243, at present the smallest legal calibre, may be considered too powerful. Even with the lighter 80 grain load, meat spoilage can reach unacceptable levels, and the thought of shooting these small deer with the heavier .270 or even the .308 calibres could be compared to rabbit shooting with a Hornet. In the present situation where there appear to be growing opportunities to stalk these smaller deer species, there is a strong case for reinstating the .22 centrefire calibres for use specifically against roe, muntjac, and possibly even Chinese water deer. Perhaps future legislation may see calibres restricted to over .240in for fallow, sika, and red deer, with the centrefire .22s acceptable for the three smaller deer species.

This type of legislation would bring Britain into line with many other countries in which calibres such as the .222 Remington are considered the correct choice for roe shooting. Certainly many of the European countries in which roe are stalked recommend this calibre for the sport.

For those more accustomed to using the heavier deer-stalking calibres, a switch to a centrefire .22 introduces them to the delights of these light weapons. The high power .22s are usually built as light and handy sporting rifles (apart from the American style varmint rifle) and are much less strain to haul about on a long day's woodland stalking. The cartridges are inherently very accurate and generally produce both low noise and light recoil. At the moment the user of a rifle in this group of calibres is restricted to fox shooting in England and Wales, but may extend his or her shooting activities to deer stalking in Scotland, and, as long as this situation exists, the centrefire .22 rifle will remain only of minority interest.

6. Deer Stalking in Britain

THROUGHOUT much of our history, the wild deer of Britain have enjoyed certain privileges not given to other species. Unlike the brown bear, lynx, and wolf, which had been hunted to extinction by medieval times, the deer species, particularly the two large breeds, red and fallow, were given royal protection. During the reign of King Canute extensive forests were set aside as hunting areas in which tree felling and settlement were rigidly controlled. The Norman kings refined this still further by establishing royal deer forests and by declaring that the deer could only be hunted by royalty. Large tracts of land were cleared of human inhabitants – evicted at best and executed for poaching at worst – so that the deer could remain undisturbed. Hunting was either by bow, crossbow, or by hounds, and an area of unfenced woodland became known as a chase, as it allowed long pursuits by the king's pack.

In later times the hunting rights were granted to nobles and clergy so that the sport of hunting deer became available to a wider number of people. Nevertheless, the deer of these forests were carefully managed and were perhaps the first of Britain's wild animals to be the subject of active conservation measures. Chases and other forest areas were later fenced to become parks in which the deer received protection while the giant forests of England, their natural habitat, were steadily cleared to make way for farmland and human settlements.

In time, the parkland deer came to be seen as creatures of grace and beauty instead of being either just meat on the hoof or beasts of the chase. This led to the fashion of introducing 'ornamental' deer to the parkland surrounding a great many country houses which, in Britain, resulted in the number of species living wild increasing from three to six. Initially these ornamental species were fairly well contained within their respective parks but two factors altered this situation and resulted in the rapid colonisation of many parts of Britain by these 'foreign' deer.

Firstly, because of the manpower demands of the military during both World Wars many of the walls surrounding the deer parks fell into disrepair. Deer escaped through these breaches to roam the surrounding unprotected countryside. Many fell prey to road traffic, poachers and dogs, but sufficient numbers survived to colonise and breed in any newly discovered safe ground. During both World Wars, the restricted access to military land allowed the deer to colonise what was, paradoxically, relatively undisturbed woodland belonging to the War Department, and thus the parkland escapees established themselves as an unrestricted deer population in many parts of Britain.

Secondly, another factor which has contributed to the rapid increase in the deer population, especially since the last war, is the way in which softwood forestry has become a permanent and integral part of the British rural landscape. In its infancy a fir plantation provides deer with ample protective cover and a good supply of food, and for the first ten years or so a plot of conifers will support a high population of deer. As the trees gain height, however, the food-providing undergrowth decreases and the surplus deer move on. In this way deer have 'leapfrogged' across the countryside from one plantation or copse to another, and where large scale reafforestation has taken place the rapid increase in deer numbers has brought about a revolution in the science of deer management and control.

As the design of rifles was steadily improved through the Middle Ages, the sport of deer stalking with firearms was quickly taken up in many European countries. In Britain, however, this did not happen and as the sport of deer hunting with hounds became unfashionable the deer population outside the deer parks was left to the mercy of the poacher and the pot hunter. It was only during the reign of Queen Victoria that a great revival of interest in deer came about and deer stalking became firmly established as a recognised sport in its own right.

Prince Albert, Queen Victoria's Consort, brought to Britain his love of field sports and he quickly took to organising small expeditions to shoot the deer of the Highlands. Suddenly red deer stalking became very fashionable and the other Scottish landowners were quick to follow the royal lead. It is from this birth of Highland stalking in the mid-nineteenth century, a sport much romanticised by such artists as Landseer, that a great many of our present skills and knowledge have developed.

The six species of deer living wild in Britain (listed in descending order of size) are red, fallow, sika, roe, Chinese water deer, and muntjac. In addition, there is one semi-feral herd of reindeer in the Cairngorms in Scotland but these are not considered quarry species. Of these species, only two are truly native to these islands. They crossed the land bridge from the continent as the last glaciation came to an end and the receding ice was replaced by extensive forests over much of Britain. The red deer and roe deer that inhabited these forests were a reliable source of meat for our ancestors, the Neolithic hunters who colonised our islands before the sea level rose to cut us off from what is now northern France. The other species have been introduced by man, at some time or another, and they have all appeared to respond well to our moderate climate and varied countryside. The fallow can claim to be semi-native as there is clear evidence that they were hunted by the Norman kings, and they may even have existed in Britain's forests at the time of King Canute. No one is certain as to when and who actually introduced the fallow to Britain but there is speculation that the Romans may have been responsible. The sika, muntjac, and the Chinese water deer were all nineteenth-century introductions and it is only since the turn of the century that these species have broken out from their original points of introduction to establish truly wild populations.

It is now generally accepted that there are well over one million deer living wild in Britain and these numbers are likely to increase still further by the year 2000 as more parts of the country are colonised. Despite determined efforts by foresters to prevent it, it seems likely that the hitherto unpopulated, extensive tracts of softwood plantation in Central and North Wales and the deep wooded valleys of South and West Wales will receive their first deer colonists within the next two decades. It will not be long before every county in Britain can claim to have a resident population of wild deer.

The six species that may be encountered in the wild state in this country can be subdivided into two groups according to their size. The red, fallow, and sika fall into the large deer category and the roe, Chinese water, and muntjac into the group of small deer. They are all very shy and retiring creatures with a strong instinctive fear of man, yet they have all displayed an ability to adapt quickly to changes in their habitats. At times they will thrive in situations which are far removed from their original environment or natural habitat.

RED DEER

The red deer is the largest land mammal living wild in Britain. At the time when this species first colonised Britain they were essentially forest dwellers and, judging by the remains of Neolithic antler tools, the lowland forests must have harboured great numbers of deer. These animals grew to enormous size and developed splendid antlers, living as they did on the abundant food supplies that exist in such woodlands. As time passed their natural habitat was cleared and their numbers declined so that now there are only relict populations of red deer in the few remaining forest areas in England. The deep, wooded valleys that fringe the moors of the south-west peninsula still harbour some magnificent red deer, and they are also to be found in the New Forest and in smaller woodlands in Wiltshire, Norfolk, Suffolk, and Sussex.

In northern England and Scotland they have displayed their ability to adapt to new conditions. In Neolithic times much of today's open moorland in these areas was covered by dense willow and hazel scrub, but from the Middle Ages this was progressively cleared to make way for sheep farming. Rather than decline as they did in the southern woodlands, however, the red deer adapted to become creatures of the open heather moorland. In doing so the change in diet resulted in the 'Highland' deer developing a more compact body with lighter antler growth. Highland red deer today are very hardy creatures which live in conditions in which only the fittest survive, and their appearance is far removed from their heavier and more ponderous brethren in the southern forests. The mention of red deer usually conjures up an image of large herds of stags or hinds and their calfs roaming the open hill in the Scottish Highlands.

A Highland red stag roaring a challenge. (*Lea MacNally*)

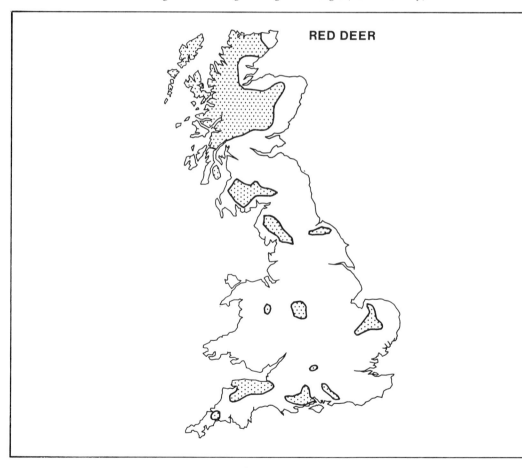

Distribution of red deer.

The final stages of the stalk often involve a stomach crawl. (*Lea MacNally*)

Indeed, this area is the population stronghold of this species and it is estimated that red deer numbers in the Highlands are in excess of two hundred thousand animals. Other large populations occur in the hills of south-west Scotland and in Cumbria and from both these the deer seem to be extending their range southwards and eastward – in time we may see other parts of the Pennines colonised by this regal beast.

The red deer of these upland areas have caused the evolution of perhaps the best known of all rifle sports in Britain. Known as hill stalking or simply deer stalking, it is essentially a form of open ground shooting which demands a certain degree of fitness on the part of the stalker as he is often required to walk many miles over rough terrain, frequently in adverse weather conditions. Put very simply, the sport revolves around selecting an animal to be shot and then approaching to within a shooting distance of it. This bald statement does nothing to explain the many hours and enormous effort required to achieve this objective. By using a powerful telescope the stalker can watch a herd of deer while remaining some miles away, and from this surveillance a deer can be selected for shooting. There then follows a lengthy and arduous stalk over the intervening ground, taking due note of the wind direction and taking advantage of any dips, hillocks, or valleys that would afford an unseen approach. The final stages of a stalk often involve a stomach crawl through wet heather and sticky black peat bog and after that the rifle has to be held steady for the shot! No experienced stalker would feel happy about taking a shot at a red deer at ranges beyond 200 yards, and the average range for this style of shooting is between one hundred and 150 yards. Red deer have perhaps the best eyesight of all deer and any successful stalker has to bear this in mind. A chosen approach route would have to avoid making any movement against the deer's skyline, even if this means adding several miles to the stalk.

The stalker has taken one stag and is 'glassing' the hill for a second. (*Lea MacNally*)

Clothing and equipment

In terms of selecting the correct clothing and equipment, the Highland stalker certainly has a different set of requirements to the deer shooter in other parts of the country. Though these mountains only reach just beyond four thousand feet, weather conditions in the Scottish Highlands are notoriously changeable. Even in the high-summer months low cloud and mist can quickly disorientate the unwary and unprepared, and on the higher slopes the temperature can often drop to below freezing. This, together with the increased chill factor of the cold rain-laden winds in these exposed places, can produce conditions in which exposure is a very real risk. With this in mind, clothing needs to be warm yet reasonably light. The perspiration generated on a strenuous stalk must be allowed to escape or be absorbed by the material of the outer clothing and therefore man-made fibres are generally considered unsatisfactory. The traditional preference is for the tweed coat and trousers or breeks and there are a number of reasons why this has remained so popular. Though not waterproof,

During the winter months hind stalking can provide an inexpensive introduction to Highland stalking. (*Lea MacNally*)

The winter hind stalker often faces extreme weather conditions. (*Lea MacNally*)

a tweed will resist showers and still remain light enough not to be burdensome. The traditional tweed colours of subdued greens and browns blend well with the landscape and above all, this material is noiseless. Nylon and even waxed cotton jackets can betray a stalker's presence from the noise generated by the sleeve catching, for instance, on a heather twig. A tweed clothed figure, on the other hand, may even be able to push his way noiselessly through gorse or briar. However, as a guard against a really heavy downpour the stalker usually carries a waterproof cape in his bag, and on wet days this is worn during the stalk and only discarded when the final approach to the shooting position is made. Bearing in mind the amount of ground covered on an average day's stalking, rubber wellington boots are impractical as they do not give enough support and strong walking boots are the only logical choice. These, and a thick pair of woollen socks, provide the feet, ankles, and calfs with the required protection and support.

During the autumn and winter months, when the stalker turns his attention to the hind cull, the weather conditions in these exposed uplands can be as

Both stag and hind stalking in the Highlands take place in magnificent surroundings.
(*Lea MacNally*)

severe as anywhere in the temperate world. At these times of year ex-military, arctic kit can be employed to advantage, and inevitably there will be many days on which stalking is impossible due to the severity of the winter weather. The few hours of daylight restrict the amount of time in which the stalker has shootable light and the frequent spells of poor visibility further reduce the stalker's chances of success. However, hind stalking is a necessary activity if the balance is to be maintained within the red deer herds. For the visiting stalker, hind stalking is one way of gaining access to inexpensive sport. It has none of the glamour of stag shooting, yet the sportsman may still gain much satisfaction from the knowledge that he is carrying out a vital task in conditions which demand that he is both fit and hardy.

Deer antlers

Red deer antlers have for a long time been prized as trophies of the chase. Like most antlered deer, the male red deer casts his antlers each year and grows a new set – in the first six years or so these antlers show a progressive increase in size until a full head is grown. A full head consists of twelve points made up of three pairs of single points or tines which project forward from the main antler stem on each side. From the forehead these are called the brow, bez, and trez tines, and the other six points, three on each side, form a small coronet at the end of each main stem. Where good feeding is available even more points will be grown so that some stags will achieve sixteen or even more points. In order to allow some favoured beasts to attain these heads a great many need to be culled in order to provide the optimum population of any given area of land. Thus the stalker's task is not to shoot the trophy stags, as they provide the best breeding stock, but to thin out the surplus prickets (yearling males), the staggies (immature stags), and the lesser adult stags.

Deer-stalking sport

Red deer stalking in the Scottish Highlands, and to a lesser extent in the southern uplands and Cumbria, is the only open ground, medium-calibre centrefire rifle sport available in Britain. Since the last war the numbers of people who stalk red deer in this way have increased dramatically as many of the social barriers have been swept away. Gone are the days when Highland stalking was exclusive to the nobility, and both stag shooting and hind stalking are available on a daily basis or on weekly lettings. Stag stalking is naturally more expensive than hind culling yet prices do vary and the prospective visitor to the Highlands would do well to shop around the many sporting agencies and hotels before buying a few day's stalking (see Appendix 1).

FALLOW DEER

Though no evidence has yet been found which proves that the fallow deer is a native species, it has been around in the woodlands of lowland England for so long that it it considered semi-native. It is the second largest of our deer species, yet in appearance it is so different from the red deer that there is little risk of one being mistaken for the other. The fallow buck's antlers are flattened and palmated with only the brow and bez tines pointing upwards and forwards. Beyond these the antlers flatten out into the palmation which has a series of small points on the rearward edge. Though a mature animal stands about three feet high at the shoulders, fallow are more slender than red deer and a buck may average around 190 to 200lb whereas a large forest stag could weigh 500lb.

In summer, the normal fallow is unmistakable in that the red-brown coat is mottled with well-defined white spots. This natural camouflage makes the animal difficult to see, particularly when bright sunlight shining through a dense canopy of deciduous foliage throws a dappled pattern on the undergrowth. The spotted coat is gradually lost through the autumn and is replaced by a thicker and darker grey-brown winter pelage. These changes in appearance occur in what are called 'normal' fallow, because this species is

127

The antlers of a fallow buck make it unmistakable. (*David de Lossy*)

A herd of normal fallow does in late summer. (*David de Lossy*)

A young and a mature fallow buck showing two of the colour variations. (*Shelagh Marshall-Ball*)

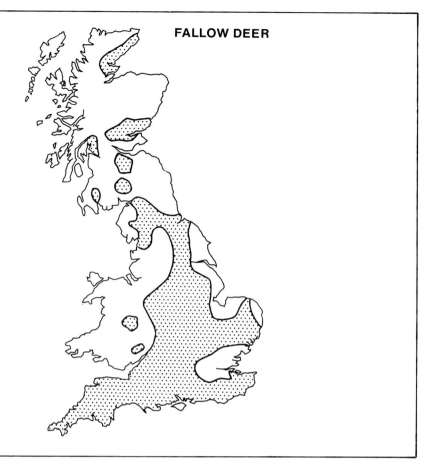

FALLOW DEER

Distribution of fallow deer.

given to far wider variation in coat colouring than any other British deer. Pure white fallow exist, as do very dark animals known as black fallow. The former has, in the past, given rise to a great many folklore tales and the White Hart – a white fallow buck – is one of the more popular public house names in the country. Another variety known as menil deer are generally lighter in colour than the normal deer and these retain their spots throughout the winter. Despite these variations in colour, however, the fallow is easily recognisable by its antler shape, and in the early summer, when these have been cast, it can be distinguished by its rather long tail, and its almost invariably white underparts.

The fallow is the most widely distributed of all British deer and is found in almost every rural English county and even in some parts of Wales and Scotland. There is a large population in the New Forest and descendants of ancient stock are also found in Cannock Chase, Rockingham Forest, the Forest of Dean and Epping Forest. Elsewhere, the wild stock has originated from park escapees, but this does not mean that they are any less wild.

Like the red deer they are herd animals and are usually found in small single-sex groups. When travelling they tend to move in single file, particularly through woodland or when negotiating an obstacle like a road or fence. This gregarious habit provides the stalker and deer manager with a more easily recognised cycle of movement around a particular herd's home range – a herd's movements are usually more easy to plot than that of more solitary species. However, it must be remembered that when farmland is raided fallow deer can do considerable damage. This resulted in the fallow being considered almost as a vermin species in the past, and like the roe, it was subjected to some fairly inhumane methods of control. Thankfully, the Deer Act of 1963 put an end to the shotgun deer drives and the population of fallow has responded by slowly extending its distribution to areas which hitherto had no deer. However, fallow are not usually found in any great numbers outside parklands or their traditional forests, and wherever crop damage reaches an intolerable level the services of a deer manager can quickly put matters right.

SIKA DEER

This final species in the group of large deer is also the relative newcomer. The sika deer was introduced into the British Isles in the late nineteenth century and wild herds have become well established over the years following the numerous parkland escapes. They are the smallest of the three larger species, an adult stag weighs up to 140lb, but they can often appear to be much larger than they really are. An adult stag emerging out of the undergrowth in a deep and shady forest can look enormous. The sika stag antlers are not palmated which immediately distinguishes them from the fallow. To the inexperienced eye this headgear can cause them to be confused with red deer but the sika is very much smaller and the antlers have a simpler format. They do not end in the crown, which is characteristic of the red deer, and the sika's antlers form a much narrower angle than the wide spread of the red stag. At the very most, the sika's antlers will show eight points and give the impression that, compared to a red stag, they are relatively straight and unbranched.

The sika's coat is also quite distinctive. In summer it is a warm brown with pale and rather indistinct spots. It is easily distinguished from a fallow because the coat darkens towards the underside of the animal whilst the fallow's turns almost white. In the winter the sika's coat turns dark grey or black but the diffused spotting is still visible. But it is mainly its size which easily distinguishes the sika from red deer, particularly in places where the two occur together. In these wooded areas the red deer can attain a height at the shoulder of about forty-eight inches, whereas the sika would average only about thirty-three inches.

There are parts of Britain where the sika is particularly numerous and a large population exists in the New Forest. These deer have also colonised all the counties on the south coast of England as far west as Devon and as far north as Avon and Berkshire. Essex also holds a sika population, and they are reasonably common in parts of northern England and north-west Scotland. Like some of the other species, the sika appears to be extending its range –

Sika stags. (*Richard Prior*)

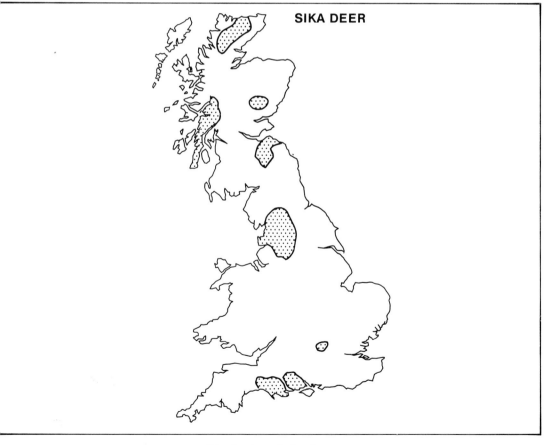

SIKA DEER

Distribution of sika deer.

though at a slower rate than either the roe or muntjac. This is perhaps because it prefers a rather more specialised habitat and is less adaptable than these other two species. The sika deer is a creature of dense and undisturbed woodland with a high proportion of thick undergrowth. As such it does not readily colonise new plantations and its scope for expansion is therefore more limited.

The sika is the most nocturnal of the three large deer species; it becomes active at dusk and usually returns to its sheltered lying-up place shortly after dawn. Though often classified as a herding animal, the sika stag tends to be a solitary creature and the groups or small herds of sika sometimes seen in the wild are usually sika hinds with their calves. Being an animal of the deep woodland, it is less often seen by the casual observer than the other two large species. This may have led to an underestimation of the total sika population and their distribution, and there are probably woodlands where they exist unnoticed and unrecorded.

ROE DEER

The distribution, habits and appearance of the roe deer are well known. The largest in the group of small deer, it is also the only other truly native, British deer species. At one time the roe deer occupied all mainland areas of Britain but the forest clearance and denudation of the countryside were significant factors in the extinction of the species in all areas except for the Scottish border country and the north-west Highlands, by the late eighteenth century. Because it is a small animal (standing about twenty-five inches at the shoulder) it lacked the stamina to be considered a beast of the chase and it consequently never received the protection afforded the red and fallow. Throughout the Middle Ages it was hunted and snared to extinction. Although reintroduced to Wimbledon Park in 1633, the real turn about in the roe's fortunes began in the early 1800s when roe were released in Dorset. Later releases were made in Windsor Great Park and at other points in southern England and Norfolk. It is from these herds that the present population of roe in southern England have descended.

It was during the First World War that roe populations really began to expand. The widespread felling of the mature forest to supply timber for the war effort left behind areas of scrub and tangled undergrowth – areas in which roe thrive. In addition, the reafforestation policy after the end of the war favoured the planting of quick-growing conifers, which, in the first years of growth, provide a similar, ideal environment. As these conifers matured the available food decreased and the surplus roe were forced to move on, thus encouraging the species to spread rapidly through the woodlands and plantations of the countryside.

The Second World War heralded the second phase of expansion for the same reasons, and the roe is now found in all the southern counties of England and as far west as Cornwall. The Thames has been a barrier to their northwards

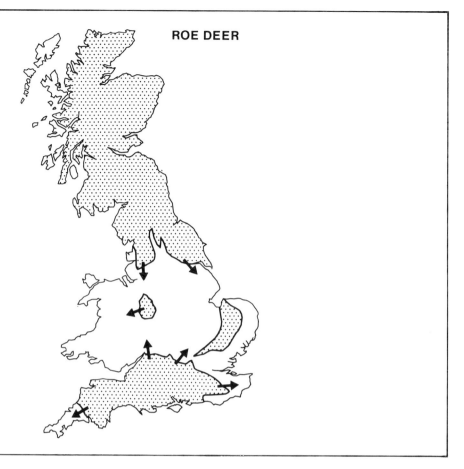

ROE DEER

Distribution of roe deer on mainland Britain. Dotted area already colonised, arrows indicate present expansion.

spread, but recent sightings in Hertfordshire will mean that the southern deer and the Norfolk population will soon meet up. Further west the roe have reached Bath and it is anticipated that parts of eastern Wales will be colonised in the future. To the north, the picture is again one of expansion. On either side of the Pennines, the population based in the border country has spread southwards into Lancashire and Yorkshire, and the large scale reafforestation programmes in the Southern Uplands and in the Highlands have provided, yet again, an ideal environment in which the roe can thrive.

A mature roe buck can achieve a body weight of 60lb although the doe seldom reaches 40lb. In summer the coat is usually a fox-red colour, though some variations do occur. The underparts are buff coloured and there is no visible external tail. These two distinguishing points immediately differentiate the roe and sika.

In winter the roe grows a heavy grey coat so that they tend to look far heavier and bulkier than their weight suggests. Throughout the winter the rear view of the animal shows a prominant white patch which is probably the

A roe doe in summer coat.

animal's most striking feature; in the buck it takes the shape of a horizontal kidney, while the doe's patch is heart-shaped with long, downward-pointing hairs. During winter the buck, unlike all other antlered species in Britain, will have cast his antlers and the white patch can be the only means of distinguishing bucks and does.

A roe's face is short and the ears have a black border. In addition, the nose is black with quite prominant white patches on the lower jaw. Again, unlike the other larger antlered deer, it is virtually impossible to estimate the age of a buck by its antlers. Sometimes even a yearling buck will develop a six point head which is characteristic of a mature animal, and the antler quantity is often a clearer indication of a buck's health than its age. A mature buck's antlers will seldom be longer than twelve inches but there can be a considerable variation in shape, thickness, pearling and the number of points between mature bucks. Even with this capacity for great variation of head quality, it is often possible to identify individual animals over a period of several years, and a good deer manager would be able to identify each individual buck in this way.

Although groups of up to a dozen or so roe may be seen together during the winter and early spring, it is not a social or herding animal. It is not really a family creature either in that its family ties are rather loose and haphazard. In early summer dominant bucks do mark out a fairly clearly-defined territory, yet if this is not within the less precise home range of a doe then he is unlikely to succeed in attracting a mate. Generally speaking though, where one finds a doe it is safe to assume that the buck is not far away. The doe's fertility is high; they usually produce twins and in some cases even triplets, yet survival of the offspring depends to a great extent on available food, farming casualties, and

A mature roe buck in flight. (*Mark Newman-Wren*)

fox predation. In my part of Wiltshire silage cutters take a toll on newly-born fawns in late May, and in areas where foxes are not controlled, these predators can drastically reduce the roe infant survival rate. However, in a relatively undisturbed patch of conifers or in a mixed woodland, the roe deer has the capacity to double its numbers each year.

More than any other species, it is the roe deer that is responsible for the tremendous upsurge of interest in woodland stalking as a sport in its own right. From before the last war up to even as late as the early 1960s, this creature was considered to be a pest and attempts to control the roe population usually came down to organised deer drives where they were killed (and more often cruelly maimed) by people armed with shotguns. In many places they were considered to be keeper's perks and were snared or shot from vehicles at night – either with shotguns or, just as bad, with underpowerd .22 rimfire rifles. Even so, there were a few pioneers who realised that this elegant and wary creature was a worthy quarry for a rifle user and the idea of proper deer management evolved out of the principle of selective culling for the general good of the roe population. Thankfully, the 1963 Deer Act put an end to the indiscriminate slaughter and inherent cruelty of the shotgun drive and the roe became an animal that, except in special circumstances, could only be pursued by the rifle user. With the outlawing of snares and the restrictions placed on the use of shotguns for deer, the way was opened for the development of woodland stalking both as a sport and as the only effective way to control a rapidly expanding deer population. Few people would argue that it was the roe's spread through both southern and northern England and Scotland that brought about the rapid development of our woodland stalking techniques.

A wary Chinese water deer. (*Roy Harris*)

CHINESE WATER DEER

Moving down the size order comes the least numerous and most enigmatic of our deer species – the Chinese water deer. Introduced into Woburn around the turn of the century, this little deer stands about twenty inches at the shoulder – which makes it appreciably smaller than the roe. Among all the deer species in Britain it is unique in that it does not grow antlers, but rather shares with the even smaller muntjac the prominent growth of its upper canine teeth. In summer these deer can be confused with the roe because their coats are of a similar foxy-red colour. In the winter, however, the Chinese water deer assumes a pale sandy-brown colour which is quite different to the grey coat of the wintering roe. What also sets these two species apart is the proportional differences in the leg length and consequent body angle. In the roe the back forms a more or less horizontal line which ends in a rather angular rump when viewed broadside on. The Chinese water deer, on the other hand, apparently has longer back legs for its size and this has the effect of tilting the body forward. Like the smaller muntjac the back line of the Chinese water deer slopes upwards from the shoulder and ends with a rounded, rather than angular, rump. At close quarters the canine teeth are quite noticeable, the buck's being longer than that of the doe, but a combination of a lack of antlers and its body shape will remain the main distinguishing features for the casual observer.

There are no dense concentrations of water deer population in any part of Britain and their distribution is still more localised than the other species. The escapees from Woburn have extended their range over much of Bedfordshire, Buckinghamshire and Hertfordshire, and other introductions have established

136

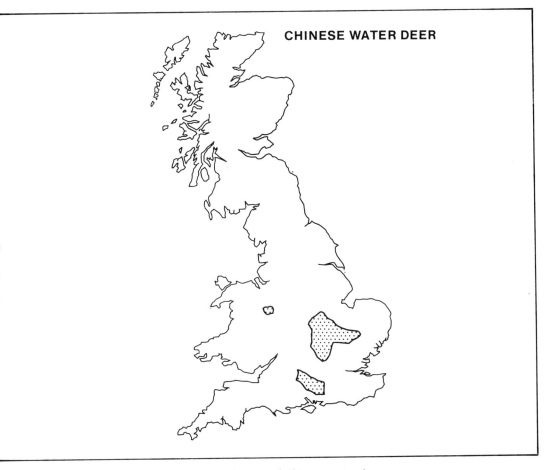

CHINESE WATER DEER

Distribution of Chinese water deer.

wild populations in Hampshire, and further north in Shropshire. Even now there is a great deal of information yet to be discovered about this species – how it has adapted to the English countryside is still a matter of continued investigation. In its natural habitat this Asian deer thrives in the reedy margins of freshwater lakes and rivers, yet in Britain this type of environment is only found in a few areas. It does appear that in England this deer has become more of an open farmland species than others on the British list and it seems to be quite happy living in open arable farming areas providing that there are occasional patches of thicket and woodland. Where reedy water margins do exist, though, it will quickly colonise the area and remain concealed for much of the time. The old gravel workings in Hertfordshire, for example, can now boast a healthy population of Chinese water deer, yet they are very difficult to observe as they seldom move out of the thick cover provided by the reed beds that fringe the gravel pits.

Because they are not found in any great numbers and their distribution range is still very limited, the Chinese water deer has yet to be given serious consideration as a quarry species. It is not afforded the protection of open and closed seasons in the Deer Act of 1963 and few people stalk Chinese water deer. However, we now have a situation where the population of this species is growing and they are slowly extending their range. When one considers the phenomenal growth of the muntjac numbers in recent years it is possible that in the future the Chinese water deer will experience a similar expansion. Should this happen, these rather mysterious deer will take their place as legitimate rifle quarry for the British woodland stalker.

MUNTJAC

Standing barely sixteen inches high at the shoulders and weighing around 30lb, the muntjac is Britain's smallest deer. It is not only its small size that makes this animal remarkable – it is a very ancient species which roamed the earth's undergrowth long before any of the other deer species had evolved from their common ancestors, and it is regarded by many as an example of a 'living fossil' in much the same way as the horseshoe crab. On mainland Britain the population of muntjac is growing so rapidly that some experts believe that it will very soon become the most numerous of all our deer species.

Like the Chinese water deer, the muntjac was introduced into Woburn around the turn of this century and it was the escapees from there that were the ancestors of our present wild stock. No other deer species has spread so rapidly from their initial escape area. Much of central England is now colonised by muntjac and each year their spread increases. To the west they have reached the Welsh borders, to the east they have been reported in Norfolk, and they are now only absent from Cornwall and Kent in the south. It seems only a matter of time before much of Wales and the Midlands will be able to claim a resident population of these small and secretive deer. The rapid growth in numbers of this species has been attributed to a number of reasons. For one thing, it is a remarkably disease-free animal. Where areas are overpopulated by roe deer, these larger animals develop a self-regulating population control method through disease and parasitic infestation. Not so the muntjac, whose main population control seems to be predators like dogs, cats and foxes. In addition, the muntjac is capable of breeding every seven months and there is no specific time of the year when a rut takes place. Fauns are therefore born throughout the year and they appear to be able to survive a normal English winter quite well. A severe winter will, however, cause widespread mortality among both young and adult animals and locally prolonged cold weather will produce a population crash. In such conditions the survivors are those that seek shelter and warmth in farm outhouses and even garden sheds. Another significant factor in their expansion is that they do little or no agricultural damage so that they have been virtually ignored by pest and deer control groups. Also, the fact that they are creatures of dense undergrowth means that their presence in an area may go undetected for some time. Much publicity has been given to animals that have adapted to an urban environment – and in many areas the

A muntjac buck. Note the humped back and stocky build. (*Richard Prior*)

muntjac has become a suburban animal. Large overgrown gardens make ideal havens for deer who have forsaken the bracken and briar of the countryside for the box hedges and shrubberies of suburbia. From these hideouts they forage the roadside verges, the vegetable plots, and the herbaceous beds of the neighbourhood gardens which provide them with a varied diet and a relatively easy living. A great many people living on the outer fringe of London would be amazed to learn just how close they are to really wild deer.

It is very difficult to confuse the identity of a muntjac with any other species of deer. They are considerably smaller than even the Chinese water deer and their stance and gait are distinctive. As an animal used to moving through dense undergrowth, it moves with a characteristic head down attitude and its back slopes upwards from the shoulders to well-rounded hindquarters. Its short tail is usually held close to the body yet in alarm it is held vertically to reveal the white underside. The buck grows small and sharply pointed antlers which are raked backwards from the forehead and covered by hairy pedicles for about half their length. Unlike other deer they are not grown and cast in any particular season, neither do they bear any relationship to the buck's ability to mate with an oestrous doe.

In summer the coat is of a rich brown, but this becomes greyer during the winter when the lack of cover means that the deer are more likely to be seen. The muntjac is a creature of the dense undergrowth – a four-year growth of brambles is sufficient to provide the necessary canopy under which it marks out a well-worn pattern of paths and tunnels. Bracken, gorse, and ornamental

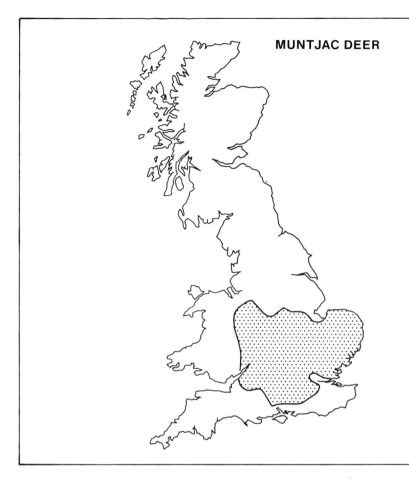

MUNTJAC DEER

Present confirmed distribution of the muntjac represented by dotted area. Actual range may be considerably greater than shown here.

shrubs also provide sufficient cover, and thorn bushes may also provide some protection from predators. As with the other small deer species, rotational conifer plantations provide secure cover and a continuous supply of food.

The muntjac is the most family oriented of all our deer species – the buck takes an active part in rearing the fauns and there have been occasions when bucks have been seen playing with their offspring! A typical family group consists of a buck and doe, accompanied by one adolescent faun and one youngster. When nearing one year old the adolescent will leave the family group, it is after all capable of breeding by this time, and these animals are generally the pioneers in the quest for new territory. When the safety of a faun is threatened both parents often indulge in threatening behaviour. There are records of humans being attacked in these circumstances, and the combination of the buck's antlers and his canine teeth is usually enough to discourage closer investigation by most dogs.

It is only in the last few years that this little deer has begun to be regarded as a quarry species. Even now, I do not think that there is anywhere in the country

A muntjac doe – the long tail of a muntjac is a useful aid to identification. (*Richard Prior*)

where a formal management policy has been developed for the muntjac, yet they certainly merit such attention. They are steady and reliable breeders and they could, in cold economic terms, provide a regular protein crop from a given area of suitable land. Though afforded the protection of the Deer Act with regard to the type of weapons that can be used on them, their continuous breeding on a seven month cycle means that there can be no set season in which either does or bucks can be culled. As a consequence, the Act does not set down any close seasons for this species and the British Deer Society can only recommend that muntjac are shot between November and February.

WOODLAND STALKING

With the exception of the red deer population in the Scottish Highlands and parts of southern Scotland and the English Lake District, all the other deer in this country are hunted by what is generally termed woodland stalking techniques. Though the Chinese water deer is at present still low on the stalker's list, the muntjac, roe, sika, and fallow deer populations are controlled by woodland, rather than open ground, stalking methods. Compared to the hill stalking techniques, the activities of the woodland stalker are far more controlled by the natural routine of the deer he pursues. While a hill stalker may be able to intercept his quarry during all daylight hours as they go about their normal daily life on the exposed slopes, the woodland stalker needs to be in a position to intercept his quarry during the limited times when they emerge from the cover of their resting places. Thus a stalker of the woodland deer species must be active when the deer are active and this is generally at dawn and dusk. When most people are enjoying the rest and peace of the early hours, snug in their warm beds, the woodland stalker must be about his woods with stick and binoculars in hand, observing and recording the whereabouts and movements of his deer. Similarly, he must forsake the company around the evening meal table to be sat in a high seat or some other vantage point to await the emergence of his quarry. Unlike the pursuit of Highland red deer, those that hunt the woodland species do not really stalk deer in the Highland sense, and the sport is essentially one of strategic prediction coupled with a great deal of luck. Whereas the Highland stalker may expect to walk many gruelling miles in the course of a day's sport, his woodland counterpart can usually measure his movements in hundreds of yards.

The woodland stalker uses two basic methods to come into contact with his quarry: active and static. Both demand a degree of knowledge of the deer population – their movements, their habits, and the way in which variations in the weather may affect these. Using this information he can predict where the deer ought to be at first light or in late evening and he then needs to get to the appropriate place to intercept them. However, no deer has ever read a book on deer behaviour and they are notoriously unpredictable in their habits! Though we can make logical predictions as to where deer ought to be at any given time, actually coming into contact with them demands a good deal of luck.

Active woodland stalking

The active sport of woodland stalking is one in which the stalker moves through a patch of woodland in the hope of seeing a shootable deer. Anyone remotely acquainted with deer will understand that this is an extremely difficult task and one which requires a very optimistic outlook on the part of the stalker. He has all the odds stacked against him. Deer have far better senses of hearing and smell than a human being and they can usually detect the presence of a person long before the human detects them. In addition, many other wildlife species will betray the presence of the stalker long before he comes into contact with any deer – on numerous occasions an early morning or late evening stalk can be spoilt by rooks, magpies, and even rabbits alerting the deer. At all times the deer are on home ground whereas the stalker is really treading in alien territory.

To set against all these natural disadvantages the accomplished woodland stalker has his own intelligence and previously acquired knowledge of his quarry. It is a sport which demands infinite patience, a good grounding in woodcraft, and the ability to concentrate all one's senses for extended periods. A walk through the wood may only involve moving a few hundred yards, yet this journey may take several hours. The stalker moves with the utmost care and stealth from one place to another, surveying his surroundings with minute attention to detail both by naked eye and through binoculars, for the merest hint of deer. The horizontal line of a deer's back behind a patch of ferns, the twitch of an ear, the odd splash of red-brown or patch of white, may all point to an otherwise concealed deer. He must pick his way through the wood, inspecting the ground before taking each step, and spending much time standing motionless scanning his surroundings. The first lapse in concentration on the part of the stalker is often rewarded by the sound of a deer bounding away through the undergrowth.

Nevertheless, woodland stalking can be an intensely exciting sport. The stalker often comes into very close contact with deer and when a shot is taken it is more often at ranges below fifty yards than above. To be out in woodland in the early hours of the morning and again in the late evening, and to move about unnoticed by the wood's wildlife is a very satisfying experience. There have been occasions when hares, foxes, and badgers have passed within feet of me and yet I have not been noticed; and I am sure that most woodland stalkers develop the feeling that they are in tune with the other creatures of the forest at such times. While it is not a physically demanding sport, active woodland stalking makes great demands on one's mental resources and powers of concentration and a few hours of stalking through woodland can be just as tiring as a long day's wildfowling or rough shooting.

Static woodland stalking

Where the area of woodland contains rides and clearings, the static form of woodland stalking is often employed. Quite simply, the shooter selects some vantage point from which he has a clear view of an area frequented by his quarry, and there he waits to ambush them as they emerge from cover.

To most people, this form of shooting conjures up images of high seats and this is the type of sport that is most readily available to the less experienced and novice stalker. Again, knowledge of the deer's habits is vital to the success of the stalker who uses the high seat as he will need to predict when the deer are likely to be on the move and where they are likely to come onto the open ground that is covered by the high seat. To this the shooter must add the ability to stay still for long periods as any movement or noise from within the hide will quickly betray his presence, and the preparedness to put up with the discomfort of sitting still in what is often a cramped or uncomfortable position.

High seats can take many forms, from simple ladders leaned against a tree trunk to elaborate and free-standing affairs more akin to the forts of the Wild West. They all serve a dual purpose in that they allow a less restricted view over a given area than would be possible from ground level, and perhaps more importantly, they allow a bullet to bury itself safely in the ground as the shot is directed downwards. For the less experienced stalker this additional safety factor is very important – it is all too easy to succumb to 'buck fever' in the excitement of a shot presenting itself, and an unsafe backdrop to the shot can often be overlooked in the heat of the moment. A high seat minimises this risk. One other aspect of high-seat shooting is of considerable importance to the novice. A well-constructed and sturdy high seat, regardless of how simple or elaborate it is, will provide a steady platform for a steady shot. Seats are usually constructed so as to allow almost bench rest conditions for the rifle and

(*left*) A free-standing high seat in a forest clearing. The steel structure has been suitably camouflaged. (*John K. Dryden*) (*right*) A simple lean-to high seat overlooking a young plantation.

a steady and deliberate aim can be taken. In contrast to active woodland stalking where shots are usually taken with only the stalking stick to steady the aim, a far greater degree of accuracy is possible from a high seat even though ranges seldom exceed one hundred yards.

Many woodland stalkers, myself included, employ both active and static methods at various times of the year in order to come into contact with the deer. I tend to use the high seat in the lead up to the roe's rut in July – a time when fraying damage becomes excessive in the young conifer plantations – or after the bracken has died away in the winter when the doe season gets under way. In early spring and autumn I tend to favour active stalking as this brings me into contact with greater numbers of deer and allows me to check on the general population level and breeding success of the animals in the woodland I manage.

Woodland stalking is possibly the fastest-growing rifle sport in Britain. Reflecting the current rapid growth in the numbers and distribution of the smaller deer species, notably roe and muntjac, woodland stalking has at last been recognised as a sport in its own right with as great a demand on the participant's shooting skills, fieldcraft, and perseverance, as any other form of shooting. The realisation that our wild deer, almost as much as domestic livestock, need to be husbanded and managed in order to maintain a healthy and thriving population has only come to be generally accepted in recent years. The need to stop unacceptable levels of damage to agricultural and forestry crops has generated a great deal of study into management techniques and much of the pioneering work in this field can be attributed to Richard Prior,

Wild (feral) goats can be an interesting diversion when stalking in the Highlands.
(*Jack Orchel*)

who is perhaps now the world's leading authority on roe deer. As a result of his work, roe deer are effectively managed and controlled over much of their range in Britain. If, as is usually the case, the need to regulate a population can be achieved through controlled rifle sport, so much the better.

DEER-STALKING CALIBRES

The Deer Act (England and Wales) 1963 defines close seasons for most of our deer species. The Act also effectively made deer shooting a rifle sport by putting severe limitations on the once widespread use of shotguns for deer control. In addition, it stipulated that the calibre of the rifle should be greater than .24in or that the muzzle energy be in excess of 1700 ft/lb. As a consequence the smallest legal calibres for deer in England and Wales are the .243 Winchester, and the 6mm Remington. The range of accepted calibres goes up to the .308 Winchester and the .30–06. When one considers that at the time the Act went through Parliament, the main deer species regarded as quarry were those upwards in size from roe to red deer, this calibre stipulation is understandable. Since the early 1960s, however, the phenomenal spread of the smaller deer species may cause some re-thinking so that the high-power centrefire .22s may become accepted again as legitimate calibres for use against roe, Chinese water deer, and muntjac. At the moment there is a growing body of stalkers in favour of this change as even the .243 can be considered too heavy for the little muntjac – it often produces an unacceptable amount of carcass damage. In Scotland deer shooting is covered by a number of Acts which stipulate the same

145

sort of restrictions as we have south of the border. The one major exception is that the Scottish stalker may use, for instance, a .222 Remington for his roe shooting and a heavier calibre for the larger species.

There are perennial arguments in the sporting press as to which is the ideal calibre for deer shooting in Britain. What seems to be overlooked by many participants of this debate is that it is the actual placement of the bullet which is far more important than the calibre of the barrel from which it came, and a badly placed shot from a .30–06 will no more knock down a deer than one from a .22–250. In general, though, it seems to be accepted that for deer species upwards in size from roe, the .243 Winchester is the minimum calibre, with the .270 and the .308 having a strong following. In Scotland the .222 Remington and the .22–250 are popular for roe. One of the best calibres in this quest for a deer rifle is often overlooked and the .25–06 has much to commend it. Its bullet weights range from 90 grains up to 120 grains which provides a suitable projectile for any of our deer species, and the calibre posesses varminting accuracy – I am surprised it is not as popular as the .270 or the 7 × 57 (.275 Rigby).

The one calibre which seems to be accepted as the all rounder by experts in this field such as Richard Prior and Lea MacNally, is one of the post-war 'mild' American cartridges, the .243 Winchester. It possesses great potential accuracy which is enhanced by its mild recoil and, compared to other calibres, quiet report. Its 100 grain bullet is sufficiently powerful to stop a large woodland red stag, yet its 75 grain light load will take a muntjac cleanly. The .243 Winchester has many supporters. My own Parker Hale rifle in this calibre is capable of taking on any deer this country has to offer although I tend to use my .270 for big fallow.

Deer stalking was once the exclusive sport of the nobility and landed classes, but since the last war it has experienced more revolutionary changes than any other branch of shooting, with the result that nowadays deer stalking is available for anyone who wishes to take part. The Forestry Commission, many private estates, and several sporting agencies offer stalking lets to suit everyone from the raw novice to the most experienced stalker. The British Deer Society runs courses in woodland stalking and deer management and the British Association for Shooting and Conservation (BASC) organise similar opportunities for the newcomer to the sport. Deer stalking is in a very healthy state in Britain, and it is likely to see even further expansion as our smaller deer species eventually colonise the remaining parts of these islands.

7. RIFLE SPORT IN EUROPE

ANYONE who has studied the sporting press in Britain in recent years could not help but notice the tremendous increase in the numbers of sporting agencies that now offer a wide variety of shotgun shooting, fishing, and stalking, in various parts of Britain. What is rather less obvious is the growth in the number of agencies and tour operators which offer the rifle shooter a wide variety of shooting in other parts of the world. Even close at hand, on mainland Europe, there are a great many opportunities for the British rifle shooter to broaden his or her horizons. The national tourist offices, the hunting associations, and the specialist tour operators of many European countries have not been slow to realise that there is a fairly important potential market for European rifle sport within British sporting rifle shooting circles. Since the establishment of the Commonwealth the sporting rifle user in Britain has developed a parochial attitude to the sport – looking at the limited shooting that is available within these islands and not really considering just what is available across the Channel. Even today this rather isolationist approach is still very common, but there is a small but growing body of rifle shooters who have sampled the sport available in Germany, Norway, or Spain, for instance, and who can be looked upon as the pioneers of British participation in the rifle sports of the European mainland.

What makes European shooting so different? Probably a combination of three factors: the wider variety of game species, the greater contrast of environments, and the different traditions of hunting that exist in each country. From the Arctic tundra of northern Norway, south through the extensive lake and conifer forest landscapes of Finland, to the high Alps and the sun-bleached shores of the Mediterranean, big-game species are hunted by devotees of the centrefire rifle, and the .22 rimfire accounts for a great number of smaller game and vermin species. There are many areas where the sporting rifle actually predominates over shotgun sports even though it was the latter which first generated the creation of facilities for the new breed of travelling shooter.

Rifle shooting in most European countries can claim a longer history and more deeply rooted traditions than Britain, and in those countries it is looked upon as the most well-established branch of shooting sports. In some areas –

the Scandinavian countries for instance – there has been a phenomenal growth in sporting rifle shooting since the last war.

For simplicity, the quarry species for the rifle can be divided into two different groups according to size and body weight. Small quarry includes the rabbit, hare, fox, and in some cases mink, capercaillie, and wolverine. It is in the category of the big game, however, that the range of species in Europe is considerably wider than we have in the British Isles. There are, for instance, nine species of deer which are hunted in various parts of Europe – from the diminutive muntjac to the mighty Scandinavian elk – and these form the most important group of quarry for the rifle shooter. In addition, the other hoofed game include wild boar, mouflon, chamois and ibex. Also, there are rare occasions when various carnivores are hunted with a rifle, so that at times the brown bear, wolf and lynx may also be added to the list of shootable species. The pursuit of any of these European big-game species will take the shooter into environments which are markedly different from those that exist in Britain.

SMALL GAME

As in Britain, the prime quarry for the .22 rimfire user in Europe is the rabbit. While not as common or widespread as it once was (myxomatosis was after all developed in France) the rabbit population still ranges from Portugal and Spain, through France and Germany, and reaches into southern Sweden in the north and Hungary in the east. Within this wide zone it has demonstrated its ability to adapt to a great many different environments. It does not colonise high mountainous areas but the rabbit will thrive in any areas where sandy soil and sufficient cover exist, and it will be found in varying numbers throughout its wide range. Although the average body weight of an adult is fairly constant throughout its range, there are areas where these animals show a considerable variation in colour. Towards the east of their range the rabbit tends to be greyer, and in places like the Carmargue in southern France a high proportion of rabbits have black fur. Elsewhere variations in colouring often derive from interbreeding with escaped domestic stock.

Moving up the scale of size, the blue hare is to be found in the colder and more mountainous areas of Europe. They may be encountered in the Alps, in the north of Denmark, and over the rest of Scandinavia. They also occur in Ireland and Iceland as well as in northern Scotland. Body size varies through its range – the largest specimens coming from the Alpine population and the smallest from Iceland. Over much of their range their winter coat is white though their ears remain black at the tips, and the summer coat varies from reddish-brown to grey-brown. Within its range it is a very popular sporting quarry species and large numbers are killed by rifle shooters. In Norway, for instance, an average of 75,000 are shot every year, yet their population appears to be stable except where they come into contact with the expanding range of their larger cousins, the brown hare.

The brown hare is slowly extending its range northwards away from its traditional habitat of open, flat country and broad-leaved woodland. As a consequence the brown hare has now colonised all of mainland Europe with the exception of the high Alps, Norway, and northern Sweden. It is distinguished from the blue hare by its larger size and rather more athletic build which makes it look much less rabbit-like than the blue hare. In the southern part of the brown hare's range a separate Mediterranean race has been identified as a slightly smaller animal with a lighter build and proportionally longer ears.

The rabbit and hares make up the edible ground game of the small-game category and as such the weapons suitable for use against them would be required to inflict a low level of carcass damage. As a result, opinions change from country to country as to whether they should be either .22 rimfire or shotgun quarry. The general pattern, however, seems to point to shotgun drives taking place where numbers on the ground require a short-term reduction, and rifle stalking where the full sporting potential of these species wants to be appreciated.

Of the non-edible small-quarry species, the fox is the most widespread and indeed, it is probably the most widely distributed of all the animals of interest to the sporting rifle user. From the extreme south west of the Iberian peninsula to the Black Sea and beyond, and north to the lands well beyond the Arctic Circle, the fox is one of Europe's most adaptable and successful predators. It has been hunted with gun, rifle and hound pack for centuries and yet the population has shown a small but steady growth rate. In many areas the actual number of foxes depends on the availability of food – there was, for instance, a reduction in overall numbers after the myxomatosis epidemic because the rabbit population crashed. But foxes are extremely adaptable scavengers and a reduced population soon recovers where a new food source is exploited.

The northern and western areas of Scandinavia are also the home range of the largest animal in the small-quarry group. The wolverine is a strange looking creature. It is related to the stoat and looks like a cross between a large badger and a small bear. It is a heavily-built animal with an overall brown coat with light patches and a yellowish stripe along its flank. The wolverine's face resembles that of a bear and the body is badger-like. During the summer it is mostly a nocturnal animal but during the winter it is active throughout the day. Despite being heavily built it is a strong animal which can jump and climb well and its diet would classify it as a carnivore. In Norway it is considered a pest and often features in the list of legitimate rifle quarry for that country. Like the other northern species it tends to migrate southwards and eastwards during severe winters so that there are times when the species may be encountered as far south as southern Sweden or on the Oslo lowlands and in south-west Norway.

The only other species of small, ground-dwelling animal which may come to the attention of the visiting rifle shooter is the wild mink. The true European mink is distributed in two general areas. One of these covers much of north-western France, and the other region lies to the east of Europe through Poland

and Finland. In the field it is practically impossible to differentiate between the European and American mink, and as the latter species is now widespread through much of Europe, considerable confusion has arisen. Certainly the American mink, an animal which has established itself from a series of deliberate and accidental introductions, is considered a pest wherever it is found. As such there are areas where determined extermination campaigns have been waged against the species, yet such is their natural tenacity that they usually recover to a worryingly healthy population within a very short time.

Finally there are two additions to the list of potential quarry in the small animal category and the first of these is also an American import. For some reason, either through accidental escapes or deliberate release, the racoon has become a firmly established feral animal in some parts of northern Germany. This strange little animal with its panda-like face is nevertheless a serious predator and is seen as a threat to the indigenous game stocks of the region. Because of this it is controlled by shooting and therefore figures in the quarry list of the rifle shooter in northern Germany.

The second addition and the only bird to feature in this group is the capercaillie, and even this is considered as a legitimate rifle target only in Czechoslovakia. There the tradition is similar to turkey hunting in North America in that the cock caper is stalked during the early spring when it is in the process of rather noisily establishing its territory. In other parts of Europe however, the capercaillie is generally considered a shotgun target and indeed many countries specifically prohibit the use of rifles in the pursuit of this species, and it can only therefore be regarded as an oddity.

There is a drawback to pursuing these smaller species with a small-bore rifle on the European continent. As far as I can ascertain, none of the sporting agencies or tour operators offer facilities specifically for this kind of shooting. Of course there will be opportunities for small-game and vermin rifle shooting on a privately arranged basis, and there is also the chance of fitting a day or two of such activities within the framework of an arranged sporting holiday or shooting package, but as yet these opportunities are few and far between.

If such an opportunity arises there are general guidelines as to the calibres that seem to be accepted for hunting the animals in this group. Quite simply, if edible game, such as rabbits, hares and blue hares, are being hunted then the most commonly used calibre is the lowly .22 rimfire Long Rifle. This round provides the ideal combination of a good knock-down blow without causing undue bruising or meat spoilage. At any range up to one hundred yards this primitive rimfire would provide all that is required for these species. At ranges up to 140 yards or so the .22 Magnum would take over from its less potent relative.

As far as the non-edible small species are concerned the .22 rimfires provide sufficient stopping power, even for animals up to the wolverine in size, providing the ranges are not stretched. Where extra distance or more power is required, however, the .22 Hornet becomes a firm favourite and it is the accepted calibre for fox shooting in most parts of Europe. In Czechoslovakia it is the recommended calibre for capercaillie – though I would question the degree of meat spoilage this produces. All these small quarry species appear to demand the use of low-powered rifles in the .22 Hornet and below category, so the .222 Remington belongs to a far larger family of calibres which seems to be acceptable for use against the larger game species. Despite the fact that there are at present no shooting tours designed specifically for the rimfire or Hornet user in Europe, opportunities for sport do exist and do appear from time to time. Anyone who has been lucky enough to hunt these small species in Europe will vouch for the great deal of enjoyment that can be derived from using these low-powered rifles in unfamiliar and often spectacular surroundings.

BIG GAME

The best of European rifle sport is concentrated on the hunting of the medium and large game species, and it is in this category that Europe far surpasses the variety of shooting available in the British Isles.

There are sixteen species that merit serious consideration as legitimate rifle quarry in various parts of Europe, and of these nine belong to the deer family. Each species occupies a different distribution range throughout the continent and with the variety in size of these animals, the contrasting environments which they occupy, and the different sporting traditions of each country, it is only to be expected that a very wide range of rifle sport is available.

As far as the deer species and deer stalking is concerned, the overall picture is one of expansion. Since the end of the last war the replanting and management of tracts of forest throughout Europe have provided many of the deer species with the conditions that make rapid expansion of their population and distribution possible. Coupled to this is the realisation that deer provide a viable revenue for the forest and woodland, and management strategies have been adopted, for the first time in many places, in order to improve the quality of the deer stocks and to provide increased sporting facilities. The countries in the eastern bloc in particular seem to be developing a wide variety of deer shooting tours which are organised specifically for the western rifle shooter, and nowadays Hungary and Czechoslovakia have a well-earned reputation for good quality hunting and for the magnificence of their trophy heads.

Hunting methods

Deer-hunting methods in Europe fall into two broad categories, originating from the two contrasting hunting traditions in the German and Gallic regions. It was probably in the vast tracts of conifer woodland east of the Rhine that woodland stalking methods were first refined and became a sport in its own right. It was here that the full stocked Stutzen was first developed as a handy and accurate woodland rifle, and here also that the high seat became associated with the German style of woodland deer shooting. It is these shooting methods, founded on the experience of deer shooters in southern Germany and Austria, that have been adapted to similar environments in other parts of mainland Europe and Britain.

151

At the other end of the deer-hunting spectrum, the Gallic areas traditionally regard deer as beasts of the chase and the sport of hunting with hounds is still strong. This sport does, however, apply more to fallow and red deer – it was the Norman kings who were first recorded as hunting fallow in this way in England – than to the smaller species and the introduced deer. The roe deer and more recently the muntjac have therefore been identified as animals that are controlled by shotgun shooting over much of northern France and there has grown a tradition of deer drives organised by groups of farmers. Modern scientific study of both roe and muntjac have revealed that this method of deer control is indiscriminate and often needlessly cruel in that many animals are maimed rather than killed, yet this form of shooting persists over much of the roe's western range.

Recently, there has been evidence of a growth in the sport of stalking with a rifle in areas where the shotgun drive has hitherto predominated, and perhaps in the future the sporting rifle will prevail in these regions. This would provide greater benefit to these areas in that the quality of the deer stock would be improved, the numbers of deer could be more effectively and humanely controlled, and the land holders would probably increase their income from the rent of stalking rights to the visiting hunters.

One other shooting method exists in the land north of the Alpine mountain chain, and this has given rise to the evolution of a special type of weapon. Throughout the forested lands of north-eastern France and northern Germany, the forest drive is a well established form of shooting. In this method the beaters work through a block of woodland, hopefully driving the game towards the waiting shooters who are positioned in strategic points to cover open spaces, fire breaks and rides. In this situation the shooter may be faced with anything from a woodcock to a red deer, and in order to cope with this the German arms manufacturers have evolved the multi-barrelled shotgun/rifle combinations described on pages 70–71. Known as drilling weapons, the range of design and calibres reflects the variety of game anticipated. Thus a typical weapon may have two shotgun barrels, one loaded with a cartridge for winged game and the other with a Brenneke rifled slug for a wild boar, while the rifle barrel might be chambered for a 7×57 cartridge loaded with a soft-point bullet for deer. In some weapons there may even be a .22 rimfire barrel for smaller ground game or vermin. While forest drives take place in many parts of Europe, it is really only in Germany where such a wide variety of game may be shot at any one time. In Scandinavia, for instance, drives may be organised for a specific species, and this is considered to be a way in which more ground can be covered safely than by an individual stalker on foot. It is also a way in which the resident population of any species can be more accurately assessed, and this in turn helps to plan the cull numbers and the hunting programme.

There are, of course, a great many variations on these hunting methods which may be dictated by local conditions, the hunting traditions of the area, and the habits of the species concerned. Over much of Europe there is usually a great deal of ritual attached to the shooting of these species, and a visiting shooter would have to be extremely careful not to cause offence through

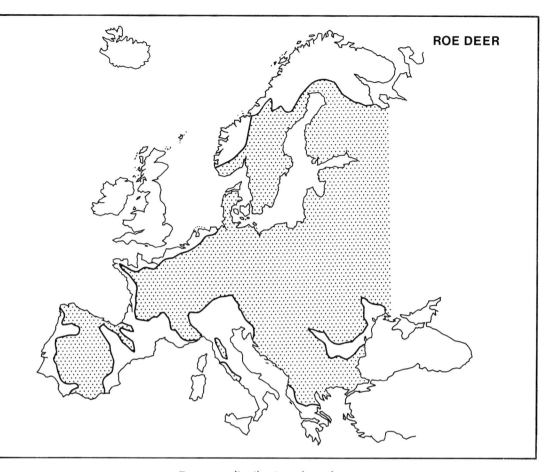

European distribution of roe deer.

ignorance of the accepted procedures. Drives are often controlled with almost military precision in order to minimise the risk of shooting accidents, and the dead game is treated with great respect. Anyone who has taken part in these shoots will know that shooting sports in Britain are conducted in a far more informal manner. The safety procedures we take for granted in this country are rigidly insisted upon in the European style of shooting, and this, perhaps, is no bad thing.

Deer species

Of all the deer species, the roe is the most widespread, with a population range extending from Spain in the south west through northern France and Germany and on into Czechoslovakia and beyond in the east. This deer species is at present extending its range, and there has been a spectacular colonisation of much of Scandinavia since the turn of this century. From a population base in south-east Sweden, the roe has spread into Norway and all round the Baltic into Finland where it has also become well established. Both the two other

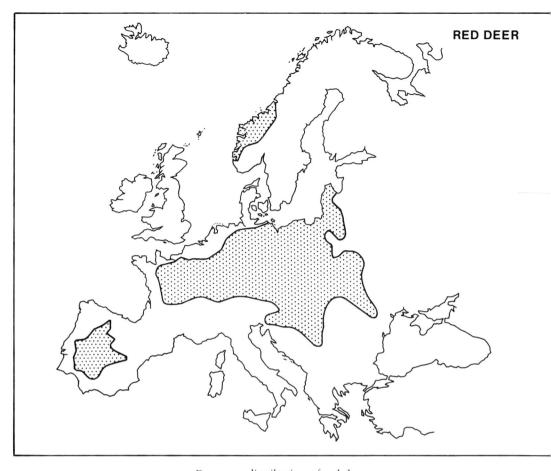

European distribution of red deer.

native species, the fallow and the red deer, have a more stable population range and are also well distributed.

Unlike the roe deer, the fallow population is centered around eastern Germany and Poland where it is relatively widespread. Elsewhere the population takes the form of isolated pockets which have colonised suitable habitat. Thus fallow can be found as far west as Portugal and as far north as lowland Sweden but their distribution is not as general as the roe.

A distribution map of Europe's red deer shows an intermediate stage between the widespread roe and the localised fallow populations. The red's range extends as far south as the fallow, but it also occurs in great numbers further north than any of the fallow's colonies. Therefore, the red deer is a prime hunting species over much of sub-arctic Norway and is the main deer species that is pursued in the extensive forests of central Europe. It is hardly surprising that the beasts of the central European forests attain great size and weight and the stags bear formidable trophy heads. It is encouraging to note that these native deer species, far from being hunted to extinction, still form the three main quarry species over most of the European landmass. All three

European deer often achieve great size, in this case a heavy-antlered red stag. (*Ake Lindau/ Arden London*)

species continue to survive and adapt to changes in their environment brought about by the activities of modern man.

There are two other deer species which, while not native to Europe as a whole, are indigenous to the northern lands of Scandinavia and which also form an important component of the quarry list of those regions.

Perhaps the best known of the two is the reindeer. Domesticated by the Lapps and subject to much Christmas folklore, the reindeer is a large animal and is unusual among the deer species in that both sexes carry antlers. The northern parts of Finland, Sweden, and Norway form the home range of this species and there are also isolated populations in the mountains of central-south Norway and in Iceland. In the Norwegian pocket it is estimated that there are about 40,000 animals and the numbers have shown a marked increase in the last two decades. A high annual cull – in 1966 over 11,000 were shot during the short season – has not halted this growth and the wild reindeer is considered to be the chief game animal within these mountainous areas. Over much of northern Sweden and Norway this animal is domesticated and reindeer shooting is understandably confined to the areas where clearly identified wild populations occur.

The other northern deer species, the elk, is the largest and it occurs in such numbers that it is considered the prime rifle quarry species throughout

The wild reindeer is an important quarry species in the Scandinavian mountains.
(*R. P. Lawrence*)

Scandinavia. The European elk or moose is an impressive animal. It weighs twice as much as a red deer stag and the bull elk can carry a formidable set of characteristically flat and palmate antlers. Also called the moose, it is the same species as its North American namesake, and it is only through the Americans calling a large sub-species of the red deer an elk that confusion has arisen. Put simply, the European elk is the same as the North American moose and the North American elk is a large red deer!

Unlike many other species of deer, the European elk is not a true forest dweller, preferring the dense willow and hazel thickets and water margins of these northern lands. Though very large they can move very quickly and it has been estimated that their characteristic fast trot can take them along at around 35 mph. They are shy and retiring animals that are hunted using a variety of different methods. In Norway, for instance, there is a tradition for using elk hounds to track·the animals and so bring the hunter into a shooting distance. At other times dogs are used to move the deer towards the waiting shooter; there are also occasions when woodland stalking methods and high seats are employed in elk hunting. Because these beasts sometimes weigh over 1000lb the Scandinavian countries impose a calibre restriction on rifles used for elk, and bullets which generate below 1500 ft/lb energy at 300 metres are considered underpowered. These regulations, incidentally, also apply to other animals on the quarry list of these countries and I would not, for example, be allowed to use my .243 on red deer in Norway.

The population of elk throughout these northern lands has shown a wide fluctuation in post-war years. At times the numbers seem to increase very rapidly and at others it has shown a marked decline. The declines have been

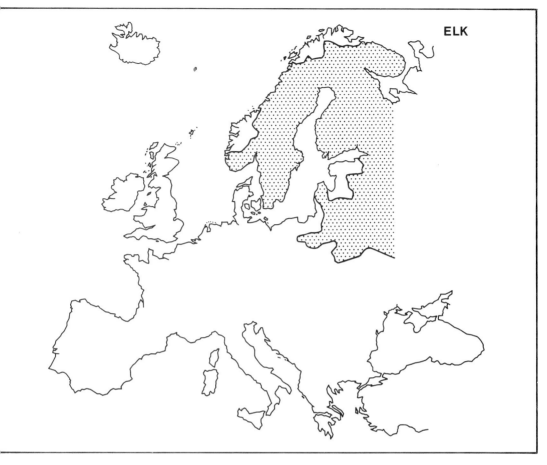

Distribution of elk.

The European elk is not a true forest dweller. (*Pamela Harrison*)

157

A bull elk in velvet. (*David de Lossy*)

partly attributed to overgrazing their food sources, and perhaps this may also help to explain why they are at present extending their range southwards and westwards through Poland and have crossed the straits between Sweden and Denmark to colonise Seeland.

Releases of foreign deer species have added variety to different parts of the European mainland. The sika, for instance, exists in pockets through northern France, Denmark, and in Germany where its range has extended southwards into the Alpine countries. Like the releases in Britain, the sika appears to thrive on the continent and there is evidence to suggest that they are extending their territory wherever they exist, and in particular there is a movement eastwards into the Eastern bloc countries.

Spreading in the opposite direction is a North American species which was introduced into southern Finland some years ago. The white-tailed deer, beloved of the American woodland hunter, have found European conditions very much to their liking and they now form an important component of the quarry list in that country. Their range is now extensive throughout southern Finland and, like the elk, they are spreading southwards and westwards.

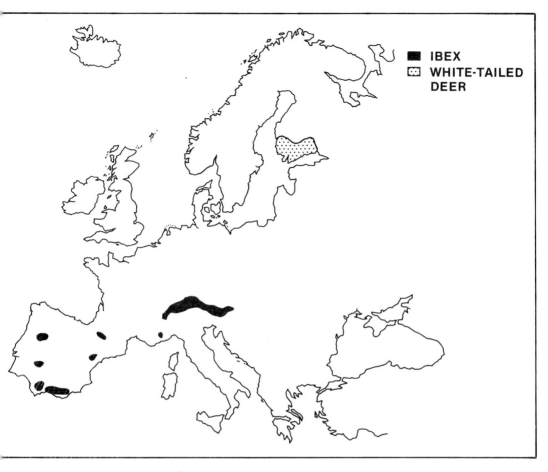

Distribution of the white-tailed deer and ibex.

Of the two small deer species that have been introduced, the Chinese water deer has still to establish a sufficiently extensive population range to be considered an important quarry species for the visiting rifle shooter. Nevertheless, there are some areas in France where they are well established and there may come a time when they will play a more significant role in the rifle shooting scene of that country.

The smallest deer to be introduced into Europe, the muntjac, is also the one that is extending its range most rapidly. The muntjac was introduced to France late last century and since the last war it has shown the same phenomenal growth that we have seen in Britain. As with most of the deer species the population of muntjac is growing and the future may well see this little deer become an exploitable resource in the areas it has recently colonised.

Other hoofed game

Apart from the nine species of deer there are also four other species of hoofed game which may come to the attention of the rifle hunter. Of these – wild

The wild boar is found throughout much of Europe. (*Mavad, Budapest*)

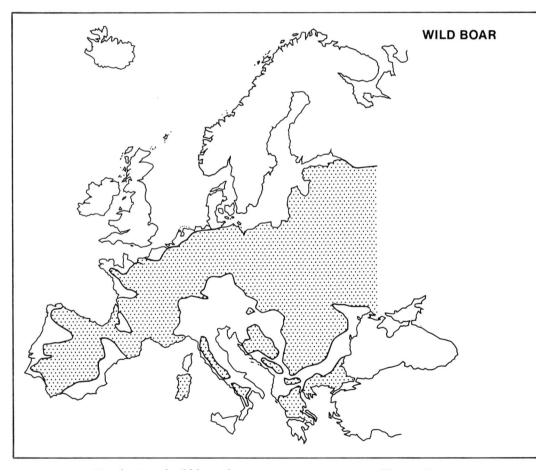

Distribution of wild boar showing approximate range in Western Europe.

160

The mouflon or wild sheep has been introduced into many locations in Europe.
(*Franz Matula*)

boar, the mouflon, the chamois, and the ibex – it is the boar which perhaps attracts the greatest attention. The mental picture of this animal is one of a burly, bristly, and sometimes ferocious animal with formidable upward pointing canine teeth. Anyone who has come into contact with a large and angry boar will testify that this does not do justice to the actual power that these animals possess.

Weighing around 300lb in the west of their range, the eastern representatives of the species tend to be even bigger. Wild boar are found throughout much of Europe from Portugal to Russia and as far south as Italy and Greece. Attempts have been made to introduce them into Scandinavia but these have met with only limited success. While there may be times when it is easy to confuse one deer species with another, it would be almost impossible to mistakenly identify a wild boar.

The traditional method of hunting the animal is by organised driving towards the waiting guns. In this style of shooting it is usual for the shooter to be suddenly confronted by a large and irritated animal at very close quarters, so the chosen weapon needs to deliver a terrific knock-down blow, though it need not possess fine accuracy at longer ranges. Thus many boar hunters choose between a shotgun loaded with a Brennecke rifled slug for accurate shooting up to about fifty yards, or one of the larger diameter rifle calibres such as the 9 × 64 where shots may be taken at longer ranges.

Over recent years there has been a growth in the number of tour operators that offer boar shooting in various parts of Europe and this reflects the present surge of interest in what can be an exciting and sometimes dangerous sport.

The mouflon or wild sheep was originally a native of Corsica and Sardinia, but it has been introduced into a wide variety of locations throughout Europe. Nowadays there are many countries in which the mouflon can be hunted but, as they are sedentary creatures with well-defined territories, their numbers are generally stable and hunting is strictly controlled. A mature mouflon ram may

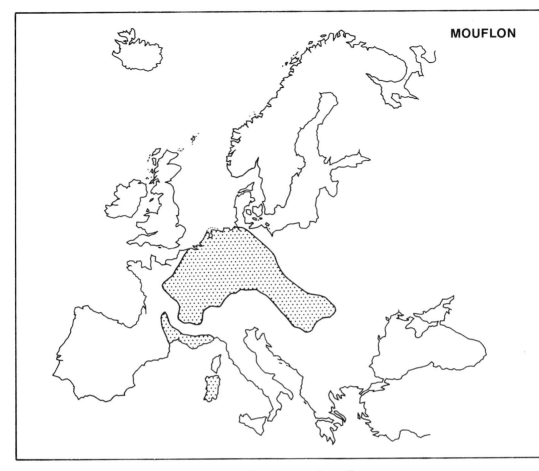

European distribution of mouflon.

weigh up to 100lb and his massive and wrinkled horns sweep in an elegant curve to the side of his head. Unlike deer, these horns are permanent features which are not shed annually. The red-brown coat of summer gives way to a darker and more sombre winter colour, but rams may also have varying degrees of grey and black around the head and chest and there may also be flank markings.

Though the mouflon occurs in certain areas of France, its real stronghold on mainland Europe lies in the north of Germany and eastwards into Hungary and Czechoslovakia. Like the wild boar, attempts have been made to establish the animal in central Scandinavia but this has met with limited success – they do, however, appear to thrive as far north as Denmark.

Within each population of mouflon the annual cull usually consists of mature rams with a slightly higher number of ewes. The mouflon is generally considered to be easier to stalk than deer because, although they are totally wild, they are naturally inquisitive. Thus an animal may stop in full flight for a few fatal moments to study the hunter, and this opportunity is often seized upon by the alert rifle shooter. In north Germany they are usually stalked on

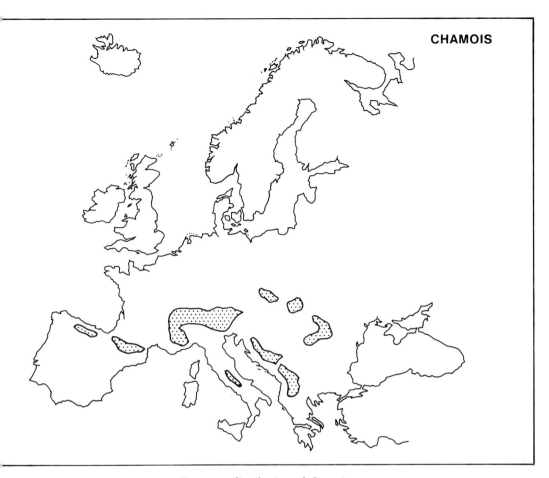

European distribution of chamois.

foot because, again unlike deer, their movements around their territory tend to be very haphazard and unpredictable. As a consequence, high seat shooting is little used – one can never guarantee that they will appear at the desired spot.

Most of the animals described so far are natives of lowland forest and scrub, but the chamois is very much an animal of the steep forest-clad slopes of the more mountainous regions of Europe. Again, unlike the other large and medium-game species, this is a diurnal animal which is rarely active at night.

The chamois is a native of the Pyrenees and it also occurs widely throughout the Alpine mountain chain. Other pockets are found in Yugoslavia and other parts of eastern Europe. The chamois has also been successfully introduced in other lower hill areas such as the Vosges and the Black Forest, but introductions in the more northerly areas have largely failed.

In some ways the behaviour of the chamois is similar to the mouflon in that they are not great wanderers and tend to stay within a home range – as a consequence their populations, once well established, will remain fairly constant. Compared to deer shooting, opportunities to hunt chamois may be few and far between, but within their areas they do figure as an important

163

The ibex is a native of Europe's southern mountains. (*David de Lossy*)

Spanish ibex can produce remarkable trophy heads. (*Spanish National Tourist Office*)

species for the rifle hunter. Within their forest environment the chosen weapon for the chamois hunter will be no different from his woodland stalking rifle, but the chamois will also range beyond the tree line onto the more exposed upper slopes of the mountains. In the frequently breathtaking scenery of these areas close approach may be impossible and the hunter and hunted may be separated by deep ravines, open, rock-strewn slopes, or dense hazel thicket, and in this situation a more powerful long-range calibre may be needed. Power and accuracy out to beyond 300 yards may demand a rifle in the .300 Winchester Magnum class such as a 7mm Magnum, one of the Weatherby medium magnums or even a .244 Holland Magnum. The chamois is not a particularly large or difficult animal to kill, and the choice of one of these medium magnum calibres is only necessitated by the increase in range over the normal woodland stalking distance.

Of the hoofed game, the final species to come to the attention of the rifle shooter is the ibex or wild goat. Unlike the feral goats that are sometimes stalked in Scotland, the ibex is a true wild species found in parts of the Alps and Pyrenees, but even in these areas there has been some interbreeding with escaped domestic stock.

These animals are creatures of the open mountain slopes and crags, and this alone sets them apart from the other hoofed game species of Europe. Their appearance is quite distinctive and a mature billy may grow a magnificent set of horns. Though there is a considerable variety in the pattern and colour of their coats, it would be difficult to confuse the ibex with any other animal because of its horns, its shape, and its environment. Ibex hunting usually takes the form of stalking, though perhaps this can be more accurately termed climbing, as a hard climb is often required to reach ibex country.

Of all the native hoofed game, the ibex is the least widely distributed and its population tends to be localised in pockets within the southern mountain chains. There are, however, opportunities to hunt ibex in northern Spain and in certain areas within the Alps – though because of its limited distribution it cannot be classed as anything but a minority species for the rifle hunter. Where the opportunity does exist, hunting takes place in magnificent and spectacular surroundings and this adds greatly to the enjoyment of the sport. Like open ground chamois hunting, the quest for ibex will also demand a long-range weapon that is capable of placing a bullet accurately up to 300 yards and beyond, and any of the calibres suitable for chamois would also serve as a good choice for ibex hunting.

Carnivores

Within Europe there are areas where large predatory animals exist in sufficient numbers, or pose such a threat to domestic livestock, that their population is controlled by shooting. Compared to the hoofed game species the carnivores all tend to show a trend of declining numbers and contracting habitat.

Just recently the wolf became extinct in Spain and it is now confined to the remote areas of central and eastern Europe. Even in the north it has been persecuted to the extent that Norway's population of wolves now numbers less than 100. To a lesser extent the lynx shows a similar fate, though their numbers are more stable. The northern lynx has its main population stronghold within Scandinavia, while the pardel lynx is still to be found in protected or remote areas of the Iberian peninsula. Both these animals are hunted within their own areas but this only takes place when livestock are endangered and hunting is carried out by the local population. In Norway, for instance, only about forty lynx are killed each year so a visiting hunter would probably never have the opportunity to go on a lynx hunt. With the current rise in concern for conservation this is no bad thing as there is little doubt that these animals could easily be hunted to extinction. I believe that the fauna of Europe would be considerably poorer without these large and beautiful cats.

Finally, the European brown bear is the one carnivore which does exist in sufficient numbers in certain parts of the continent to warrant the attention of the rifle shooter. Though some bears are shot in Scandinavia each year, it is in eastern Europe that the opportunity exists for bear hunting by the visiting shooter. Yugoslavia, in particular, is the present centre for bear shooting tours and is recommended for those who seek this rather enigmatic and unmistakable animal. Bear shooting usually takes the form of drives whereby the animal is moved towards the waiting hunter by a team of beaters and dogs, but there are occasions when they are hunted by woodland stalking methods. In either case a rifle suitable for boar will also be suitable for brown bear. The bullet construction needs to be fairly fragile in order to allow rapid expansion within this rather soft-skinned animal.

The European continent offers a potential sixteen species of medium and large game for the visiting rifle hunter. While predator shooting does exist, the accent is on hoofed quarry and within this group the wild boar and various species of deer predominate. Shooting in Europe can take the hunter from the burning and arid foothills of the Mediterranean countries to the frozen Arctic wastes of northern Scandinavia, with landscapes as flat as the extensive lake and forest areas of Finland or dramatic and breathtaking as the higher slopes of the Alps. The variety of species that are available for hunting reflects these contrasts in the hunting environment. Bearing in mind that the deer population of the European continent is following a trend of expansion and colonisation, and that hunting opportunities are being developed at an ever increasing rate, the future of rifle sport in Europe holds great promise.

PART THREE

RIFLE OWNERSHIP AND USE

8. OWNING A RIFLE

THE 1968 Firearms Act brought both shotguns and rifles under police control. Shotguns could only be owned by the holder of a shotgun certificate issued by the police, and the legislation regarding the ownership of Section 1 firearms – rifles, pistols, etc. – reinforced the previous system of control under the issue of firearms certificates for specified weapons and ammunition. This Act highlights two important differences between shotgun and rifle ownership. Firstly, a shotgun certificate allows the holder to possess any number of shotguns – with no limit to the calibres, or the quantity of ammunition allowed on the certificate. A firearm certificate, on the other hand, allows the holder to own only the weapons and ammunition stated on the certificate. In addition, the latter certificate must be produced and an entry made on it each time ammunition is purchased, and the details of the weapon must also be carefully entered.

The second important difference brought about by the 1968 Firearms Act is that everyone has the right to a shotgun certificate, and if the police refuse a shotgun application the onus is on them to justify their refusal. For a firearm application however, the reverse is true. That is, the onus is very firmly on the applicant to prove that he has good and justifiable reason to own and use a sporting rifle – and his reasons must stand up to detailed investigation by the police. Only when they are satisfied that the applicant's reasons are sound will a firearm certificate be granted.

The first step towards rifle ownership, then, involves an application for a firearm certificate for the weapon and calibre of your choice. In order to be successful a good deal of groundwork and preparation is needed before you even fill in the application form, and a methodical approach here will minimise the risk of refusal later.

APPLYING FOR A FIREARM CERTIFICATE

The most obvious starting point is to decide on the quarry you wish to hunt with a rifle. Very few people come into rifle shooting as raw beginners, and most potential users of a sporting rifle will have a background in some other branch of shooting. Many will come up through the ranks of sporting air-rifle users as the law in this country limits non-certificated air rifles to a muzzle energy of only 12 ft/lb. The revolution in air weapons' technology over the past decade has shown just how effective air rifles can be against vermin up to the size of rabbit, but the aspiring firearm owner may wish to extend his range beyond the average forty yards air-rifle limit and to increase his quarry species to include hares, foxes, and even deer.

Others may come into rifle shooting from the shotgun world – they may wish to obtain a weapon that will cause much less disturbance when controlling vermin, or they may even require a more humane and effective weapon for killing either foxes or deer. With the background knowledge already acquired, the potential rifle user can decide the calibre needed to pursue his chosen quarry species. Within the British Isles this choice would fall into three broad categories. For vermin control at moderate ranges the choice would lie between the two rimfire calibres: the .22 Long Rifle or .22 Rimfire Magnum. The specialist fox shooter may, on the other hand, opt for one of the potent .22 centrefire rounds, while those wishing to take up deer stalking would need to select a calibre in the range from .243 up to .30–06.

Having decided on the quarry species and the appropriate calibre, the next stage is to find land on which you may be allowed to use the rifle in pursuit of your chosen quarry. To a novice this often presents the biggest problem which can only be overcome with tact, diplomacy, and time – attaining this goal will only be accomplished in gradual stages over a period of months or even years. For example, a friend once obtained permission to shoot rabbits and pigeons with either shotgun or air rifle on a local farm. Over a period of about a year he proved to be effective in this task and the farmer also found him to be a trustworthy sportsman who respected the game stocks on the land. Word soon spread through the locality and he slowly gained access to shooting on other farms in the area and his shooting territory began to increase. After some time he approached the farmers with the idea that a .22 rimfire would be a more effective anti-rabbit weapon which would cause less noise disturbance about the farmland, and he readily obtained the authority he needed for his firearm application. From the farmers' point of view he had proved himself a safe and trustworthy shooter and the addition of a .22 rifle increased his effectiveness. While air rifles and shotguns are weapons of rather limited range, the carrying power of even a rimfire .22 means that the landowner must be asbolutely sure that the authorised person is a safe shooter. Written authority for the use of a rifle is not given lightly and is the result of the build-up of trust between the shooter and the farmer.

Another friend has been a keen rough shooter for many years and his two well-trained Labrador dogs ensure that he is welcomed on many local game shoots as a reliable picker-up on their driven days. Over the last few years he has come to know the gamekeepers very well and it is through their encouragement that he applied for his firearm certificate. Not only did he obtain a rimfire .22 for vermin control, (he had the necessary written authority from the keepers) but he also obtained a .243 stalking rifle as he was asked to

AUTHORITY DOCUMENT

Mr. A. Landowner,
Anyfarm,
WILTSHIRE.

DATE: ....

TO WHOM IT MAY CONCERN,
            This letter confirms that ....(name).........................,
of ....(address)..,
has my full authority to use a .22 rifle for the purpose of vermin control on
the lands of Anyfarm, Wiltshire, subject to the terms and conditions agreed
between myself and ....(name)................................,
on the above date.

            Signed ....
                    (A. LANDOWNER)
                    ANYFARM,
                    WILTSHIRE.

A simple authority letter will satisfy police requirements.

lend a hand with the roe cull. Again, once the police had checked out his
documents he experienced no trouble obtaining his certificate. As a final
example I can quote my own rough shooting syndicate. For years we had
experienced problems in controlling our vermin numbers, then three of our
members obtained .22 rimfires for vermin control and our efforts became that
much more effective. In this instance the letters of authority came from the
landowner who was very sympathetic to our cause and had grown to trust the
judgement of our members.

As very few people come into rifle shooting 'cold' it is fair to assume that the
great majority of those wishing to apply for a sporting rifle certificate will
already have some contacts which may help them with their letters of
authority. Once you have obtained the written authority to use a rifle of
suitable calibre for your chosen purpose, you need only to decide on a secure
storage place for the weapon before you can set the application wheels into
motion. As far as Section 1 firearms are concerned, most police forces now
insist on some form of steel security cabinet for the storage of the weapon –
look at the advertisements in the sporting press as there are a great many
different types of steel gun-cabinet on the market. These are an easy and
practical solution to the safe storage of any weapon and, bolted to a wall, they
will satisfy most police authorities except possibly those in the more sensitive
inner-city areas where they may insist on the addition of various other devices
to increase the security.

Having now obtained your letters to prove your legitimate need for a rifle,
and with a safe place to store the weapon, the next step is to fill out the
application form and hand this, together with your authority letters, to the

police. One or two points are worth remembering when filling out the form. On it you are asked to state the calibre and type of weapon you require – your chosen calibre should be entered here, together with the words 'sporting rifle'. If possible avoid narrowing down your options by entering such descriptions as bolt action, auto-loading etc. The simple term 'sporting rifle' will allow you to sample whatever types of weapon within this category you may fancy.

You will also be asked the amount of ammunition you require, and this is broken down into two sub-sections. Firstly, the maximum number of rounds you wish to buy at any one time, and secondly the maximum quantity you wish to hold in store. Whatever figures you arrive at it is useful to allow yourself double the purchase figure for storage. In this way you should never be caught 'short' on, for example, a target and zeroing day when you may need to fire off a great many rounds. For a .22 rimfire user you should enter figures which are multiples of fifty as this is the smallest quantity you can buy and for a centrefire calibre the ammunition comes in boxes of twenty so your ammunition requirements should be in multiples of twenty.

When you hand over your letters and completed application form to the police you will also have to pay the appropriate fee and they will then set their own investigations in motion. The officer processing your application will visit your home to check on your security arrangements for the rifle, and he will also ask for police visits to be made on your landowners. During these visits the police will assess the suitability of the land for a rifle of your chosen calibre and they will also discuss with the farmer the existence of any footpaths, lanes, or dwellings in the immediate area. They will look at any other factors that may have a bearing on safety and on this evidence they will report back to the processing officer, giving approval or rejection of the land. When these investigations have been completed the processing officer files his report to the firearms department at headquarters and, if the majority of the land is suitable, the applicant is of sound character, and his need for a rifle has been demonstrated, then the application is approved. Processing an application takes from four weeks to three months, depending on the police force, and it seems to be standard practice for the processing officer to deliver the new certificate to the applicant by hand.

At last, after weeks of doubt and anxiety you have your own firearm certificate in your hand. Sign it in ink and study the details carefully. On the front side of the certificate you will find details of the calibre you have been granted and below this the quantities of ammunition you will be permitted to buy and hold in store. Under this is the section which outlines the particular conditions applying to your certificate. Notes here stipulate a secure storage for the firearm and ammunition when not in use, and the need to notify the police on loss, theft, or change of address. Finally, there are conditions which relate to your use of the rifle. Here you will find stated the purpose for which you may use the rifle and also where you may use it. These are called the territorial restrictions as it will often state precisely on whose land you may shoot. Initially you should find this quite satisfactory, but as you expand your shooting territory you may need to increase the entry on your certificate. The cost of a firearm certificate 'variation' is almost as much as the initial application but this is only charged if you are asking for additional firearms – there should be no charge made for merely increasing the territory. Some police authorities cut costs by issuing an open certificate once the owner has held a certificate for a certain period – for example in the case of the Hampshire police this is three years. An open certificate is one without territorial restrictions so that the shooter is at liberty to use his rifle wherever he is given permission to shoot without first having to seek police approval.

On the reverse of the certificate there are two tables, the first of which will contain details of the rifle, to be written up when you purchase or acquire it, and the second requires an entry each time you buy any ammunition.

JOINING THE BRITISH ASSOCIATION FOR SHOOTING AND CONSERVATION

Compared with all other forms of shooting, sporting rifle users are in the minority, and this makes us one of the prime targets for those who wish to impose further restrictions on firearms ownership and sporting shooting. In order to ensure that they will not succeed in restricting your shooting even more, I recommend that you become a member of the British Association for Shooting and Conservation (BASC). This is the one national body which looks after the interests of all sporting shooters and it is the organisation through which the voice of the rifle user can be heard. As well as helping to ensure the future of our sport, a number of other services offered by BASC membership may be useful to the prospective firearms user. The cost of membership includes third party insurance liability up to £1 million, and a number of landowners insist on this safeguard before allowing the shooter onto their land. Membership of the BASC infers that you are a responsible sportsman and this may, at times, influence a landowner in your favour. Amongst all the other services offered by the BASC, perhaps their firearms and legal advisory service is the most useful. If, for instance, your application for a firearm certificate has been refused on grounds that you consider to be unreasonable, then the firearms officer at BASC headquarters may offer legal advice and even support. There are many instances when the BASC has supported an appeal against a refusal and has won a reversal of the decision. Should your application be unsuccessful, therefore, your first recourse as a member would be to ask for legal advice from national headquarters. There are also a whole range of other services and facilities available to members and the annual subscription is the best investment you can make for the continuance of your sport.

CHOOSING YOUR WEAPON

In choosing your weapon, you will need to consider the type of shooting you anticipate, the average range at which you expect to shoot, and the state of your bank account. Each person coming to rifle shooting for the first time will

173

probably have some idea of the style of weapon he would like to use, but some brief observations may help to clarify the options open to a prospective purchaser.

If your certificate allows a .22 rimfire, you should first decide which rimfire – the .22 Long Rifle (LR) or the .22 Rimfire Magnum. The majority of rimfire rifles are used primarily for vermin control, with the occasional hare thrown in when the opportunity arises. The choice as to which rimfire then comes down to the range at which you intend to do most of your shooting. At ranges up to one hundred yards the .22 LR is the best choice, particularly if you hope to eat the rabbits and pigeons you shoot. In addition, you have the advantage of being able to vary your power by using a variety of Short and Long Rifle ammunition and in this way you can attempt to minimise the risks when shooting in a fairly populated countryside. If, on the other hand, you expect that most of your shooting will be done at distances from fifty to 150 yards, then the .22 Magnum is the better option. The higher velocity (approaching 2000 fps) and flatter trajectory of this calibre will produce good accuracy and instant kills on anything up to the size of a fox at these ranges. Between the two rimfire calibres, therefore, the choice really is one of shooting distances, but there is also a cost factor to consider. Good, accurate .22 LR rifles can be bought very cheaply in most gunshops whereas a .22 Magnum is often far more costly, and for those on a limited budget this can be an important factor.

Having decided on your rifle calibre, the next question is what type of rifle? You have a very wide variety to choose from and faced with this bewildering selection it would simplify matters if you decide what you want from your rifle. If accuracy is your overriding consideration then you will require a weapon which has a positive and precise lock-up mechanism which holds the cartridge case firmly when the rifle is fired. It is generally recognised that a bolt action or Martini action provides this positive lock-up and these are usually the most accurate rifles. This also explains why practically all target rifles in .22 calibre are built around bolt or Martini actions. Lever and pump action rifles come a close second in the accuracy league, while the auto-loaders generally score rather badly. For serious work then, a bolt action rifle is by far the most popular choice and the other rifles are often consigned, unfortunately, to the status of 'plinkers'. This is a great pity as many lever actions, pumps, and auto-loaders are finely-made weapons which, in the hands of a competent shooter, can give sterling service. I think that for shooting with a .22 LR up to about seventy yards, any well-made rifle would provide sufficient accuracy. If you wish to kill consistently beyond that distance, however, then you should opt for a bolt action to provide that extra precision.

This need for fine accuracy is even more important to a person who is granted a certificate for a centrefire .22 for fox control. Here the distances are far greater – a .22 Hornet will kill a fox at about 180 yards, the .222 Remington will extend this to around 250 yards, and the .22–250 and the .220 Swift will go all the way out to beyond 350 yards in the hands of a skilled shot. Whichever calibre you have chosen, the selection of an accurate weapon really comes down to either a bolt action or a rifle with a falling block mechanism in the

Martini or Farquharson design. Second-hand Martini action varmint rifles do sometimes appear on the market and the Ruger No. 1 single shot rifle is an updated and modified Farquharson. These, together with the many bolt action rifles available in the .22 centrefire calibres, stand head and shoulders above the other repeaters in terms of accuracy over long ranges.

The newcomer to deer management and stalking will probably have opted for one of three calibres: the .243, the .270, or the .308, and these are available in a wide variety of rifle types. Bearing in mind that the majority of woodland stalking involves shooting at fairly close range – most of the deer I have killed have been at ranges from fifteen to eighty yards – and even moorland stalking traditionally limits shooting to below 200 yards, varmint rifle accuracy is not so important in a deer rifle. Accuracy, therefore, is good whether the rifle is bolt actioned, lever actioned or a single shot, so your choice may be based on other considerations. All deer have very acute hearing, and in the pursuit of such creatures a rifle that can be handled silently gives a decided advantage. Most bolt actioned weapons, and the Ruger single shot rifle, score well on this – the only time they generate mechanical sounds is on reloading after a shot has been fired, and at that time it is not often crucial. The increasing number of moving parts in the other forms of repeating rifles do make them more prone to rattle. While a stalker may get away with the sound of a twig snapping under a careless foot, the sound of a metallic rattle from his rifle will quickly send any nearby deer away.

One further point which may cause the novice rifle user some confusion lies in the variety of trigger mechanisms that are available. Single triggers usually take the form of either single-pull or double-pull types. The single-pull mechanism is one in which there is little or no movement in the trigger before increasing finger pressure fires the rifle. Similar in feel to a shotgun's trigger, the single-pull trigger is found on many stalking rifles and a fair proportion of the better rimfire weapons. The double-pull is one in which initial pressure from the trigger finger moves the trigger backwards against a weak spring until a firm stop is felt. Increasing pressure then overcomes this to fire the rifle. Those coming into rifle shooting with air-rifle experience will probably be more familiar with this type of trigger.

As a general rule, rifles with double triggers or single set triggers should be avoided by the novice rifle shooter as they add further complications to the process of shooting. In a rifle fitted with two triggers the weapon is fired either by pulling on the rear trigger only, but this is often a long dragging pull against fair pressure, or the hair trigger device is activated. To do this the front trigger is first pulled to set the rear, and the rifle can now be fired by the slightest touch on the rear trigger. A rifle equipped with a single set trigger operates on the same idea but in this case the trigger is set by first pushing it forward. Double and single set triggers can really come into their own when the sport allows time for careful and deliberate aiming. In Highland stalking, for example, where shots are often taken from a prone position, this type of trigger mechanism can be an aid to precision shooting.

On other occasions, however, the more complex operation can be a hinderance and the single or double-pull trigger is to be preferred. For someone coming into rifle shooting from a shotgun or air-rifle background, the familiar feel of the single or double-pull trigger will help him attain accurate shooting skills more easily.

One further point on choosing a rifle concerns left-handed shooters. As a left-hander myself, I have found that on many rifles the stock design is such that they cannot be fired comfortably from the left shoulder – any right-handed rifle with a roll-over cheekpiece is almost impossible to use from the other shoulder. If you are left-handed you will have to confine yourself to using a rifle with a straight stock, or you could have the stock altered by a gunsmith. In the case of my .243 the cheekpiece and roll-over were removed and a straight Monto Carlo comb was fitted to bring my eye up to scope level to be perfectly satisfactory, and my other rifles have 'classic' straight socks. In practice I have found this to be perfectly satisfactory. Some left-handers experience problems with auto-loading rifles that eject the spent cartridge to the right of the action. When fired from the left shoulder the empty case passes across the face and this can be quite disconcerting. True left-handed rifles are available from a number of manufacturers but they are generally more expensive than the standard models. With practice a left-handed shooter should have little difficulty in adjusting to a rifle with a right-handed bolt, but if a problem does persist he can opt for a top-loading single shot or a level action rifle which can be operated from either shoulder with equal ease and efficiency.

BUYING YOUR RIFLE

The next stage in the process of acquiring your own rifle is to decide where you should buy it and whether you should buy new or second-hand. Apart from the differences in price, there is very little to choose between a new rifle and a well cared for second-hand weapon. The propellant powders used in most rifle ammunition have been formulated to actually protect the internal bore from corrosion, so unless a rifle has been sadly neglected or been 'shot out' from many years of hard use, the rifling should be in good order and the bore free from any pitting. In the case of .22 rimfires, you could spend several hundred pounds on a superb weapon from Anschutz or other top quality maker, and yet really accurate bolt actioned rifles can be picked up second-hand for as little as £20.

Centrefire rifles, which generate far higher muzzle velocities, tend to shoot out their rifling more rapidly than the rimfires and more care is needed when choosing a second-hand centrefire. As a general rule, the calibres that suffer most from barrel wear are those that produce the highest velocities. Therefore the prospective buyer of a .17 Remington, a .220 Swift, or a .22–250 should be on particular lookout for this. However, a well-cared for centrefire rifle should last, even with regular use, for many years and you will be extremely unlucky to find a poor example. If you buy a new rifle it may need a 'running in' period to work out any stiffness in the mechanism. Careful lubrication in the right places and plenty of dry practice will work in a rifle very quickly.

Sporting rifles can be purchased or acquired from three main sources. The classified columns of the sporting press often carry advertisements from private individuals wishing to sell their rifles; a number of well-established sporting auctions are held in different parts of the country and these often sell a variety of Section 1 firearms; and finally there is the retail gunshop. Unless you are obtaining your rifle from a relative or friend, in which case your weapon will have a known history, by far the best option is buy your firearm from a reputable gunshop. The majority of gunshop owners will have a sound working knowledge of sporting rifles and will be able to offer unbiased advice on the weapon most suitable for your needs. Where possible, though, go to a gunsmith who is himself a keen sporting rifle user rather than a shotgun or pistol specialist – he will really understand your needs and will be in the best position to help. His specialist knowledge will ensure that you do not end up with a worn-out or unsuitable rifle and he should be able to offer some form of guarantee or option on changing the weapon should you discover, after trials, that it is unsuitable.

Buying a rifle at an auction of sporting weapons should be avoided unless you really know what to look for. Without specialist tools it can be very difficult for a private individual to be sure that the weapon is in good condition. Moreover, a number of auction houses are reluctant to sell any firearms to people other than registered dealers so that the private buyer is automatically excluded.

ACCESSORIES

Once you have made your choice and are the proud owner of your first sporting rifle you will be eager to try it out with the ammunition you have also bought. Before doing this you should consider the accessories that you will need for your newly-acquired firearm. The most important of these concerns the sighting system. The majority of rifle users will automatically assume that a telescopic sight is essential, but this may not necessarily be true (see pages 52–4).

In practice a telescopic sight is not essential if all your shooting will be at ranges below about fifty yards. In addition, if you intend to shoot at moving targets occasionally then a scope can be a hinderance. A great deal of sport can be had from, for example, using an auto-loader rimfire with open sights for close-range ratting or rabbit shooting. When as a young boy I witnessed my father knock down six bolting rabbits with six shots from his Savage .22 auto without taking the rifle from his shoulder, the ranges varied from about twenty to forty yards, and such rapid shooting would have been impossible had his rifle been fitted with a telescope.

At more extended ranges, however, the telescopic sight really comes into its own and your choice will depend on many factors (outlined on pages 55–7). In addition to the telescopic sight itself you will need lens caps to protect the exposed front and rear lenses when not in use (these are usually supplied with

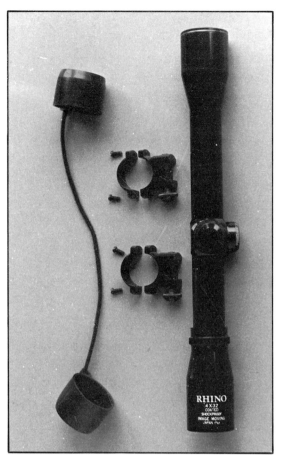 

(left) As well as the scope, you will need lens caps and mounts to fit your rifle. *(right)*
Accessories illustrated here include rifle sleeves, knives, roe sack, scope sight, stalking stick,
binoculars, rifle sling and swivels.

the sight) and you will also require a set of split-ring telescope mounts to fit
your rifle. The dovetail grooves vary in width from one rifle to another so your
scope rings should be matched to your rifle. The method for mounting and
aligning the telescopic sight is described on pages 185–6.

If you intend to carry your rifle for long periods then you will probably find
that a sling is almost essential. This should be of leather or other material that
will not fold or stretch so that the weight of the weapon is evenly distributed on
your shoulder. Rifle shooters in North America have developed the use of the
sling as a steadying device for shooting to a fine art, but in this country the
rifle sling is generally considered to be merely an aid to carrying the weapon.

For transporting your rifle to and from the house or car you will need a rifle
sleeve, often referred to as a gunslip. If you intend to fit a telescopic sight then
make sure that your sleeve has sufficient width to allow plenty of room for the
rifle and sight so as to avoid any strain on the scope mountings. A tight-fitting
sleeve will at best throw the sight off zero and at worst may even bend the

Binoculars can be steadied on a stalking stick. (*Shelagh Marshall-Ball*) Note; I find this method of carrying my rifles most comfortable when woodland stalking alone but would never use it when in company.

scope tube. One word of caution here; never store your rifle in its sleeve as this will promote very rapid rusting – the sleeve is merely a means of covering the rifle while it is being carried in a public place.

So much has been written about choosing suitable binoculars for different purposes that I will not dwell on the topic here. A great deal of rifle shooting takes place in the early morning, the late evening, or during the winter months – when poor lighting conditions prevail. Your choice of binoculars should, therefore, be based on twilight performance, and over the years the most popular for this purpose have proved to be either the 7 × 50 or the 8 × 40 models.

The final accessory is one you can select from the woodland or the hedgerows on your land. I find a stalking stick essential to my rifle shooting and I am surprised how few novice rifle users take advantage of this great aid to accuracy. Choose a straight hazel stick and cut it to a length which approximates to the distance from your eyes to the ground. The top of the stick then comes to eye level and if it is an inch or so thick it will not bend when used as a rest for rifle or binoculars. A rubber stopper on the bottom will help to silence its use as a balancing prop when creeping through the woodland on a still evening. The stick has two main purposes. Firstly, binoculars can be rested on the top of the stick which allows for a much more controlled and detailed survey of the surroundings than would be possible if the binoculars were merely hand held. If the stick is of the correct length the binoculars will come naturally to eye level. Secondly, its use as a steadying device for a rifle shot can make all the difference between a clean kill and a miss. I use the stick for both my vermin shooting and deer stalking, held at arm's length in my right.hand (I am left-handed) the stick steadies the fore-end of the rifle and eliminates any up-and-down movement of the aiming point. Practice helps to cut down on the sideways wobble and the result is a far steadier shot than would have been possible off-hand.

9. Theory into Practice

DRY FIRING

Before you ever fire a live round, you should spend some time getting to know the feel of the rifle so that you become familiar with its handling characteristics – how it comes to your shoulder, how your cheek beds down on the stock, and its general balance. Experiment with holding the fore-end in different places so that you can arrive at the most comfortable, and therefore the steadiest grip. Dry firing is an essential part of this familiarisation routine. While most shotgun mechanisms can be damaged by pulling the trigger on an empty chamber, fewer rifles have this tendency and dry firing serves as a very valuable training. If in doubt, practise firing on an empty case as this is the only way to become really familiar with the trigger pull of your particular rifle. Get to know exactly how much pressure is needed to fire the weapon, and the amount of movement the trigger has before it activates the firing mechanism. In a sport which requires precise timing with the weapon discharging when the sights are exactly on target, familiarity with the trigger is essential. Practise dry firing the rifle through a steady increase in pressure on the trigger – all too often a novice will yank at the trigger and, having developed this unconscious habbit, will wonder why he never achieves any degree of accuracy. There have been many occasions when a rifle has been blamed for an inconsistent performance when in fact it is the shooter who throws his aim by a hefty tug on the trigger. Get into the habit of firing the weapon through a steadily increasing pressure and it will pay handsome dividends later. Dry firing and handling practice are a continuing activity; you cannot become over-familiar with your rifle and even after years of shooting, practice will still help your steadiness and accuracy.

SIGHTING-IN YOUR RIFLE

The next step is to sight-in the weapon so that you are producing a reasonably consistent and accurate performance. To sight-in your rifle you will need to fire a number of live rounds so you must find a safe place to do this. Here most people will have two options open to them: they can either set up a makeshift range on the land over which they have authority to shoot, or they can make use of one of the established rifle ranges that are dotted about the country. Safety arrangements are tightly controlled on these outdoor ranges, but if you choose the former option there are a number of points you must remember.

Firstly, you must obtain the landowner's approval and it may be wise to ask his advice on selecting a safe site for shooting. The landowner's advice is important as there may be areas on his land where farming activities would rule out rifle shooting, or perhaps areas where you may disturb breeding game birds. He will probably direct you to an area that will be reasonably free from disturbance so you must now decide on your actual shooting range. Try to ensure that you are shooting into a bank or hillside and that there is no livestock nearby. Once you have this safe dead ground to receive the bullets you can then set up your range. The initial targets need not be elaborate – sheets of card with a simple aiming mark are ideal – and you will need a stick or two to hold them upright. Site your target against a safe backdrop and you can pace out your first shooting distance.

Open sights

Many novices, on buying their first rifle, quickly slap on a telescopic sight and zero in with this having paid no attention to the open sights already on the weapon. This is a mistake as the open sights can be used in an emergency if they have been properly aligned. This point was brought home to me quite forcibly some time ago when I was out for an evening's rabbit shooting. Crossing the top of a grass bank I slipped and gave my .22 rimfire a hefty knock. A careful look through the scope showed that the crosswires were well out of alignment and my shooting sortie could have come to an abrupt end. I was too close to the rabbit field to re-zero the rifle without disturbing the quarry, it was too late for me to retrace my steps to a more secluded area on the farm to re-align the sights, and in any case I had only brought sufficient ammunition for the rabbits I anticipated. The fact that I had also sighted the rifle on open sights meant that I simply removed the scope mounts and continued on my way. That evening I confined my shooting to ranges below fifty yards and I had a very enjoyable time. Some months later I mounted a larger scope on the rifle but this necessitated the removal of the rear sight and I still miss the reassurance of having the open-sighting system on the rifle.

The most consistent shooting accuracy you will be able to attain is from what is known as the bench-rest position. Ideally, you should sit on a solid seat with a firm table on which to rest your elbows as you hold the rifle. The aim can be further steadied if you support your leading hand by placing a box, cushions, or other prop underneath it. Having settled into a comfortable position you will probably be able to hold the rifle rock steady, and you should also be able to repeat this shooting position consistently for every shot. If you do not have a sturdy table, the bonnet of a car, or a fallen tree trunk will provide the necessary support for your elbows, but you must be sitting comfortably to avoid any body shake. Fire your first sighting shots at close range – about twenty-five to thirty yards – and use the same aiming mark for

A bench-rest position will give you the steadiest aim for zeroing a rifle. (*Shooting Times*)

each shot. After using about ten rounds, inspect the sheet to see where the bullets have printed the target. If your aiming and firing have been consistent all the bullet holes should be grouped close together, although they may not be anywhere near the aiming mark. If you fail to achieve this close grouping make another mark and shoot to this, taking deliberate care over the sighting and trigger pull for each shot. With careful shooting this close grouping should be achieved quite quickly. This shows that you are aiming and shooting consistently – the rifle sights cannot be aligned if the person behind it is shooting erratically!

If careful shooting still fails to produce a close group then there may be a number of factors that need checking. Make sure, for instance, that your method of holding the rifle is consistent and ensure that the fore-end or barrel is not resting on any hard object. When a rifle is fired the barrel vibrates in a similar way to a tuning fork and it must be allowed to do so if it is to produce reliable accuracy. Any solid rest will interfere with this natural resonance in the barrel and will produce inconsistent shooting. If this is not the cause check the tightness of all the screws that hold the barrel and action to the stock. Most rifles are firmly bedded into the stock by a strong, mounting bolt just forward of the breech. Beyond this, the barrel is often in free float, that is, not in contact with the fore-end. Should a twig or piece of grit become lodged between the barrel and the fore-end this would also cause the rifle to shoot badly. Finally, check the sights to ensure that they are not loose – I once spent some time examining my own shooting technique and the rifle's mounting bolts only to

A simple zeroing frame made from scrap timber.

discover that the rear-sight moved every time the rifle was fired!

Fire off your grouping shots in batches of five then rest the rifle for a minute or two. Some rifles, especially in the centrefire calibres, overheat rapidly and this can also produce inaccurate results. After shooting off a good few rounds you will have satisfied yourself that both you and the rifle are producing good tight groups at close range. The next stage is to make the point of aim and the point of impact coincide. You will now need to rest the rifle in such a way that it is firmly held while the sights are adjusted. A vice is ideal for this purpose, but a simple zeroing frame will also do the job well. You can make a zeroing frame out of scrap timber in about five minutes. Position the rifle so that the sights are exactly on the point of aim and, while it is held firmly, adjust the rear sight to bring the sighting plane onto the point of impact.

Using the bench-rest technique (do not fire the rifle in the zeroing frame) fire another group of shots and you will find that these are now much closer to the aiming mark. All you need to do now is to repeat the process so that you can fine tune the rifle to shoot exactly to the point of aim with open sights at your chosen range. If possible, lock the sight in this position and you can move your bench rest to different ranges so that you can record the point of impact at any shootable distance. With one brand of ammunition my BSA .22 rimfire shoots to the mark at twenty-five yards, it will then be about one inch high at fifty yards, and it is again spot on at about sixty-five yards. It must be remembered that open sights are only a back-up should your scope fail, so this simple sighting-in method will be perfectly adequate.

Telescopic sights

Once you have gained the experience of aligning your open sights, mounting and zeroing in a telescopic sight will be that much easier, and in fact the final adjustment of the scope is far simpler than any iron sight.

The first stage is to separate the two parts of each split-ring scope mount (they are usually held together by small screws on either side of the ring) and to fix the bases onto the dovetail grooves on the top of the rifle's receiver. Looking along the top of the barrel, check that they are aligned before screwing them in firmly. Resting the rifle in the zeroing frame, ensure that it is firmly held and upright and then place the telescope onto the mount bases and adjust the exact position in two directions. With your shoulder to the stock, move the scope backwards or forwards until your eye sees the full field of view when your head is in the most natural shooting position, and at the same time ascertain that the scope does not interfere with the working of the bolt or any other mechanism. The second adjustment is to rotate the sight to ensure that the horizontal crosswires are actually horizontal. This can be gauged quite accurately by the human eye, but as a final check you can draw a horizontal line on the target with the aid of a spirit-level and point the scope at this. Once these two adjustments have been made the scope is now ready for clamping down. Before doing this, check that the adjustment knobs are on the top and on the right-hand side of the rifle – if not then the sight is 90° from upright.

When screwing down the top half of the scope rings you must ensure that each side is tightened evenly otherwise the mount may produce stress points in the sight which could eventually harm the optics. Having finished this you now have your telescopic sight firmly attached to your rifle. Spend some time bringing it to your shoulder to make sure that the scope is at the correct distance from your eye each time you mount the rifle. If it isn't you will need to loosen the clamp screws to re-adjust the sight. Getting the correct rear lens-to-eye distance is very important for two reasons. Firstly, you must be able to pick up your target the moment the rifle touches your shoulder. You will only get this if you have a full sight picture. Secondly, if the scope is set too close on a centrefire rifle there is a very real risk that the shooter will suffer a 'Weatherby eyebrow' – a crescent-shaped cut above the eye made by the rear end of a scope under recoil.

The sight is now mounted in the correct place on the rifle, but it will probably still be way off alignment with the barrel. Even before any sighting-in shots are fired, the next stage is to bore-sight the telescope. The principle behind this is simple, but some rifle designs can make it quite tricky. Essentially, the idea is to point the rifle at an aiming point so that this point can be seen by looking through the barrel. If you have a bolt action or falling block rifle this is a simple matter, but with many lever actions, pumps, and auto-loaders, you will need to use a small mirror, wedged in the breech, to give you a view down the barrel. With the rifle held firmly in its zeroing frame, and with the aiming point visible through the bore, the scope adjustment screws are turned so that the crosswires also come to the aiming point. As with open

Scope mounting sequence. a) (*top*) Rifle with bolt removed. If the rear iron sight interferes with the scope tube, remove this as well. b) With the rear-sight removed, fix the bases onto the dovetail grooves on the rifle's receiver.

sights, it is advisable to initially bore-sight a telescope at close range and then fire your first sighting shots at this range. Fine adjustments can be made after the first few shots and then you can zero your rifle to your anticipated shooting distance.

If you have not done so before, in the final adjustments to your zeroing you must use the ammunition you plan to use for hunting. By experimentation and

c) (*top*) Place the scope on the bases and adjust until the crosswires are horizontal and the position gives a comfortable eye relief. d) Screw down the top half of the scope rings, taking care not to move the scope. Once the rings are on tight, the dial covers are removed for initial bore-sighting.

experience you will realise that each brand of ammunition will produce a different point of impact – so you should stick to the make and type of ammunition for which your rifle is zeroed. Many .22 rimfire shooters, in particular, are guilty of often changing their ammunition with no attempt to re-calibrate their sights – and then they wonder why their shooting is erratic.

You should always carry out the zeroing of a rifle on a relatively calm day.

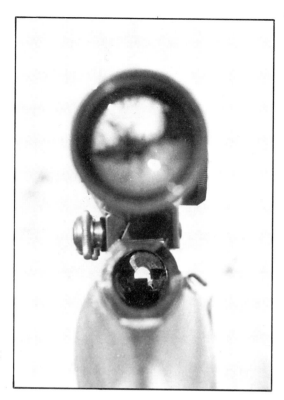

Bore-sighting a bolt action rifle is a relatively simple matter of adjusting the crosswires until they point to what you can see through the bore.

Even a 15 mph crosswind will blow a rimfire bullet about to such an extent that zeroing is a pointless exercise. High velocity rounds are more prone to wind deflection than slower ammunition, so you cannot overcome a crosswind by a higher bullet speed!

You have now zeroed your rifle for a specified range, but as a sporting rifle user you must become familiar with the trajectory of the bullet from your particular rifle. Unlike a target shooter who always shoots at a target at a fixed distance, the user of a sporting rifle is likely to encounter his quarry at a variety of distances and he will need to know the impact point of his bullet throughout the usable range of the rifle.

Trial and error has shown me that with my favourite brand of .22 rimfire ammunition in my small rifle zeroed at seventy yards, it will shoot one inch high at fifty yards, and about three inches low at one hundred yards. My .243 is sighted-in for 120 yards so that the 100 grain bullet is one inch high at fifty yards and three inches low at 180 yards. With the trajectory memorised and the range well estimated, the rifle shooter should be able to place his bullet exactly on target at any distance within the rifle's effective range. Now that your rifle and scope combination is accurately zeroed, you must put in a good deal of practice both in dry firing and by using live rounds before you venture out on your first real sortie. So far you have only fired the rifle from a comfortable bench-rest position but the occasions when you can do this in the field are few and far between. What you must practise now is accurate shooting from a variety of stances.

(*left*) Practise using your stick to steady your shooting – here, a standing shot. (*right*) A stick is also useful for a kneeling or sitting shot. (*Shelagh Marshall-Ball*)

PRACTISING ACCURATE SHOOTING

A stalking stick is a great aid to accurate shooting and now is the time to take up both stick and rifle so that you develop the technique of holding the rifle steady. Always remember that the rifle should be held alongside the stick and should not come into contact with it. You therefore need to find the most comfortable grip to support the rifle while using a finger to act as a buffer between weapon and stick. For the majority of my vermin shooting and woodland stalking I have to take standing shots. At other times I may shoot from a kneeling or sitting position, and in all these cases a stick is very useful, and I would advise a novice to practise using a stick from all these stances. Only when lying prone or when using some form of natural bench-rest can you dispense with a stick, so the more practice you have the better. A stalking stick can also be used as a prop for the rifle and to avoid fatigue. Once when I was out after fallow deer I spotted the rear half of an animal barely twenty yards away behind some undergrowth. I slipped the sling off my shoulder and mounted the rifle to point it at the place I hoped the deer would emerge. I had to wait at least five minutes before the deer broke cover, exactly where the rifle was pointing, and once I had identified it as a shootable beast I aimed and fired. The young buck dropped in his tracks. Now, had I not been using a stick

Shooting from the prone position provides the steadiest shot. (*Shelagh Marshall-Ball*)

I could not possibly have supported the rifle at my shoulder for that length of time. I would have had to raise the rifle as he broke cover, he would have seen my movement, and he would probably have escaped.

While you are working up your rifle accuracy, try also to improve your range estimation. Bear in mind that the certain kill area on a rabbit is only a two-inch diameter circle, on a roe it is only four inches, and on a grey squirrel it is less than one inch. A poorly-judged distance can therefore easily put your bullet outside the kill zone and result in a wounded animal. Good range estimation only comes with practice and experience but the novice should train himself as much as possible before shooting at any live quarry. If your scope sight has a Dual-X reticule there is one way that the sight can be used to estimate range. In this type of reticule the central section of the vertical and horizontal crosswires are very fine lines. By experimentation you can find out how much of this fine section is taken up by your quarry at various ranges. A rabbit shooter, for instance, can cut out a life-sized silhouette of a rabbit and view this through the scope at different distances. If he then makes a note of the image size compared to the thin section of the reticule he will be able to gauge the approximate range of every rabbit he shoots at. Of course all quarry species vary in size from one individual to the next, but this crude method does at least give some indication of range. In the field, however, you must be very aware of the risks associated with using the sight in this way. Wherever you point your scope you are also pointing a loaded rifle, so this form of range estimation must only be used after the target has been identified (through binoculars), and after you have made sure that you have a safe backdrop for the shot. Only then do you mount the rifle, estimate the range, adjust your aim accordingly, and fire.

FIRST SHOOTING SORTIE

Having developed your skills with the rifle to the stage when you can be reasonably certain of killing cleanly and painlessly anything you shoot at, you can venture out for your first real rifle shooting sortie. Although you are more than likely to be on farmland that is not open to the public, you will be using a potentially lethal weapon in areas that may include public roads, footpaths, or even dwellings. As a consequence you must understand that your first and most important consideration is that of safety.

You must know the ground well before you ever venture out with your rifle. Before I take my rifle out onto any piece of land for the first time, even if I have shot over it many times previously with other weapons, I make a few observation visits when I produce a rough map of the ground. On this I note all the danger areas where, if a shot was fired, either the bullet would not go to ground or it would pass too close to footpath, lane, or house. If there are any areas where the shooting potential looks good, the location of a rabbit warren perhaps, or a number of roe deer fraying stocks, I make a note of the concealed approach routes and any possible vantage points from which I can shoot in safety. Looking at an area of land from a rifle shooter's point of view will highlight many factors which you may not have previously considered, so preliminary visits are essential if you are to use your rifle safely.

As a matter of courtesy, as well as safety, let the landowner know whenever you plan to be out on his land with a rifle. By this arrangement he is forewarned of your presence and he can warn you of any farming operations which may interfere with your sport. He may also have good reason to ask you to stay away from certain parts of his land. He may have a lambing field, or there may be people camping on his ground, or any number of other reasons why the day you have chosen or the area you plan to shoot is unsuitable. By the same token he can warn other users of his land to avoid the area in which you plan to operate – this arrangement is very much a two-way flow of information.

After all the preparation, the day finally arrives when you are on the land dressed in your shooting kit with binoculars round your neck, ammunition and firearm certificate in your pocket, stick in one hand, and your rifle slung over a shoulder. You have discarded the rifle sleeve, checked that the barrel is clear and the magazine is empty. Now is the time to load the magazine and work the action to slip the first round into the chamber. Make a mental note of the number of rounds in your rifle and top the magazine up to this level each time you fire any shots. A habit like this will add to your safety drill. I invariably load four rounds into my .22 and three into the .243 so that whenever I need to unload I can check out the rounds again. This in turn minimises the risk of a forgotten cartridge remaining in the rifle.

Having worked the first round into the chamber you apply the safety catch, slip the rifle sling onto your shoulder, and set out for your first live target. How you carry your rifle is largely a matter of personal preference but you must be able to take the sling off your shoulder and mount the rifle with the minimum of movement. My preference is to carry my rifle on my left shoulder with the muzzle pointing upwards and forwards. I can then control the direction in which the rifle is pointing at all times and moving it from this position onto my left shoulder for a shot is a simple forward and upward movement with a half twist. Others find it more convenient to carry the rifle muzzle down, while there are many who like to carry it in a more traditional way – slung behind the shoulder with the muzzle upwards, and in fact I use this method at all times when stalking in company. Whichever method you find easiest, that is the one you should use.

First live quarry

Sooner or later you will be presented with a potential target. You must, before all else, identify it as your legitimate quarry species and then take a good look at its background to ascertain that it is in a safe position for a shot. It is all too easy in the heat and excitement of the moment to forget these two simple and absolutely essential checks. If it is a suitable target and a safe shot, then you must consider the approximate range and ask yourself honestly if you can kill it cleanly. Having gone through a good deal of target practice you should have a fair idea of your own and your rifle's limitations, and you can also assess how your shooting position will affect your accuracy – will you be able to get off a steady shot. On both sporting and ethical grounds you must give your quarry the benefit of any doubts in your mind and refuse to be tempted by a shot you know to be beyond your ability. If, however, you feel that the shot is possible, gently slip the rifle from its carrying position. As you mount the rifle make a final check on the target's surroundings, and if all is well push off the safety catch just before the rifle touches your shoulder. Steady the weapon with the stick or other support, make a final estimate of range through the scope, adjust your aim, and gently squeeze off the shot. After the hours of dry firing and target practice the sound of the rifle's discharge will be followed by the sight of your target collapsing in its tracks. As a sporting rifle shooter, you have arrived!

You will notice that shooting at your first live quarry is a very different proposition to shooting at inanimate targets. The thrill of the stalk and the enjoyment of actually being out in the field with the rifle in your hands will sometimes bring about an increase in heartbeat and an unsteadiness in the hands that you never experienced in target practice. Whatever you do, you should never fire a shot while you are in this condition – sheer excitement has resulted in more wounded and missed animals than anything else. If you are using a stick to support your rifle you can afford to hold in readiness until you are sufficiently calm to take a steady shot. Deer stalkers refer to this condition as 'buck fever', but it occurs in all branches of sporting rifle shooting and it can afflict the person shooting his first grey squirrel just as much as one lining up on his first red stag. Be aware, therefore, that it can happen to you, and avoid shooting until your pulse is back to near normal.

POINTS TO REMEMBER

When carrying your rifle, always carry your firearm certificate as well. The police, after all, are empowered to confiscate your weapon if you fail to produce the appropriate documents on demand and this can result in a spoilt shooting day and a lot of needless aggravation. While out in the field, keep the certificate in a plastic bag or other protective case so that it is not affected by rain, snow, or condensation.

As for your ammunition, you should never carry it loose in your pockets. Dust and grit will be picked up on the surface of the bullet and when the round is fired these particles can make a terrible mess of your precision rifling. Far better to keep your cartridges in their box until needed or, if this is too bulky (in the case of centrefire calibres) or too fiddly (in the rimfires) then you can either buy or make some form of ammunition pouch or wallet. For my deer stalking I always carry eight rounds – three in the rifle and five in a leather pouch. A .22 rimfire user can obtain a wristoleer which is a wide leather wrist-strap holding ten rounds, and keep further supplies in his pocket. In this way he has ammunition quickly available for reloading and all the rounds are kept clean and safe from knocks and dents.

Even after you become a regular rifle hunter, you still need to keep up your target practice and, in particular, you will need to check the zero of your rifle at frequent intervals. Very occasionally different batches of the same brand and type of ammunition will produce different trajectories, and you will certainly need to re-calibrate the sights if you change your brand of ammunition.

Make a habit also of checking the tightness of the screws on your rifle. Those that bed the barrel and action firmly to the stock should be tight, and those on the scope mounts should allow no play in either the mounts or the scope. Quite often these can work loose through the vibration caused by the rifle being fired regularly and they are frequently overlooked when a shooter is trying to work out the reasons for a string of misses. Telescopic sight mounts that are not firmly tightened are capable of creep, that is, the whole assembly can move either forwards or backwards along the dovetail grooves through the effects of recoil. This can be very difficult to detect and it is worthwhile marking the rear scope mount and the receiver in such a way that you can check for any subsequent movement.

When you consider that a sporting rifle is a precision instrument, cleaning and maintenance are very simple tasks and these divide neatly into external

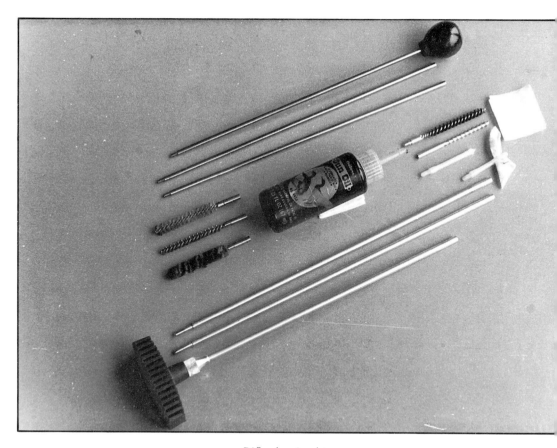

Rifle cleaning kits.

lubrication, and barrel care. Every time you use the rifle, get into the habit of giving it a quick wipe down before replacing it in its safe container. For the majority of rifles all you need is an oily rag and a can of WD40 or similar oil. Give the barrel and action a once-over with the oily rag to remove moisture and fingerprints, open the bolt and if possible wipe this down as well. An hour or two standing the rifle in a warm atmosphere will get rid of any moisture, but should any persist in the nooks and crannies of the action a quick squirt of WD40 will get rid of it. At the same time give the stock a rub down to remove any mud or dried blood, and you have completed the basic cleaning drill.

Since the advent of modern primers and propellant powders for rifles, severe corrosion on rifle barrels has become a thing of the past. Modern primers and powders actually contain compounds which, when left as a residue in the barrel after the round has been fired, protect the bore from corrosion. With the addition of modern bullet lubricants, lead fouling has been virtually eliminated even in the rimfire .22s. So barrel care comes down to a scrub out with a bronze wire-brush once every month or two just to make sure that all is well. However, be careful. Any oil left in the bore or on the breech face when the rifle is fired can set up dangerous pressures and will produce a wild trajectory. If you have oiled your barrel and bolt, you must give them a wipe out with a dry cloth before you set off for a spell of live firing.

Looked after in this way, even the most simple sporting rifle will last for many years and will still produce an accurate performance after firing many thousands of rounds. Always store the rifle unloaded, and for greater security lock the removable bolt and ammunition in a separate container away from the rifle.

Finally, as your experience of sporting rifle shooting increases, you may well find it useful to write up a shooting log to record your observations, successes and failures, in the field. Over the years this will form a useful store of information about wildlife in general and your quarry species in particular; and a shooting log is also an excellent memory jogger. The log may be as detailed as you like, but it is helpful if you enter the date, weather, wind strength and direction, your approach route and the times of your arrival and departure. Among your observations you can enter the type of shots taken, the ranges, and the quarry brought to bag. Such an account makes fine leisure reading, and vivid memories will spring to mind as you leaf through the pages by the fireside on a long winter's evening.

APPENDIX 1

USEFUL ADDRESSES

Major shooting organisations, government bodies, and other sources from which information on rifle shooting sports may be obtained:

British Isles

The British Association for Shooting
  and Conservation (BASC)
National Headquarters
Marford Mill
Rossett
Clwyd LL12 0HL

Everyone who wants to use any sporting weapons in Britain should be a member of the BASC.

The British Field Sports Society
59 Kennington Road
London SE1 7PZ

The British Deer Society
Church Farm
Lower Basildon
Reading
Berkshire RG8 9NH

The Game Conservancy
Burford Manor
Fordingbridge
Hampshire SP6 1EF

St Hubert Club
The Apes Hall
Littleport
Cambridge

Deer-stalking rights may be rented through a variety of agencies and other organisations. Prices vary, so shop around.

The Forestry Commission
National Headquarters
231 Corstorphine Road
Edinburgh EH12 7AT

The BASC (address above)

Game Finders
Tyning Wood
Gare Hill
Frome BA11 5EY

Weald Game
Coldharbour Cottage
Three Leg Cross
East Sussex TN5 7HN

Cowley and Fell Sporting Agency
Cree Cottage
Woodland Head
Yeoford
Crediton
Devon

Sportselect Ltd
Great Edstone House
Kirkbymoorside
York YO6 6PE

Spain
Spain Safaris
Box 752
Santiago
Spain

Instituto Nacional para la
 Conservacion de la Naturaleza
(ICONA)
Madrid
Spain

France
French Government Tourist Office
178 Piccadilly
London W1

West Germany
The German National Tourist Office
61 Conduit Street
London W1R 0EN

The German Hunting Association
Deutsches Jagdschutz Verband,
Schillerstrasse 26
D–5300 Bonn
W Germany

Hungary
Danube Travel Agency Ltd
6 Conduit Street
London W1R 9TG

The Hungarian Hunting Bureau
MAVAD
1014 Budapest
Uri Utca 39
Hungary

Poland
Polish Travel Office
313 Regent Street
London W1R 7PE

The Polish Hunting Association
Polski Zwiazek Lowiecki
00–029 Warsaw
Nowi Swiat 35
Poland

Norway
The Norwegian Government Agency
Direktoatet for Vilt og Ferskvanfiske
Trondheim
Norway

The Norwegian Hunting Association
Norges Jeger og Fiskerforbund
Hvalstadasen 7
Norway

Africa
Hunting Safari Consultants
83 Gloucester Place
London W1H 3PG

UK Field and Stream
Birchensale Farm
Salters Lane
Redditch
Worcester B97 6QB

The one monthly publication in the UK that caters solely for the sporting rifle shooter is
Stalking Magazine
48 Queen Street
Exeter EX4 3SR
(available on subscription only)

APPENDIX 2

THE LAW AND THE RIFLE SHOOTER

There are two categories of laws relating to the ownership and use of firearms in Britain. Regulations on the possession and use of firearms are governed by the Firearms Act of 1968 with amendments and additional conditions imposed by the Deer Act (1963) and the Firearms Act (1981).

The second category concerns the quarry species that may be shot legally, either within their open season or, in some cases, throughout the year. These are described in the Ground Game Act (1880), the Protection of Birds Act (1956), the Deer Act (1963) and its amendments, and the Wildlife and Countryside Act (1981).

Different laws apply in Scotland and in Northern Ireland, but the regulations are broadly similar to those of England and Wales. A shooter in Scotland or Ulster needs to find out from their local police or firearms dealers how the restrictions of these countries vary from those described below.

CATEGORY 1 OWNERSHIP AND USE OF SPORTING RIFLES

A Ownership Regulations
i)   A person may not own or have in his possession a sporting rifle or ammunition without holding a firearm certificate pertaining to that weapon or ammunition. Application must be made to the appropriate police authority for the issue of a certificate before a person may acquire a firearm, and details of the weapon must be entered on the certificate on taking possession of the rifle.
ii) Ammunition – The firearm certificate states the amount and calibre of the ammunition the holder is allowed to purchase and store at any one time. An entry must be made on the certificate each time ammunition is purchased.
Note – Before the issue of a firearm certificate for a sporting rifle the police will wish to ascertain to their own satisfaction that the applicant has:
a) Good and justifiable reason to own a firearm,
b) Adequate safe ground upon which to use the weapon,
c) A secure place to store the rifle and ammunition when not in use.
    They will also need to ascertain that the applicant is of good character and is not likely to endanger the public if granted a firearm certificate.
iii) Conditions of Issue –
    a) The holder must, on receipt of the certificate, sign it in ink with his/her usual signature. The holder must inform the police immediately of:
    b) any change of address,
    c) theft or loss of the certificate,

    d) any change of weapon, stating to whom the original rifle was sold and the source of the new firearm.

B Conditions of Use

i)   Shooting near a Road – It is an offence, without lawful authority or reasonable excuse to shoot within fifty feet of the centre of a highway *if* as a consequence someone on that highway is endangered, interfered with, or injured.

ii)   Shooting on Public Footpaths – Providing a person has the right to shoot on land over which a public right of way exists, he may shoot on or near the right of way.

iii) Trespass – A person commits an offence if, while holding a firearm, he enters on any land without authority or reasonable excuse.

Note – Police powers. A constable may seize any firearm if the shooter fails to produce upon demand a valid firearm certificate for the weapon and ammunition in his possession. It is also an offence for a person to refuse to declare his true name and address when asked to do so.

CATEGORY 2 SPORTING RIFLE QUARRY

With the exception of deer, all other species of wildlife are now protected by the terms of the Wildlife and Countryside Act (1981) which in effect drew together all the previous Acts concerning the quarry species. Under the terms of this Act, only certain quarry species may be shot by authorised persons at all times of the year, and the others in the quarry list have a statutory open and close season.

A 'Small' Quarry Species

i)   Vermin – The following species may be shot at all times of the year except on Christmas Day and on Sundays where Sunday shooting has been expressly forbidden: Woodpigeon, Magpie, Rook, Jay, Carrion/Hooded Crow, Collared Dove, Rabbit, Fox, Rat, Feral Mink, Feral Coypu.

ii)   Hares – This species may be shot at any time of the year except on Christmas Day and Sundays. They may not, however, be offered for sale from March to July inclusive, and you must also remember that hares are classified as game so to shoot them you will need a Game Licence.

iii) Game Birds/Wildfowl – Although no law expressly prohibits the shooting of game birds (pheasant, partridge, grouse, etc.) with a rifle, the British sporting traditions would affirm that they are definitely not on the rifle user's quarry list. The same can be said of all the species of wildfowl and waders which form the legitimate quarry for the shotgun user.

iv) Rabbits – This species occupies a rather peculiar position in law. For an authorised and legal shooter they are classified as vermin, but a person who is apprehended while poaching rabbits may also be charged under the game laws for taking game.

Firearms Permitted for Killing Deer in the United Kingdom

	ENGLAND & WALES	SCOTLAND	NORTHERN IRELAND
RIFLES	Calibre of not less than .240 ins or Muzzle energy of not less than 1,700 foot pounds	Calibre of not less than .236 ins
RIFLE AMMUNITION	Bullet must be soft-nosed or hollow-nosed	*Roe deer*: Bullet of not less than 50 grains AND Muzzle velocity of not less than 2,450 feet per second AND Muzzle energy of not less than 1,000 foot pounds *All deer*: Bullet of not less than 100 grains AND Muzzle velocity of not less than 2,450 feet per second AND Muzzle energy of not less than 1,750 foot pounds All bullets must be designed to expand on impact	Bullet of not less than 100 grains AND Muzzle energy of not less than 1,700 foot pounds Bullet must be designed to expand on impact
SHOTGUNS	Not less than 12 bore *See important NOTE 1 below*	Not less than 12 bore *See important NOTE 2 below*	Not less than 12 bore *See important NOTE 3 below*
SHOTGUN AMMUNITION	Rifled slug of not less than 350 grains or AAA shot	*All deer*: Rifled slug of not less than 380 grains or Shot not smaller than SSG *Roe deer*: Shot not smaller than AAA	Rifled slug of not less than 350 grains or AAA shot
PROHIBITIONS	Any air gun, air rifle or air pistol	Any sight specially designed for night shooting (The above ballistic requirements eliminate all handguns and all air and gas weapons)	Any handgun, air gun, air rifle, air pistol or gas weapon Any artificial light or dazzling or night sighting device
	NOTE 1 A shotgun may be used only by the occupier and certain others, who must be able to prove serious damage (see Deer Act 1963, as amended, s.10A)	NOTE 2 A shotgun may be used only on arable or enclosed land and only by the occupier and certain others, who must be able to prove serious damage (see Deer (Firearms etc.) (Scotland) Order 1985, No. 1168).	NOTE 3 A shotgun may be used only by the occupier and certain others, who must be able to prove serious damage (see Wildlife (NI) Order 1985, No. 171, art. 20).

Statutory Close Seasons for Deer in the United Kingdom
(All dates inclusive)

Species	Sex	England and Wales	Scotland	Northern Ireland
Red	Male Female	1 May–31 July 1 Mar–31 Oct	21 Oct–30 June 16 Feb–20 Oct	1 May–31 July 1 Mar–31 Oct
Sika	Male Female	1 May–31 July 1 Mar–31 Oct	21 Oct–30 June 16 Feb–20 Oct	1 May–31 July 1 Mar–31 Oct
Red/Sika hybrids	Male Female	*1 May–31 July 1 Mar–31 Oct	21 Oct–30 June 16 Feb–20 Oct	1 May–31 July 1 Mar–31 Oct
Fallow	Male Female	1 May–31 July 1 Mar–31 Oct	1 May–31 July 16 Feb–20 Oct	1 May–31 July 1 Mar–31 Oct
Roe	Male Female	1 Nov–31 Mar 1 Mar–31 Oct	21 Oct–31 Mar 1 Apr–20 Oct	

The British Deer Society also recommends that both sexes of Chinese Water Deer and Muntjac be given a close season from 1st March to 31st October.

Exemptions – Deer may be killed outside the open season in order to:

a) Prevent suffering, i.e. dispatching an injured animal

b) Prevent serious damage to crops. In this instance permission must be obtained from the appropriate government department.

Note – Night Shooting. As a general rule, only foxes, hares and rabbits may be shot by authorised persons during the hours of darkness. With the exception of hares, no other game species may be taken at night. Deer may not be shot at night.

(The above tables were compiled by John Hotchkis, Hon. legal adviser to the British Deer Society, by whose kind permission they are reproduced here.)

THE LAW AND THE YOUNG RIFLE SHOOTER

i) Aged under 14 years – A person in this age group may not possess a firearm certificate and may not carry or use a Part 1 weapon except in the following circumstances:

a) if he/she is a member of an approved club.

b) if he/she is using a miniature rifle (i.e. a .22 Short RF) in a shooting gallery.

c) when carrying a firearm and ammunition under the instruction of a certificate holder for his/her use for sporting purposes.

ii) Aged 14 to 17 years – While in this age group a person may apply for a firearm certificate to own a Part 1 rifle. He/she may be given or lent a weapon and ammunition to which the certificate applies, but may not purchase either.

When using a firearm, a young person should be supervised by a person over 21 years old.

iii) Aged over 17 years – A person may apply for a firearm certificate and may purchase the firearm and ammunition described on the certificate.

Appendix 3

BALLISTIC TABLES

Ballistic tables based on the average performance for each calibre.

GROUP 1 The Rimfires					
Name	*Bullet Weight**	*Velocity fps*		*Energy ft/lb*	
		Muzzle	100 yards	Muzzle	100 yards
.22 Short HP	27	1125	900	74	48
.22 Short solid	29	1090	900	76	51
.22 Long Rifle HVHP	36	1285	1008	130	80
.22 Long Rifle Subsonic HP	36	1050	872	90	62
.22 Hyper Velocity	32	1550	1090	170	87
.22 WRF Magnum	40	2000	1390	355	170

GROUP 2 The .22 Centrefires					
.17 Remington	25	4020	3290	900	600
.22 Hornet	45	2690	2030	720	420
.222 Remington	50	3200	2660	1140	785
.223 Remington	55	3300	2800	1330	955
.22–250 Remington	55	3810	3330	1770	1360
.220 Swift	48	4111	3610	1877	1448
5.6 × 57 RWS (.224)	74	3410	3050	1910	1530

GROUP 3 Deer Calibres					
.243 Winchester	100	3070	2790	2093	1729
6mm Remington	100	3190	2920	2260	1890
.25–06 Remington	120	3120	2850	2590	2160
.257 Roberts	100	2900	2540	1870	1430
7 × 57 Mauser (.275 Rigby)	150	2756	2539	2530	2148
.270 Winchester	130	3110	2850	2800	2390
.280 Remington	150	2990	2670	2800	2370
.303 British	150	2720	2440	2465	1983
.308 Winchester	150	2860	2570	2725	2220
.30–06 Springfield	180	2700	2494	2914	2485

* Weights given in grains

GROUP 4 The Medium Magnums

Name	Bullet Weight	Velocity fps Muzzle	100 yards	Energy ft/lb Muzzle	100 yards
.244 H & H Magnum	100	3500	3230	2725	2320
7mm Remington Magnum	150	3260	2970	3540	2945
6.5 × 68 mm	93	3937	3389	3183	2360
.300 H & H (Super 30)	150	3190	2870	3390	2740
.300 Winchester Magnum	180	3070	2859	3770	3250
8 × 68 mm	185	3080	2761	3896	3132
.338 Winchester Magnum	200	3000	2690	4000	3210

GROUP 5 The Heavy Calibres

Name	Bullet Weight	Velocity fps Muzzle	100 yards	Energy ft/lb Muzzle	100 yards
.358 Norma Magnum	250	2790	2493	4322	3451
9.3 × 74 mm	285	2365	2260	3530	2578
.375 H & H Magnum	300	2530	2140	4330	3450
.404 Jeffrey	300	2600	2360	4500	4250
.416 Rigby	410	2350	2150	5010	4250
.425 Westley Richards	410	2350	2120	5010	4100
.458 Winchester Magnum	500	2130	1910	5040	4050
.470	500	2125	1910	5030	4060
.500 Nitro	570	2125	1880	5730	4490
.505 Gibbs	525	2300	2020	6180	4760
.577 Nitro	750	2050	1730	7020	5000
.600 Nitro	900	1950	1690	7610	5720
.460 Weatherby Magnum	500	2700	2330	8095	6025

GROUP 6 The Brush Calibres

Name	Bullet Weight	Velocity fps Muzzle	100 yards	Energy ft/lb Muzzle	100 yards
25–20 Winchester	86	1460	1180	405	265
32–20 Winchester	100	1290	1060	370	250
30–30 Winchester	150	2410	1960	1930	1280
44–40 Winchester	200	1310	1050	760	490
.444 Marlin	240	2400	1845	3070	1815
45–70 Government	405	1320	1160	1570	1210

Index

Page numbers in *italic* refer to illustrations